A WORLD OF WORK

A World of Work

Imagined Manuals for Real Jobs

Edited by Ilana Gershon
Afterword by Jean Lave

ILR Press
an imprint of
Cornell University Press
Ithaca and London

First published 2015 by Cornell University Press
First printing, Cornell Paperbacks, 2015
Printed in the United States of America

Library of Congress Cataloging-in-Publication Data
World of work (Gershon)
  A world of work : imagined manuals for real jobs / edited by Ilana Gershon ; afterword by Jean Lave.
     pages cm
  Includes bibliographical references and index.
  ISBN 978-0-8014-5393-9 (cloth : alk. paper)
  ISBN 978-0-8014-5685-5 (pbk. : alk. paper)
  1. Work—Cross-cultural studies.   2. Occupations—Cross-cultural studies.   3. Vocational guidance—Cross-cultural studies.   I. Gershon, Ilana, editor.   II. Wendland, Claire L. How to be a doctor in Malawi. Container of (work):   III. Title.
  GN448.5.W67 2015
  331.7—dc23   2014049157

Cornell University Press strives to use environmentally responsible suppliers and materials to the fullest extent possible in the publishing of its books. Such materials include vegetable-based, low-VOC inks and acid-free papers that are recycled, totally chlorine-free, or partly composed of nonwood fibers. For further information, visit our website at www.cornellpress.cornell.edu.

Cloth printing   10 9 8 7 6 5 4 3 2 1
Paperback printing 10 9 8 7 6 5 4 3 2 1

Printed with Union Labor

For Rivka Ben-Amos

CONTENTS

Acknowledgments

For years I have sworn that I would never edit a book. It is a tribute to all the authors in this volume and to Fran Benson that I have not regretted breaking my vow for a single moment. Because of my authors, this project has been a delight from the first email I sent to a potential contributor, asking Clare if she would be willing to write an imagined job manual on being a costume designer in Bollywood. It took me many conversations with people to decide to put this book together, and I want to thank the following people for encouraging me: Elizabeth Dunn, Kim Fisher, Paula Girshick, Richard Katz, Lauren Leve, Caitrin Lynch, and, most of all, Fran Benson and Alma Gottlieb. Several people gave me thoughtful advice on how to write the introduction, with insightful suggestions on how to make sentences more graceful: Amy Cohen, David Fisher, Jane Goodman, Caitrin Lynch, Ethan Pollock, Diane Rezendes, and Matt Tomlinson. I am particularly indebted to Amy Cohen who suggested paragraphs I could write when I was so tired and bereft of ideas. Finally, my gratitude to Stanford's Center for Advanced Study in the Behavioral Sciences, which provided me with the time to stray in such an unlikely direction.

A World of Work

INTRODUCTION

Ilana Gershon

Wondering what kind of job you want? Wondering what you would need to know to be a magician in Paris? Or a salmon farmer in Norway? Or a professional wrestler in Mexico? Think about the work you have done. You generally need a complicated mix of skills to do any of it well. You often have to learn some tacit knowledge and have some direct training, you need to show social competence and master some physical skills—all specific to that particular occupation. To be a magician in Paris, you need to know how to perform tricks without much room to maneuver because you might have to do it in a restaurant. But you also need to know how to negotiate with a French government bureaucrat so that you can get a government stipend for being a creative artist. Some of what you need to know can be taught through books, some you can learn only after observing and practicing on the job itself, and some you learn from your mentors and co-workers. This book compiles imagined job manuals for real jobs. These manuals provide a sense of the different kinds of knowledge one would need to do a wide range of jobs from all over the world—from being a cell phone repair person in Washington, D.C., to a ballerina in London.

This book offers fourteen imagined job manuals written by scholars in response to a "what if" thought exercise: What if a crime scene technician in Sweden or a journalist in Siberia decided to explain what it means to do their work well? There are chapters about occupations in Africa, Asia, Europe, Latin America, the Pacific Islands, and the United States, although the majority of chapters describe work in Europe and the United States. All are contemporary occupations—these are jobs you could have right now if you want. But these aren't lines of work that you can do without training. Some of the manuals detail work that requires a lot of physical dexterity, others describe jobs that demand social finesse or years of schooling. Many of the authors are anthropologists who have spent years observing and talking to people with these occupations, and a number of them have decided to coauthor with practitioners from their field sites.

I was inspired to create a collection of imagined job advice by a book I love to teach: *A World of Babies: Imagined Childcare Guides for Seven Societies,* edited by Judy DeLoache and Alma Gottlieb. Their book is also a "what if" collection—if every culture had a version of a Dr. Spock manual for how to raise a baby, what would these manuals look like? I was walking home one day after teaching the manual on how an Australian aboriginal grandmother would advise her granddaughter to raise her great-grandchild, and I started to wonder: What happens to all these babies when they grow up? What kinds of jobs will they get? And what social challenges do they face in these jobs, whether the job is repairing cell phones or designing costumes in Bollywood?

As the editors of *A World of Babies* point out, manuals are not a universal genre. Some manuals will lay out how to do a job in a way that might be familiar to anyone who has read a book like *Rookie Teaching for Dummies.* Some can't conform at all to this genre because of the nature of the work, or the cultural context. A village magistrate in Papua New Guinea might never have come across a job manual—or ever dreamed of writing one. But there are invariably moments in a job where someone with experience is explaining to someone new how to do the work well. The authors chose a voice, a perspective, from which to impart sage advice about the ins and outs of a particular occupation. There might be no job manuals in Papua New Guinea for being a judge, but village magistrates will often explain in eulogies what their work is like and especially how difficult it is to do their work well. A Mexican trainer might only think to describe the life of a professional wrestler when talking a young woman, one who wants to become a *luchadora,* as she visits different gyms trying to figure out where she should train. The imagined job manuals collected here evoke many different genres—advice letters, gossipy emails, sermons, words of wisdom spoken in a bar—alongside more traditional entries. The authors use this wide range of genres to showcase the cultural diversity at the heart of this collection.

When people think of job manuals, they often think of technical how-to guides or professional self-help books. Not so in this book. These chapters are possible because of the paths cleared by earlier lyrical nonfiction narrators of American work lives, writers such as Studs Terkel and Barbara Ehrenreich. Because the authors are mostly scholars writing about lines of work they have studied, these pieces are ethnographic fictions. Even when one of the authors is a professional practitioner, most of the pieces are written in the voice of a fictional character offering a perspective based on research and using a composite of many people's experiences. But fictions are not always entirely fictional. These manuals are also ethnographic—which means that they are based on the authors' years spent observing and analyzing particular livelihoods. At the same time, the authors have taken some creative license in how they frame the chapters and the words used to describe work practices. The manuals are both ethnographic and fictional because they represent the workplace practices of the people they have studied as accurately *and* as engagingly as possible (see Narayan, p. 142).

The authors all focus on how culturally specific every job is. They pay careful attention to the fact that people pass along knowledge and skills in contextually specific ways—how a musician in Bolivia might teach a boy to play the charango will be different than how a Japanese musician will teach a geisha to play the shamisen. And people have their own culturally specific ways of talking about work, talking about having a career, talking about skills that can be passed on to others, talking about the unique challenges that arise in each workplace. A professional organizer in the United States might worry about becoming friends with her clients, of mixing the personal and the professional too much, while a journalist in Buryatia might think that helping those you are friends with or related to is the way to express what is most human about you, to enter into the web of obligations is the main way that people get anything done in Buryatia. For an organizer in the United States, becoming professional means drawing boundaries with one's friends and potential friends so that your obligations are clearly demarcated. For a journalist in Buryatia, becoming a professional means treating friends and relatives as well as possible so that they will be in your debt when you need a favor or information. In this comparison, people have different understandings about how to treat relationships that are simultaneously personal and professional, and how being too personal or too professional can affect people's ability to get the work done.

Communities of Practice

Each job manual is a written invitation to a would-be practitioner to join a group of workers who have different degrees of experience. Everyone in the workplace is connected by a series of loosely defined tasks and dilemmas they must face with some degree of coordination. In short, people enter what Jean Lave and Etienne Wenger call a "community of practice" (p. 56). These job manuals often adopt the perspective of a very experienced person, the voice is of an old-timer explaining to the newcomer some aspects that can be openly stated about what it might mean to be part of this community of practice.

Lave and Wenger might caution readers not to cling too tightly to the dichotomy between those with experience and those without it. Many people participate in workplaces with varying degrees of experience and different perspectives. The vet who visits the salmon and the salmon farmers on a Norwegian domestic salmon farm has a lot of experience tending to the fishes' health, but the farmers have their own experiences and insights. Together the vet and farmers collaborate. At the same time, they are collaborating in such a way that someone who just joined the farm a week ago can also participate. Indeed, newcomers to the salmon farm can often notice things about the daily practices that will, over time, change how things are done there. All these authors, in some way or another, show that jobs change in doing them, and the communities of practice change as people move from being newcomers to old-timers as new ideas get put into dialogue with earlier notions and practices.

All jobs are social and bring social tensions with them. Newcomers are always joining a cohort of fellow workers, not all of whom have the same duties. Many of these manuals will point out that doing your work well sometimes puts you in conflict with other people in your community of practice who are equally intent on doing their own work well. In his book *Postmortem,* which helped inspire some of the pieces in this collection, Stefan Timmermans writes about how forensic pathologists have an occupation that almost always puts them in conflict with the emergency medical workers or the funeral home morticians with whom they come into contact while investigating the cause of a death. The pathologists are invariably frustrated by the emergency medical workers, who may well have destroyed valuable evidence while trying and failing to save the dying person. But pathologists themselves often make morticians' tasks more complicated, since pathologists sometimes disfigure the corpse in an effort to ascertain cause of death while morticians want to make the corpse as presentable as possible for the funeral. These kinds of tensions will be present when one joins a workplace in which people with different jobs have responsibilities and functions that contradict each other in practice.

In short, the pressures and demands of one line of work will often put people in conflict with the pressures and demands of other peoples' lines of work. The chapter on costume designers in Bollywood shows how designers want to make sure that characters are dressed the same way in every shot of a scene or dressed appropriately for the time period. They have difficulty achieving this because the directors will make last-minute decisions for creative reasons or insist on a schedule that leaves little time for the costume designer to find the proper fabric or to sew the costume so that it looks as though the character has worn the outfit for years. The director wants to be able to shoot a scene on a particular day, and actors cannot afford to spend too much time on a single film. The end result of all this time pressure and creative wrangling is that the costume designer has to rely on the goodwill of local merchants to produce outfits that look good enough, and to do so in ways that sacrifice perfection for completion. In this case, the costume designer is working toward the same common goal as the director or the actors—they all want to make a film. But they might have different ideas about what makes a successful film, and each of their contributions will be evaluated differently by audiences when they see the final result. This too can create social tensions as people try to do their jobs alongside others. All of the manuals in this volume trace the social dilemmas that are part of a job, addressing the social sophistication and adeptness that are required when dealing with other people and dealing with other people's job conditions.

What you need to know to join a community of practice, all the tacit knowledge you acquire, can't always be described in a job manual. If you think about workplaces as communities of practice—there are always things that a manual has to leave out, bodily and other implicit knowledge that you gain over time. Some of these chapters provide glimpses of the bodily knowledge you have to acquire to succeed at a particular occupation. Working in a needle factory in Massachusetts means that you have to learn a particular rhythm for picking a needle up, putting the needle in a machine, and pressing the drill down to create a hole. You stop the drill when it bottoms out, but you know that it has bottomed out because you know what the machine feels like when this has happened. You know because you have done this a hundred or five hundred or several thousand times before. Many tasks can't be explained with words alone. You learn all sorts of specific ways to hold your body, to sense exactly when to start a motion and when to stop it thanks to touch, smell, hearing, and sight. Unlike other job manuals, these not only explain what can be written down about doing a job but also discuss some of the skills you can gain only by doing the work, when being told what to do in the abstract is not enough.

Jobs All around the World

Does the country you live in affect the way you work? Do you need different skills to be a doctor in Malawi or the United States? Many of the authors discuss how important government regulations and local infrastructure can be. For instance, doctors in Malawi face significantly different challenges than doctors in the United States or in Germany. In the chapter on being an African physician, a doctor points out to her younger brother, who just finished his residency, that surgical threads for sutures might not be easily available, so her brother may have to make do with fishing thread. Electric generators break down often and, as a result, a doctor has to do regular favors for a talented local electrician so that he will reliably fix the generators in a pinch. Medical textbooks written in Europe or the United States often assume an infrastructure—medical and pharmaceutical supplies and equipment, especially—that don't exist reliably or in predictable quantities in Malawi. Doctors there have to come up with creative alternatives that compensate for the lack of infrastructure. In doing so, people will often form communities of practice to address the problems the larger infrastructures present to them—doctors join with local electricians, international aid agencies, and patients' relatives to come up with imaginative alternatives for the supplies that are not easily available in Malawi. The chapters that follow show how people deal with the demands of a job in other countries. This draws attention to the resources and institutional structures readers might be taking for granted that, in fact, are not in place everywhere.

The global range of this collection also shows how much a country's legal or economic policies can affect people's daily work lives. Depending on your occupation, it can matter how your country's constitution defines the relationship between church and state. In the United States, chaplains who work in prisons and hospitals try to define their practices in broad spiritual terms instead of specific religious terms because government chaplains don't want to be seen as proselytizing. The chaplains are concerned that if they are denominationally religious in these contexts, this could be a violation of their clients' First Amendment rights. Government chaplains in the United Kingdom don't struggle with the same dilemma. There is no comparable legal restriction in Great Britain, where the Church of England has long been established as the state's religious partner. In this chapter, the authors compare government chaplains in the United States and the United Kingdom and show in detail how much the legal system can influence people's daily lives, down to the kind of spiritual care available to them in a hospital bed.

Similarly, when taking paying jobs, magicians in Paris have to make different economic calculations than magicians in other countries do. The French government offers creative artists what is called an "Intermittence du Spectacle," a yearly government stipend based on the amount they earned in the previous year by performing. To get this stipend, magicians have to perform a certain number of times in a calendar year. And magicians aren't always sure if they will be hired to perform enough times that year. But they also want to have as many high-paying jobs as possible so that they have a good stipend the following year. Magicians thus have to make certain complicated calculations when they are offered a low-paying gig. If they take too many low-paying gigs, their stipend for the next year will be low too. But if they don't have enough gigs in a given year, they won't get any government support at all the next year. Bureaucratic regulations force French magicians to evaluate what it means to perform differently than magicians in other countries who are facing a different kind of bureaucracy. A country's government policies can affect people's daily work lives to such an extent that they influence whether or not a magician performs at a child's birthday party.

All this is an important reminder of how much national and cultural context matters at a moment when market analysts all too often describe the world of work as flat and homogenous. In today's global economy, labor market observers optimistically claim that labor is supposed to move freely and jobs are supposed to be so standardized that a computer programmer in Iran could just as easily be working in Bangalore or Silicon Valley. Yet people's on-the-ground experiences show that this is not true. Even ballerinas discover that this isn't true, although ballerinas everywhere are supposed to learn the same repertoire of ballet steps so that a ballerina in London should be able to fill in at a moment's notice for a dancer in Stockholm or New York. Yet dancers in London have contracts with the Royal Ballet company that have to be renewed every year. They feel far more vulnerable than the dancers in a Swedish company, where the government insists that dancers have contracts that last until retirement. As a result, ballerinas in London are much more worried than their counterparts in Stockholm about injury and are much less likely to start a family until they are at the end of their careers in their early forties. Ballet steps may be the same the world over, but the conditions under which the ballerina dances and when she or he starts raising a family depend on the country in which the dancer lives. The following chapters provide many more examples that this belief in the ever-increasing similarity of workplaces is misplaced. Yes, the legal and economic conditions of a nation shape the contours of work. But just as importantly, every single chapter describes how culturally specific a job can be. When a line of work is culturally specific, it means that all the social interactions are context-dependent, and so are the range of solutions that might fix a situationally specific occupational dilemma.

Postscript

I have so many students who don't know what they want to do when they graduate, who don't even know what kinds of jobs are possible. They think mostly of the jobs that their parents and their parents' friends have, or the jobs that they see on television. They often wonder how to even begin to dream of other ways of living, of other kinds of work that they would enjoy. This collection is a graduation gift to my students, a bouquet of possibilities so that they can start thinking in concrete detail about what they need to know to do many different kinds of unusual jobs. Here it is: a world of work for all those who have wondered, "What careers could I dream of having? What would it be like day to day to be in a different line of work? And what are the range of things that go into doing *that* job?"

Suggested Readings

For an inspiring collection of imagined advice from an anthropological perspective:
Judy S. DeLoache and Alma Gottlieb, eds., *A World of Babies: Imagined Childcare Guides for Seven Societies.* Cambridge: Cambridge University Press, 2000.

For a theoretical lens on apprenticeship, learning, and communities of practice:
Jean Lave and Etienne Wenger, *Situated Learning: Legitimate Peripheral Participation.* Cambridge: Cambridge University Press, 1991.

For a sophisticated discussion of ethnographic fiction:
Kirin Narayan, "Ethnography and Fiction: Where is the Border?" *Anthropology and Humanism* 24, no. 2 (1999): 134–47.

For another rich ethnographic investigation of many of the analytical themes in these chapters:
Stefan Timmermans, *Postmortem: How Medical Examiners Explain Suspicious Deaths.* Chicago: University of Chicago Press, 2007.

1

LETTER TO A YOUNG MALAWIAN DOCTOR

Claire Wendland and Chiwoza Bandawe

The citizens of Malawi share a proud tradition of peaceful coexistence among ethnically mixed people. Their southeast African nation is well known for its beautiful lakes and mountains, and for its friendly citizens. It is also known for its poverty. In recent years, some things have changed for the better. Electrification and cell phone coverage have reached more and more parts of the country, for instance, and both primary and secondary education have expanded. Still, most people remain quite poor: Over 90 percent of Malawians get by on under two dollars a day.

Western-style medicine has been present here for over a hundred and fifty years, since the earliest Scottish missionary doctors reached what is now northern Malawi. The country's first postcolonial president was a Malawian physician, Dr. Hastings Kamuzu Banda, who had trained in the United States and practiced for years in Britain and West Africa. (Dr. Banda, referred to near the end of the letter below as "Kamuzu," maintained a very tight grip on power for three decades before the country's mid-1990s transition to multi-party democracy.) Doctors are still relatively few and far between outside of the country's few large referral hospitals, however. Malawi's medical school is relatively new—it only graduated its first fully domestically trained doctors at the turn of the millennium—so the rural district hospitals still may have only one or two doctors on staff. Nurses, midwives, medical assistants, and "clinical officers" (whose training is a bit like that of physician assistants in the United States) provide the great majority of Malawi's primary health care. The nation's poverty, and government budget restrictions imposed through international economic policies, mean that salaries are low, medications often run out, staffing is limited, and supplies are inconsistent in the threadbare public hospitals where most patients seek care. The hypothetical "six million" hospital budget mentioned in the letter may sound fine, for instance, until one recalculates from Malawi kwacha to dollars: it would be a little over fifteen thousand dollars for a year. Given these limitations, relatives provide much of the basic nursing care, and for this and many other reasons, maintaining good relationships with one's relatives is crucial. Doctors have to be flexible and creative to do their work well. Many also supplement that work with research jobs or part-time employment in private clinics.

When Wendland studied among medical students and interns at the University of Malawi College of Medicine years ago, she often asked them, "If you had a little brother or sister who wanted to become a doctor in Malawi, what would your advice be?" Some students, especially very junior ones, were enthusiastic. Most were cautious, advocating a long conversation about the pros and cons of medicine so that their siblings might make well-informed decisions. Some, including most of the interns, advised against the whole idea. These discussions were often illuminating and surprising. And so we have imagined here an older sister, long finished with her medical training and with several years of experience as the sole doctor in a district hospital in Malawi, writing a long letter full of advice to her younger brother, who is about to begin work as a District Health Officer (DHO).

Dear little brother,

You have asked for my advice as you finish your internship and begin work at Wathanzi District Hospital. I am not sure why you want it now: You never listened to my advice when I told you to find some other kind of work! I said, the white coat and stethoscope, you may admire them, but they are not for everyone. We have one doctor in the family now that I am working in Chakumpoto. One is enough. Think about all the other kinds of work you could pursue, maybe the law, maybe teaching. But you were not deterred. You had to continue on this path!

I am teasing, little brother. Of course if you have a heart for this kind of work, it is what you should do, despite the trauma and the cost. You know already, from your five years at the medical college and your year and a half of internship, how it will challenge you. But I am happy to give what advice I can. In my eight years at Chakumpoto District Hospital, I have learned a few things.

I have never seen Wathanzi, but my colleague Thokozani used to work there before she got her position with that Johns Hopkins project. I asked about it when I came to the city for a training session last month. The place is quite nice for a district hospital, she says, rebuilt in the 1970s and well maintained. It sounds a bit like my hospital—a women's ward, a men's ward, pediatrics, the maternity wing, around eighty beds in total, although sometimes you will have many more patients than beds, and some will need to stay on the floor. There is a surgical theater and the outpatient block, X-ray and a small pharmacy. All of these are laid out in a compound surrounded by a metal fence. The district health officer's house—your house, soon—is just outside the compound, close enough that anyone from the hospital can walk there in an emergency and knock on your door. It has a nice garden where you can cultivate some tomatoes and greens and keep a few chickens. On the hospital compound there are several well-grown mango trees. That's good, as your patients will need some shade—and perhaps a nice snack of mango—while they are sitting on the grounds waiting for the clinic or the pharmacy to open. Oh, and of course there is a guardians' shelter at the back of the compound, with a tap and a concrete basin, where relatives cook meals and wash clothes for those in hospital.

Figure 1.1 The patient entrance at a district hospital in Malawi. Photograph by Mary O'Regan.

The district health officer position has been vacant since Thokozani left last year. A clinical officer, Mr. Mpeni, runs the hospital, along with the matron Mrs. Mapilisi. They are both very sound, said Thokozani, but they will be slow to trust a new doctor—they have seen so many come and go over the years. (Thokozani sounded regretful about that, but she said her salary at the project is much better, and that she had to think of the school fees for her two boys and the seven children her sisters left behind.) Only about half of the nursing posts are vacant, so you will have more staff than most of the districts—but of course not as many as your patients actually need. The pharmacist is skilled and honest. Thokozani never had to worry about medications finding their way to the market in Wathanzi, as I have struggled with here in Chakumpoto. Of course there are many, many times when the pharmacy runs out of supplies. You'll have gotten used to these stock-outs in your internship, I know, and will have a sense of what other drugs you might use when the best ones run out, or which you can ask your patients' relatives to go buy at a private pharmacy. Oh, and Thokozani also said Wathanzi's X-ray technician died last year, but he had been training an assistant already when he got sick and that one is taking pretty good films.

Being in Charge

It will be strange for you, I know, starting as the DHO in charge of all of these people when you have just finished your internship. Do not worry. You are the doctor, and they will respect your training and your knowledge—after all, we are known as the brains of the Malawian educational system! It took some time for me, a woman and a Chewa coming up to the North. I had to learn ChiTumbuka quickly. And I had to be very authoritative at first. This stern manner will not be necessary for you. You are a man, and you will be working in the Central Region, where we are from.

I have been thinking hard about how to advise you on being Wathanzi's only doctor. We can hope this situation will not last long: The College of Medicine is so large now that most of the districts shall have three or four doctors eventually, and Wathanzi is not so remote, or so hot, or so troubled, that it will be hard to staff. But for now, you will be alone. That has some advantages, and it poses some challenges.

You can make a positive impact quite quickly, if you show you are willing to work hard and to be stubborn on behalf of your patients. The leadership of a single committed doctor can be powerful.

But: There is no one to check your excesses. If you stop seeing your patients as humans and just work through the line without exchanging a kind word, no one will correct you. If you become angry and fatalistic, there is no one to restore your spirits. If you feel this happening, call me, little brother. I have been there, and I can help. If you stop keeping up to date and practice only the medicine that you learned in school, who will notice? (There is a balance to be struck. You want to learn enough to stay up to date, but not so much that you are always away from the hospital at a training session!) The burden is on you to keep learning, to keep thinking, to keep caring, to keep being the best doctor you can.

You must be available—always. When an overloaded *matola*[1] blows a tire and flips over and everyone riding in the back is badly injured, when an *azamba*[2] brings in a woman after two days of obstructed labor out in the village, when cholera breaks out during the rainy season, you will be the one on the spot. You must be careful about getting too tired. You must be restrained about drinking beer—yes, I heard stories about your time at the college. Mr. Mpeni the clinical officer can help, but you are in charge each and every moment, and you will need to stay sharp.

Chronic Illness

As you know, many of your patients will be infected with HIV. Dealing with HIV is not quite a simple thing for a doctor here! In the days when I was training—before Malawi finally got the money for antiretroviral medications—we used to say it was better not even to test. Yes, a negative status was a great relief. But to tell patients that they were positive was like giving a death sentence, telling them to give up hope. The government promoted voluntary counseling and testing, but my colleagues and I didn't test ourselves, and we rarely recommended testing for our patients. (And at any rate, the test reagents were often unavailable.)

Now things are different. I find that most pregnant women want to get tested. We can easily get them medicines to prevent transmission to the infant, and now, with the new policy, we shall even be able to treat the mothers afterward. Some will be afraid, and your nurses will have to speak with them gently. Sometimes if a woman tests positive, the whole family will blame her even when it is obvious that it is the man who has been "movious" as we say, moving from girlfriend to girlfriend. Here in the North wives can be put out of the house when

---

1. A *matola* is a pickup truck that takes on paying passengers, who are typically loaded in great numbers in the back; it serves as a form of informal public transit.

2. An *azamba* is a person, usually lacking formal medical training, who attends births in homes or village settings.

the blaming gets bad. In Wathanzi District, of course, you have matri-lineal families: it's the wife's house and the wife's family's compound where the married couple stays. Still, she can fear for her livelihood, or for abuse.

I find the men harder to test. Many will not come until they are quite sick, because they think a positive test will sap them of their will to live, and to work, and to earn for their families. We have had better success in recent years once a few of the hospital staff let it be known quietly that they themselves were taking ARVs. Word got around fast. When everyone could see that our ambulance driver was getting fat and driving almost every day—he had been as thin as a maize stalk and had not come to work for months, although I did not let him go because then how could his family eat, so sometimes I drove the ambu-lance myself and more often one of the sisters who had a driving license did . . . where was I?—ah, then some of the men began to come in for testing too.

Testing is not the only difficulty. Sometimes dealing with so much HIV is dull: Skin rashes are HIV, chest infections are HIV, sore throat is candidiasis from HIV. You can get so bored that you don't pay atten-tion, and you miss the time when a sore throat is actually diphtheria and what looks like a chest infection is actually asbestosis. (Down in Wathanzi you'll still have some old men who worked in the South African asbes-tos mines.)

Also, you cannot be afraid of the knife when you are a district doctor. I know they like to say that getting HIV at work is rare, but you and I know it is not. Not when we still sometimes run out of gloves and have to re-boil them so often that they fall apart in surgery. Not when we re-use nee-dle drivers until their teeth are dull and the needle dances and twists and stabs us. But you must put aside the fear and do your work in the surgi-cal theater.

What of yourself? Take care, little brother. Do not think, "Of course I will get it, so there is no hope" and become careless with needles and scal-pels: That is dangerous for yourself, for your patients, and your nurses. (Do not be careless in your own life either. It is not proper for me to speak of these things to you my *mlongo,* but we are doctors, so I will say this much: you have heard people say "You can't eat sweets with the wrapper on," no doubt.[3] Nonsense. I say find yourself a good and faithful wife, as I have found myself a good and faithful husband, and until then if you must eat sweets, leave the wrapper on.)

Everyday Challenges

Do not become lost in administration. A never-ending flow of paperwork will find its way to your desk. We already had ledgers, and now there are new computer programs. But the ledgers have not gone away, as they are useful for when the computers fail or the electricity is out, so now you have two places to note everything. Two? I should say many. Every donor who contributes something to keep the hospital running expects some kind of form to be filled out on its use. So if GIZ gave the ophthalmoscope, and NORAD gave the X-ray machine, and USAID is supporting the antiretrovirals, but only for pregnant women, and . . . you get the idea.[4] And the Ministry of Health requires many of its own records. Add it all up, and it becomes quite a lot. You could spend all your time doing this kind of thing. Sometimes perhaps it is a bit tempting to do so. After all, you can't kill anyone with paperwork, at least not in the obvious ways that you can with a scalpel. When you are feeling unsure of yourself, you may wish to leave the wards and the theater to Mr. Mpeni. Don't let that happen, little brother. Unless your clinicians are very different than most humans, they will soon begin to take advantage of you. And the people in your district will see what is happening, and they will feel wronged.

Do you remember our parents speaking of *uMunthu?* That is what you must keep in mind: how we Malawians realize that all people are human beings and that we are all connected to each other through our

---

3. *Mlongo* is a sibling of the opposite sex. In this case, as a woman is writing, it indicates her brother.

4. The three acronyms represent bilateral aid organizations active in Malawi: GIZ is the Deutsche Gesellschaft für Internationale Zusammenarbeit from Germany, NORAD is the Norwegian Agency for Development Cooperation, and USAID is the U. S. Agency for International Development.

humanity. I am because you are, dear brother, and you are because I am. The people you work with and those you serve expect you to be treating them as fellow human beings: with kindness, respect, hospitality, loyalty, sociability, sympathy, and endurance. In the work of a doctor, all the more so, my dear! I remember one of our senior lecturers explaining that *uMunthu* is the collective consciousness of the African people, shaping our behavior patterns, our expressions, helping us to know what being an ethical human is, and what we need to grow spiritually and find fulfillment. In the work that you do you have an opportunity to feel the most vital needs of others: to live all the characteristics of *uMunthu*.

You may have an opportunity to teach it, too. Wathanzi is not so terribly far from the city, so you may have *azungu* who want to volunteer in your hospital.[5] We get a few even as far north as Chakumpoto. Two I can think of in the last several years were really wonderful, a midwife from Scotland and an intern from America. Both of them stayed for several months, worked hard, learned enough ChiTumbuka to get by, and consulted with me regularly when they had questions. I would welcome either one back! (In fact, Dan the intern promised to return when his training is done.) Others were more trouble than they were worth. We had one German medical student who did not want to put in drips or even catheters because she was so frightened of HIV—she just wanted to watch us work, as if Chakumpoto were a zoo. And I remember two American students who thought they could do anything they wanted, even surgery, because this was Africa. Do not be too quick to say yes to volunteers, and when they arrive talk to them seriously about your expectations. You must help them to understand that not only do they have something to give to Africa but they also have something to receive. Apart from the work in the hospital, they can learn *uMunthu* in action, to learn the value of a lesser emphasis on individualism and a greater one on communal cohesion—and to realize that the Malawian *uMunthu* concept of togetherness is a powerful way of life that we

---

5. *Azungu* (singular: *mzungu*) are white foreigners.

Africans can teach the world. Do you remember when grandma died, the whole community came together and they mourned with us? It was the whole community that felt broken, it was not just left to our family.

And while I am on the topic of people who can be both a blessing and a challenge . . . ah, relatives! I know that you rejoiced when you got the news of your posting at Wathanzi, only two hours by minibus from our family home. Yes, in many ways that is a very good thing. Our parents will be proud to have their son the doctor nearby. I think our mother will be taking you to her standard-eight classes as an inspiration to her students every time you visit![6] And father will no doubt hang a picture of you in your white coat on his wall at work, near the president's picture, and that old family photo where we are all so young and serious-looking.

There is a difficult side to relatives too. Someone will come to the hospital who says, "Ah, I am the son of your daddy's brother's wife's sister, and we have not met, but I have this problem" . . . and then they will expect you to drop whatever you are doing and escort them through the hospital. And probably expect you to buy their medications or bandages when it's all done. This is a challenge. You must take good care of them, or people will say you have lost your culture and become like a *mzungu*. But you must not let them take from your work too often, either, or your patients will grumble that you are favoring your family and neglecting everyone else.

You may also find many relatives who ask you for support, school fees for their children, to take in orphans, or to help them with capital to start a small business or such. With all your schooling, you count as a senior person in the family, young as you are. And people do think that because we are doctors we are rich! If they only knew how little we actually earn. I mean, it is much more than the average Malawian, true. But it is not enough to pay for school fees for every Jack and Jim, so you may have to think carefully about how to manage your relatives—and your salary.

---

6. Standard eight is the equivalent of eighth grade. It is the final year of free public education.

Resourcing

Where you must be most clever is in resourcing. We are a poor country, you know, we are just developing. Still, there *is* money to be had, there *are* drugs, there *are* supplies . . . but you must learn how to get them.

When you deal with district officials, do not give in too quickly. Say you ask for a budget of six million, and they give you two point eight. Do not just say "chabwino, I will do what I can."[7] Say "fine, I will have to close the hospital." They will be unhappy. They may say you are rude. But they will at least find a way to make a few more hundred thousand appear—better than you would have had if you had just said yes right away!

There are donors too. Many of them deal directly with the Ministry of Health, but if you can make your hospital's reputation strong, then more of that money may come your way. And some donors you can deal with directly. It will be good if you can ask Thokozani about them—she was very good about arranging for donations! She told me, send them pictures of starving children, yes, that is often what they need to see. But send them pictures too of white-coated doctors working among them. It should not look too hopeless, both for our pride and for their pocketbooks. They all want to make a big difference with a little money. So your hospital needs to look like a place where everything is all ready to get better if only some helpful donor would provide an ambulance, or some autoclaves, or whatever.

You can be creative not just with funds but with people, and with things. Find out what people are good at. Maybe you have a medical assistant who is too slow in OPD, but he handles medicines well and can step in when the pharmacist must attend a funeral. Up here we had a wonderful senior nurse whose arthritis became so bad she could no longer get around the wards quickly. Now she handles much of the paperwork for me, and she is my staff disciplinarian. One stern lecture from her and a misbehaving worker mends his ways!

As for things, of course you know already how to sterilize fishing line for suture and to turn a used intravenous drip into a catheter. Not ideal, and

---

7. *Chabwino* means okay.

we should not have to do these things. But it is better to do them, I think, than to have no catheters and no sutures at all. Find the district's most ingenious metal-worker and its best electrician. Learn from them. When you have something that needs repair, ask them to show you how to fix it. We've made our autoclave last years beyond what it should have up here in Chakumpoto, and the ambulance too.

Community Work

As DHO you will need to lead community outreach projects. I can share with you a few things about how the community operates—for there were some unforeseen lessons I learned the hard way.

Zeal of Key Players Is Critical

In my first year here we established health clubs in two local schools. Two teachers offered to be patrons. We provided them with basic health education training and a set program for weekly club activities. The first year went well. During the second year, though, one of the patrons, Woyamba Mphunzitsi, left the district for three months. Michael Thandizani stepped in, saying that he would run the club. I spent as much time as I could spare training him on health education basics. He tried hard, but he was a novice, and he was dutiful but unenthusiastic. The club floundered and struggled, and meetings grew intermittent. It was only after Woyamba returned that the health club picked up again. He came back with an energy and momentum that quickly re-established the club on a sound footing.

I learned a powerful lesson: Regardless of how meticulously an intervention is planned, its success depends upon the zeal and preparation of key players. When recruiting leaders, ensure that they have passion for the task or you will find difficulties.

Do Not Play Favorites

In my second year we held a health education display at one of the schools. The function went off very well; the students and community drama group performed admirably. When it was my turn to make speeches, I took the opportunity to award the best male and female participants with a backpack for their efforts. I announced the recipients of the prizes, and to the crowd's applause they came forward. Soon after the ceremony was over, several health club members—including the chairperson—approached me, very upset. They complained bitterly that they had worked hard on the displays and had expected a prize. I explained that only one male and female could get the prize—and that the prizes were not intended to denigrate any of the other participants but rather to encourage the club members. They were not appeased. In fact, they threatened to quit the club altogether, and boycotted the after-party of soft drinks and biscuits. One of the schoolteachers, having observed what transpired, called me aside. She advised that in future, I should not single anyone out. The presenting of ballpoint pens or some small gift that included everyone would be more effective than giving out individual prizes.

This event highlights an important downside to community living. Do you remember the psychology professor's lecture on the "pull-down" motive? It's really true that individual achievement can have high social costs; I have seen it up in the north often and Thokozani tells me it is even more an issue in Wathanzi. If everything and everyone must be equitable for a community to hold together, the one that succeeds "leaves" the group. You know already that when someone in Malawi excels at work or in business, he or she is more likely to receive discouragement than praise. That is why we used to joke that "PhD" stood for "pull him down." You will get a lot of this, dear brother. In the community, remember that when you can maximize equity, you minimize trouble.

The Community Always Asserts Itself

I remember we once held a music and drama display at one of the schools. After selecting the date to ensure minimal disruption to the school program, the headmaster had told all the pupils and teachers that classes would be cancelled. The school was to gather by the big tree under the hill to watch the display. The pupils all came—but instead of the usual turnout of many teachers, there were only two. After only a few songs and poems there was suddenly a mass exodus of pupils. Shocked and embarrassed, the headmaster put the program on hold and tried to find out what was happening. It turned out that some of the teachers had sent a message to the students that they would be writing mock exams, and that any pupil who did not come right then would fail the year. The students all heeded the call and rushed to their classrooms. With half the audience there—and an apologetic headmaster—we finished the program. When I followed the issue up later it emerged that some of the teachers were feeling resentful toward the health club: its patrons received a very small allowance, which was perceived as depriving other teachers. Money issues are very sensitive in a space where poverty reigns supreme.

It is sensitive, too, where nongovernmental organizations with loads of funding make the rules. Some give remuneration, which becomes expected of all programs. I remember as we were designing our vaccination outreach in Chakumpoto we brought together interested parties, including the chiefs, to share their concerns. When a health assistant visited the villages to follow up later, he was castigated by the chiefs. Having not been paid for their time in attending the meeting, they felt cheated and were furious to the point of threatening not to cooperate with the vaccination program. Yet the underlying rule of the program was never to pay: neither to pay the chiefs to attend a meeting, nor to pay the assistants who would go from village to village administering injections. The rationale was that if the community is involved in a project that it benefits from, then without a financial incentive, the program stands a better chance of being sustained.

Ah, how to instill voluntarism and community cooperation when money is so scarce? Brother, involve the community right from the start if you want a real "community-based" intervention. In the design of the vaccination program, funding was never discussed with the community. When the budget was drawn up, the external coordinators of the program determined who would be paid (mostly their consultants) and who would not (health workers and village leaders). There thus was a clear inequality that went against the ethos of *uMunthu,* which we had intended to be an important framework guiding this intervention.

The community made it clear that these differences were important. What I learned is that the "pay me!" stance the villagers insisted upon in this intervention was an attempt to rectify an imbalance, to reassert human dignity and social identity. It was a recognition of the distortions of development and donor practices. You know what, dear brother, at one level aid or assistance is perceived by recipients to be an undermining experience in which something is taken away by aid providers (time, self-respect, pride, dignity, and collective autonomy). Hence, in line with the norm of reciprocity—an integral component of *uMunthu*—the loss must be repaid somehow.

The desire for restitution will sometimes put you in uncomfortable dilemmas. You may be administering health projects run by NGOs that provide no payment, yet expect much extra work from health personnel. Your staff may expect that as a fellow Malawian you will be more sympathetic to their situation and more generous with allowances. In the case of the vaccine program, I was able to approach the Ministry of Health for additional funds. My staff were very pleased to receive this recognition of their efforts and participated enthusiastically.

Why to Stay

There will be times when you think, "I cannot stay working here any longer. I am a doctor. I am trained in medical sciences, I can explain the molecular pathways of oncogenesis and the full life cycles of twenty parasites. Yet here I am, wards overflowing with sick patients, working with four antibiotics (on a good day), no pregnancy tests, a microscope with a broken 100x lens, and chiefs demanding payment. What is the point? Should I not look into finding work in London, or Dubai, or at least Durban?"

I can tell you, my dear, that I have been in this same place many a time. If someone had come at the right moment and offered me a position in (say) Cape Town, I would have said yes. Indeed, some of my friends from the College of Medicine emigrated. You know that Margaret went to Adelaide to train in radiology and never came home, and Dalitso is in Manchester. We keep in touch. I know they have cars and nice houses and that they enjoy their work. (Did I tell you that Dalitso married an Englishwoman?) But it is clear to me too that in some ways my life is more satisfying. I know every day that I make a difference. They mostly work with old people who have many chronic diseases. I work mostly with children, often acutely ill, and if I can treat a cerebral malaria case effectively, then I have changed the course of someone's life—and that of his family too.

A doctor's status is not so high there as it is here, and sometimes foreign doctors are treated with suspicion. Dalitso and Margaret both say that the everyday racism they encounter in the *mzungu* world is wearying. Here everyone's eyes dilate with admiration when I come into the room, and my word is accepted as truth. Even in church! Truly that can be tedious with old friends, but it is useful around town—I can easily get credit with the local businesses, and sometimes they offer small gifts. At the *chigayo* the mill owner will sometimes give an extra sack of *ufa* to the doctor.[8] That's nice, given my salary and how often it is "delayed" for one reason or another.

Our status is also useful politically. A doctor in Malawi can have real power. When we speak about what it will take to heal the nation, people listen. We may not have the money and advanced technologies that our brothers in rich countries have, but we have authority and status, and if those things appeal to you, then a district practice in Malawi can be richly rewarding indeed.

And that brings me to my last point in this very long letter. I know that our parents urged us to stay clear of politics. I understand their fear. Grandfather was never the same after his years in prison under Kamuzu. I am not, myself, blind to the dangers. But we are doctors now. Sometimes when people have it made, they are making a good income, their family life is happy, they can become blind to the suffering of others. Insulated. You and I? That can never happen. A doctor here in Malawi would have to sit behind her desk all day without seeing patients to think that all is well in our nation. A doctor would have to be very stupid not to see how poverty and political malfeasance and lack of high-quality education are

---

8 A *chigayo*, or maize mill, grinds up dried corn into flour—*ufa*—that is used to make the staple stiff cornmeal porridge most Malawians eat daily.

at the bottom of so many of the problems we see. And I know you are not stupid. Drugs are vital! Surgery is important! Health knowledge is critical. But you cannot help but see that medicines and operations and health education alone are not going to be enough. A healthy country needs good roads and traffic enforcement so that these terrible *matola* accidents end; environmental safety measures so that children don't die of pesticide poisoning; decent agricultural policies so everyone has nourishing food to eat and seeds to plant; an end to corruption so that the drugs intended for our hospitals stop going to the markets instead; strong leaders who push back against pharmaceutical prices so high that cancer treatment cannot happen in the districts—and can rarely happen in the capital city. So you may choose to use your status as a doctor to exert political pressure. This could be in small ways, as when you talk with the district about your budget. It might be in more risky ways. Perhaps you will even pursue elected office someday. (If you become president, can I be your Minister of Health? I think I would be a very good Minister of Health.) You may have a heart for the people, and perhaps working with them in the hospital as a healer will be enough. But if you want to heal our nation, you may need to work beyond the hospital as well.

Good luck and good health, my brother. I have faith in you.

Acknowledgments

Both authors wish to express gratitude to the many Malawian medical students, interns, and doctors—as well as nurses, midwives, clinical officers, and others—who have shared their experiences with us over the years.

Suggested Readings

On medical and nursing work in a southern African hospital, see:
Julie Livingston, *Improvising Medicine: An African Oncology Ward in an Emerging Cancer Epidemic*. Durham, NC: Duke University Press, 2012.

On medical training in Malawi, see:
Claire Wendland, *A Heart for the Work: Journeys through an African Medical School*. Chicago: University of Chicago Press, 2010.

On community participation challenges, see these articles:

Lisa C. Jordan, G. Anne Bogat, and Gloria Smith, "Collaborating for Social Change: The Black Psychologist and the Black Community." *American Journal of Community Psychology* 29, no. 4 (2001): 599–620.

Stuart Carr and M. MacLachlan, "Psychology in Developing Countries: Reassessing Its Impact." *Psychology and Developing Societies* 10 (1998): 1–20.

On *uMunthu*, see:

Chiwoza Bandawe, "Psychology Brewed in an African Pot: Indigenous Philosophies and the Quest for Relevance." *Higher Education Policy* 18 (2005): 289–300.

Augustine Shutte, *Ubuntu: An Ethic for a New South Africa*. Pietermaritzburg: Cluster Publications, 2001.

2

What You Need to Know to Be a Fish Farmer in West Norway

Marianne Elisabeth Lien and John Law

Spearheading the so-called Blue Revolution, Atlantic salmon have recently been domesticated on a massive scale. In just a few decades, they have become husbandry animals. More than 95 percent of the world's Atlantic salmon alive today has been raised on a fish farm. But even so, they are still in many ways "newcomers to the farm." Norway has taken a lead role in the industrial domestication of salmon. Here, salmon farms are often locally owned, and aquaculture provides an important source of employment in remote coastal villages, where a traditional livelihood has generally relied on a combination of fishing and small-scale farming. Today, the reliance on fish farming has increased. With a production of more than a million tons of farmed salmon per year, Norway is the largest producer of farmed salmon worldwide. But Norway is also home to the largest remaining population of wild Atlantic salmon. Accommodating both farmed and wild salmon in the same waterways is a difficult balancing act that involves protective measures of many kinds. In this chapter we trace the workday of a salmon farmer in West Norway.

In the dark the car drives itself. Three minutes, down the hill, carefully because the road's icy. The parking lot is brilliantly lit. I pull on my woolly cap and step out of the car. A chilly wind is cutting around the corner of the warehouse as I bang the door shut behind me and walk into the workshop. They're there already, three of them. Sitting. Standing. No one is talking. It's too early. Too dark. Now the manager arrives. There are brief greetings. "*God morgen.*"[1] It's all very informal. It's quiet. It's Norway. Rural West Coast Norway. Everyone knows, or is related to, everyone else. You know where they come from, and you have to get along. But you don't need to talk much. Especially not in the morning.

So what's on the agenda for today? Well, says the foreman, the vet's visiting. She will lead a workshop on fish welfare, and some of us will need to sign up for that. It's mandatory now. And then the nets need to be rotated. We need to do that today. As we do endlessly. Net rotating. "*Tromling.*"[2] And then there is a new apprentice this week. Vidar. A lean young man, shy among his new workmates, barely 18. He is assigned to me. Otherwise, well, nothing special. Just the usual things. I'll come out, says the foreman, around lunchtime.

Okay, it's time to move. I pick up one of the lights, a big hefty underwater lamp, and we walk out into the dark in a procession. It's a hundred and fifty feet down the quay to the motor boat, it's bitterly cold and still dark out. The boy, Vidar, undoes the mooring ropes while I lift the engine canopy and put the fuel on. Thank goodness, he knows how to pilot boats in the dark and needs only minimal instructions. I dive into the cabin, fumble the key into the ignition, and start the motor. Soon the engine coughs and bursts into life. Vidar releases the last of the ropes as I put the boat into reverse. Now we're both in the cabin with the door shut. I back the boat away from its mooring, turn the rudder, put the engine into forward gear and we're off. Around the end of the jetty I take us, slowly, and then I head directly for the farm. Barely visible, it's out there in the middle of the fjord, but the boat knows the way. I push the throttle forward and sit down on the swivel chair. We're banging along now, against the waves in the choppy water. And dawn is just beginning to break, a distant blue beyond the mountains to the east.

---

1. Good morning.
2. Net rotating.

It doesn't take long, five or seven minutes, and the farm looms up. Ten square pens, smaller, in the rigid part of the farm. And then, at the far end, the raft with the warehouse and the control room. Like a two-story house in the middle of the fjord. I slow the boat as we pass the pens. There are half a million salmon out here, and there is no reason to scare them. Then I slow down more as we get to the raft. Choppy it is, the boat is bouncing up and down. Vidar is out on the deck reaching for a mooring rope. On his second try he grabs it, and he's cleating it down while I've turned off the engine. Vidar has climbed up onto the raft deck—it's ten feet above the water. I wait for a moment while he disinfects his boots—biosecurity is important, though the birds don't sterilize their feet, that's for sure—and then I pass him the light. Now I climb up, fish out the key from its hiding place and open the door to the lobby. In we go, shutting the door behind us. I drop my bag near the computer. I'll settle in properly in a bit. But first I need to get the generator running. Nothing will happen until we've got power. And then we can make a cup of coffee. That's pretty urgent too.

I turn into the warehouse. In the half-dark there are ghostly bags of fish feed on my right that reach all the way to the ceiling. In the far corner there's the new generator. Like the boat it takes a moment to kick in. And then there is a roar. It's rumbling. And it's going to go on rumbling for the next eight or ten. The lights blink on in the warehouse. The fish farm is coming to life. I return to the lounge and sit down at the desk. There are two computers, but I'm interested in the one that controls the feeding. Now that there's power, I can boot it up. Waiting, watching as it goes through its impenetrable routines, and then I move the mouse. I hear the familiar "click" as the screen lights up with an image of our four feed silos underneath the warehouse. Hmm. There's enough feed in the silos for now. Then I start the blowers to get the feed moving. Three more clicks. There we are. The program is running. The blowers are on. And the pellets are starting to rattle down the pipes and rain down on the heads of the salmon. Out there in the breaking dawn salmon are starting to feed. Hopefully, at least. That is the idea. But we won't know that for sure quite yet.

It is time for coffee. Vidar has got the coffee maker going. That's a good sign. I reach for my mug and fill it up. While I blow on the hot surface, I think about what to tell him. I need to give him some idea of the jobs that are waiting for us. He's a newcomer to this city of fish. I am an old-timer. But where do I begin?

What do I need to know to be a fish farmer? I need to be able to drive a car. I need to be able to pilot a small boat in the icy pre-dawn waters of a fjord in West Norway. I need to be able to tie that boat up safely. All this goes without saying. Like most boys from around here, Vidar knows all this already. I need to know about engines—small ones like the motor in the boat, and large ones like the massive generator set that powers the farm. I need to know something about computers too. I need to know a little about the software that does the feeding. I need to know how to make a cup of coffee. I need to know when to work and when to rest, when to relax and when to be worried. I has to know what signs to look for, to pick up on the signals coming from deep down where the salmon swim. But how can I explain all this to this young man who knows hardly anything about salmon? It has to be learning by doing. So I finish my coffee, and tell him that today he will collect *"daufisk"*—dead fish.

Daufisk

Here is what you need: a wheelbarrow, a clipboard, a sheet of waterproof paper, and a pencil on a string. Vidar carries the inscription devices, while I push the wheelbarrow. We walk single file, about two hundred feet along the walkway dividing the rows to the pen at the very end. We can hear the rattling sound of feed flowing through pipes and the splash of a salmon breaking the surface. Good. The fish are feeding. It's soon light, and it's going to be a beautiful day, crisp and clear. Then I open the stop-valve on the air pipe. I tell Vidar to watch out. The hissing starts. Then there's a rumble and a fat blue pipe bobs to the surface in the pen. It's pointing at the deck close to where I'm standing. For a moment it lies still, and then it starts thrashing around like a demented sea serpent. I'm hoping that it hasn't gotten blocked. If this happens it will mean trouble, we'll have to haul it up and clear it, and that can take several hours. Vidar asks: *How does it work?* Over the hissing sound of the water I shout that the air is

Figure 2.1 Ethnographers collecting *daufisk*, the dead salmon at the bottom
of the fish enclosure. Photograph by the author.

driving a pump way down at the bottom of the pen. And the pump is
sucking water from the bottom of the pipe to the top, close to where we're
standing. Suddenly a torrent of water pours out. Vidar gets showered before he jumps to one side. And then they come: dead salmon sucked from
the bottom of the pen. Bang, bang, bang, they spurt out of the end of the
pipe and hit the blue plastic container, slithering around before they come
to rest. Three, four, five of them, and then a couple of lively wrasse, *leppe-
fisk,* placed in the pen to eat the sea lice, accidentally sucked up the tube.[3] I
throw them back into the water.

Why do they die? It is Vidar again. But who knows why they die? There
are fifty thousand fish in this pen. A few of them will die each day. It is inevitable. And we need to take them out. We're the undertakers here. The
caretakers too. The two jobs go together. And that's what the pipe is for.

---

3. Wrasse are a type of small fish that feed on invertebrates.

So that the dead can be removed, and the rest stay healthy. I watch the torrent of water, there's six, seven, eight, and nine, and then they stop coming. I turn the stop-valve and the flow starts to tail off. I ask Vidar to get the clipboard, and I make a note in the right column. Pen number one: "9." That's okay. Not too many. No need to worry. A sign that the batch as a whole is doing OK. Next pen. But first we need to pick up the nine corpses and put them in the wheelbarrow.

How do you pick up a salmon? Even more to the point, how do you do this efficiently? You're going to pick up dozens each day. So how do you minimize the effort you need to put in? I give Vidar a demonstration. You do it one-handed. You grab them very firmly by the tail. Wrap your fingers round them. And then you just lift them up, all ten or so pounds. And then you can toss them into the wheelbarrow. That's it. Simple. All in one movement. So long as you know how to do it. He watches while I do a few, and then I leave him to do the rest. And then we move on to pen number two. By the time we have finished pen number four, Vidar is doing OK. I leave him to do the rest of the pens and go back to the control room to do some paperwork.

What do I need to know to be a fish farmer? I need to be able to push a wheelbarrow. I need to know what all the pipework is on the farm: big pipes and small, for water, feed, pressurized air, and the electric system. I need to know how the "*daufisk*" routine works. I need to know how to pick up fish that are heavy and slippery. I need to keep out of the way of torrents of water. I need to remember to take a note of the number of fish that flop down at my feet and then to enter the numbers into our computer. I need to be able to diagnose what's happening when things start to go wrong or when too many fish are starting to die. I need to know what counts as "too many." But I don't need to know why each single fish dies. I need to know fish as a collective, as a group or a batch or a pen. That is how I need to know the fish. Not as single individuals.

Ingenuity: Engineering a Crate

Stupidity makes for more work. If you're at the far end of the farm and you've forgotten to bring the box cutter or the pliers, then it's a long walk back to the workshop to get them. But then again, some of the things that we do—some of the ways that we work—also make for extra work. Quite unnecessarily. Collecting the dead fish in the wheelbarrow? Vidar found it easy today. No wonder. If you're only getting ten or twelve out of each pen, then you only need to make two or three journeys with the wheelbarrow. That's not so bad. But from time to time the fish start dying in larger numbers. Epidemics occasionally sweep through a fish farm. If things are going badly there may be thirty or forty dead fish coming out of each pen every morning. Then it's a different matter. You're sorry for the fish, yes, but you're sorry for yourself too. It's hard work, carting off all those fish in the wheelbarrow and emptying them into the tank filled with formic acid. So then there's the question: Isn't there a better way of doing things? That is what I ask myself. Time and again. And the answer is usually: yes.

For instance, there's the forklift truck. And then there are the large oblong polyurethane containers. Six feet by three feet by three feet. More or less. They're made to be picked up and stacked by forklifts. So I started to think. Could I adapt one of these containers? Was there any way we could avoid the business of manhandling all those fish? And the answer was: Yes, there was. It took a while, and it was a bit of a jumble, but it worked just fine. First I cut out one of the walls of the container, most of the way up to the corner. Then I got a piece of pipework that would serve as a hinge and ran it along the top of the side I'd just cut out, from corner to corner. Then I attached the missing side to the pipe so that it hung down to cover the space I'd just cut it from. And then I made a catch—this took several tries—to keep this flap shut. Because we didn't want the fish flopping out. Except, that is, when we actually wanted to deposit them in the formic acid tank. And there, that was it. A new kind of device. If you're interested you can see it, over there. Ready for the next lot of daufisk.[4]

---

4. Dead fish, or morts.

What do I need to know to be a fish farmer? I need to be able to solve practical puzzles. Puzzles that, if I can solve them, will simply make the job easier. So puzzle solving, that's the first thing. Though, no, I correct myself, it isn't the first thing. First I need to be able to see that there's even a puzzle there to solve. I need to ask myself the question: Is this a good way of working? Or is there something about it that could be made easier? So that's number one and number two. Here's number three: It helps if I am a little bit lazy. Not really lazy. It's not a question of shirking. But it helps to be lazy enough to want to make the work a bit less back-breaking, a little bit quicker. Perhaps it helps, too, that I'm not the young man that I was. Some things get more obvious in middle age. There's quite a lot of heavy lifting and it's nice to find ways of cutting this down. And then, here's number four, I need to be able to think about the puzzles mechanically. This isn't anything to do with theory. This isn't even design, if by design you mean doing something with a pencil and paper. It's in my head and it's three-dimensional. The question is: What kind of a device, what kind of a physical object, might I engineer up to solve the puzzle? With, and this is important, the bits and pieces at hand on the fish farm. Because we don't have a machine shop—that's back on the shore. All we've got is a workshop—the tools are okay but they're not limitless—and the bits and pieces that end up out in the middle of the fjord, one way or another. I need to know what I can get my hands on. And then, number five: I actually need to be able to *do* the job. I need to be able cut through polyurethane, to make workable hinges out of pieces of pipe and jubilee clamps with their worm threads. I need to be able to do things with my hands. And then finally, I need the time. I've no complaints about the company. It's fine. But the fact is that if everything's going okay and you're doing what has to be done, out in the middle of the fjord nobody is looking over your shoulder and barking orders. So, and this is number six, I need to be able to spend a bit of my time on a project like this. These are some of the things I need to know if I want to solve practical problems on the fish farm.

One forklift, one container, the germ of an idea, and quite a bit of fiddling around with whatever the materials are to hand, that's what it took. Yes, it's not a thing of beauty, and you sometimes need to work on the hinge or the catch. But it works. It's made life easier. And Vidar? He listens politely. Perhaps one day he'll understand why it's worthwhile, this kind of lash-up.

Feeding

My stomach is rumbling. Sure enough. It is time for lunch already. In the damp changing room I step out of my clogs and pull off my red coveralls. Hands under the warm water. That feels nice. I peek into the kitchen and see that Vidar has set the table for three. Kristoffer, the foreman, must be on his way out. Everything seems to be there, bread, butter, salami, canned mackerel in tomato sauce, smoked salmon, smoked mackerel, and *seilaks*—the canned pollock dyed red so that it looks like salmon, a throwback to the 1960s, when salmon was still expensive. And there are cheeses too, goat cheese and gouda. Lunch is heavily subsidized by the company. We pay a small sum each month—it's deducted from our salaries. But it's a great deal, one of the fringe benefits of working for the company. Vidar has even emptied the dishwasher. Good boy. That is one of the things we need to know how to do too. We need to know how to take care of ourselves, which includes keeping the kitchen tidy. Or tidy enough. No one else is going to do this for us.

Kristoffer arrives. We sit down to eat, and he wants to know how things are going. Are they, the salmon, feeding properly? Are we giving them enough to eat? Or are we feeding them too much? The managers constantly worry about these questions. They know the figures, they know our profit margins. Feeding, they say, counts for 60 percent of the cost of raising salmon. If you overfeed them, then you're throwing money into the ocean. And if you're not giving them enough, then they won't grow as quickly as they should. And that will affect the margins too. When you get down to it, it's all about money, of course. The salmon put the food on our tables, while we drop feed on their heads.

But then again, there is more to feeding than cost. Because feeding is also a way of knowing how well they're doing. If they're eating less than they should, it could be a sign that something is wrong. You start to ask yourself: Did I get the numbers right? (It's easy to miscount.) Or has disease gotten into the pen? We've got estimates for the total weight of salmon in each pen, and we know how much they are likely to eat. But, of course, we could be wrong. On the other hand, if we've got the weights right, then perhaps there's something wrong with the salmon. And then you start to worry. So how do you know what's going on? How do you know that you're giving them the right amount to eat? It is actually quite complicated. How can I give Vidar a sense of this?

While we're clearing the table I ask him to follow me up onto the gantry when we're through. "We're going to check the feeding," I explain. "*Sjekke foringa*."[5] "It won't take long." "But aren't they feeding already?" Vidar asks. Of course they are. We can hear when the feed lines come to life. There's a shrill ringing as the feed pellets blow down the line to the pens. And then, equally suddenly, there's a deafening silence when the quota has been reached and the feed pump automatically turns itself off. But right now they're all on. That's what Vidar can see. But this doesn't stop us hand feeding, to check their appetite. . . .

I grab a scoop and a bucket, fill it with pellets. Then we climb the steep steps. Up here on the gantry, it's windy. Noisy too. Not a place for conversation. But we get a good overview of the pens. Now we're above pen number six. I fill the scoop, and with a casual movement of the wrist I flick the pellets at the surface of the water. The response is instantaneous. Suddenly the water is simmering with life. It's almost as if the water is boiling. We can see the salmon jumping, we can hear their tails flapping as they break the surface. Good! They are hungry! Or at least some of them are. Some of them? Yes, because from up above we can only see what's happening near the surface. Even so, it's looking good. We decide that pen six is in good shape.

There are other ways of checking the feeding. You can watch your computer screen. Because you can lower a camera into the pen and see the fish swim past. You can see the pellets of feed falling through the water, and how

---

5. "To check the feeding." The expression refers to regular monitoring of fish by checking their appetite and usually involves hand feeding.

the fish react. You can sip your coffee at the same time, and follow Facebook on the corner of your screen, though that's a job for the younger generation. You can stay out of the wind. It all sounds easier. But I tell the younger farm-hands it is not the same. You need to have a *sense* of the fish. You need to be near them.

"What are you looking for?" Vidar shouts through the wind. "This," I reply. "This is good. They are feeding. No disease. No waste. Let's go and check the next pen."

"But what if nothing happens? What if they don't react when you drop feed on them?" It is Vidar again. He's good at asking questions. "Well, then something is probably wrong," I shout back. Though only probably. Because it's difficult to see what's going on in the pen. If the wind is blow-ing, if the surface of the water is choppy or the light is wrong, you really

What do I need to know to be a fish farmer? I need to know how to "sense" the fish. I need to know what it looks like when things are okay in the pen and when they're not. I need to watch them. A lot. And I need to be able to see things that I can't see, deep down there in the pen. Sensing fish is about seeing, but it's also more than seeing. There's science here too, and numbers. Fish nutrition. "Feed conver-sion ratios"—how much feed it takes to make a pound of fish. The number of fish in the pen, their average weight, the biomass swimming around beneath my feet. But then it's also more than scientific mea-surements. It's an art as well. The art of seeing. But also the art of feel-ing. That educated sixth sense that things are going well. Or not. Is this knowing? Well, perhaps it is. But it's a kind of knowing that is corpo-real, depends on vision and sensory skills, and draws on experience. On all those other moments that were similar. The cues that something might be wrong are subtle. A sign of disease may come in just a hint of a change. It's not easily put into words. Regardless of the noise up here on the gantry. Vidar will just need to watch as I do this. One day he will get it. Or he won't. There's not a whole lot that I can do about it.

can't see very much at all. And even if it's all perfect, how far can you see down into the pen? Five feet? Ten? Not very far. But it's enough to get a sense of what's happening. So we do it every day. We do it lots of times each day. *Sjekke foringa*. It's important. It's constantly on our minds. And it's an art, not a science. You get a feel for it. Hopefully. It is learning by doing.

Domestication and Care

It's late afternoon. Vidar, Kristoffer, and I have been moving the nets, *tromling,* since lunchtime. Why? What's the need? The answer is that after a while the nets get heavy with algae. You need to stop it growing. You need to kill it. And how to do this? The answer is—you leave the nets to dry. It sounds simple enough. Indeed, it is simple. But there's a snag. The nets are doing a job. They're there setting boundaries. They're there to stop all your expensive fish from swimming off into the wide blue yonder. No nets, no fish, no income flow. And, by the way, they're also there to stop your precious salmon from reproducing with their distant cousins, who are still swimming in rivers nearby. So what do you do? Well, the answer is pretty straightforward. The net is far longer than it needs to be. Only half of it is in the water at any given time. The other is wound around a huge cylinder. So when it's time to clean the net, you start to unwind it. You turn the cylinder and let the net drop into the water. And then you go to the other end of the pen and start to pull in the part of the net that's been underwater. You pull it in and wind it around the other cylinder. None of which is much fun. It's heavy work. Lines need to be disentangled. At the same time it is a pretty smart invention. Like so many things out here.

But now we're done and we're having another cup of coffee. And eating chocolate too, another of the firm's fringe benefits. Soon we'll get back to work. We need to catch a few fish for Anna. She's the young community vet, and she's on her way out. It's time for her scheduled inspection. Though that makes it sound very formal. Which it isn't. Yes, it's serious, and she comes regularly. But her inspections are welcome too. Every time she comes I learn something from her. There is always something that we didn't know about. It's forty years after the first successful attempts to raise salmon in saltwater pens, and the fish are still "newcomers to the farm." And we, their caretakers, are mere beginners. At least, that is often how it feels. Because there's always something to worry about, and it's hard to know whether you are doing things right. I mean, how can you know fish that come in shoals of fifty thousand to the pen when you don't go in the water yourself?

One way, as Anna keeps telling us, is by taking samples. Today is the day for the fortnightly sea lice count. Sea lice are nasty little parasites that have always been attracted by salmon. And we've got so many salmon that our pens give them plenty to feed on. So much so that the sea lice are flourishing in the Western fjords. And they're becoming a threat to the salmon outside the pens as well. The wild salmon, the smolt that hatched out in the river last year, come down the river. And on their way to the Atlantic they swim past the salmon farms. And then they catch sea lice. Or at least, that's what the authorities tell us. And the authorities know because they add up our lice counts and publish their aggregated statistics. At any rate the result is now an almost zero-tolerance policy for sea lice in the pens. The threshold for treatment has never been so low. Good for the wild salmon but more work for us.

There is a slight drizzle as Vidar and I head back out to the pens. He's carrying the dip net and the metal clipboard with its waterproof paper, while I carry the bucket. There's water in the bucket and liquid anesthetic. Again, the hissing sound of pellets being blown through plastic pipes stops us from talking. But Vidar is a keen observer and doesn't need much instruction. Soon, he's able to catch the salmon himself. He's holding on firmly while ten pounds or so of lively fish desperately thrash about inside the net. He lifts the net, edges it over the handrail, and empties its contents into the bucket. The fish is still splashing and flapping like crazy, but within seconds it calms down. It "goes to sleep," as they say in medicine. Then I lift it up to examine it for lice. Squatting, I lie the salmon across my thighs and start looking. Sea lice are tiny creatures, and they come in different categories, or at least that is how we report them: "young," "mobile," and "female." If they're female then they've taken up residence on the salmon's scales and they're about to reproduce. Most salmon have none. But occasionally, we spot one or two. Slowly, we fill the slots on the paper grid. We need to check twenty salmon from each pen. A random sample of the fifty thousand in the pen.

What do I need to know to be a fish farmer? I need to be able to lift and hold heavy lively fish at a difficult angle. I need strong upper arms. I need to recognize a sea louse and to distinguish females from young ones that are still crawling around. I need to know how to write the right numbers in the right boxes on the chart and how to enter them into the computer. And I need to be able to work quickly because we don't want to keep the fish in the bucket for too long. I need to throw them back into the water before they have become too drowsy. In other words, I need to know how to inflict some (but not much) discomfort on a few fish, in order to care for the population as a whole. And sometimes—this happens when the sea lice count gets too high—I also need to know how to medicate our salmon because we need to keep their wild cousins healthy and happy.

Welfare

Happy? Who knows? Anna has joined us now. And while she helps us to finish the sea lice count, she asks me: "Have you signed up for the fish welfare workshop?" She reminds me: It's mandatory. And it's next week. And then, as she speaks, I remember that since last year salmon have been subject to Norwegian animal welfare legislation. They have rights now, pretty much like cows and pigs. Like four-legged farm animals, they're even stunned before they're slaughtered. Much of the salmon slaughterhouse was rebuilt as a result. No more suffocating with CO_2. Things are changing.

But, I'm thinking, next week I have a million better things to do. I dread the thought of spending two whole days inside a classroom, looking at PowerPoint presentations and listening to people talking about legal regulations. I've been working with salmon for twenty years! I don't have anything against letting Vidar take part, but do I *really* have to do this? "Yes," she says. She looks at me kindly but sternly. The look in her blue eyes leaves no room for doubt. "Precisely because you have worked with us for so long," she insists. "Your experience is crucial. It's really important." I look at her and I raise my eyebrows. "You see," she continues, "it's not only us teaching you. It's you teaching us as well. You'll be asked about practical routines. About how to do things differently, and better. You will talk about salmon as sentient beings. Because they probably are. It is just we don't know them yet. Or rather, we are all learning." Anna takes her knife from her belt and picks a sleepy anaesthetized salmon from the bucket by its tail. With a swift move, she cuts its throat. Soon she will take it to the laboratory room next to our kitchen and check its inner organs. Her specialty. I wouldn't have a clue, but she sure does, and sometimes she sends samples to a proper lab for further analysis.

What do I need to know to be a fish farmer? I need to know the difference between what I need to know and what I don't need to know. I need to know when to ask for advice. I need to be able to judge the many by examining the few, and vice versa. I need to know the limits of what anyone can know in this business, but sometimes, just sometimes, I need to press those limits, to push a bit further. Because, in the end, life is a journey and we are all in this together, salmon, people, sea lice, wrasse, and whatever else. Sometimes our lives intersect, like here, on the platform. And then, all we can do is do our best, and perhaps, now and then, find ways of making life a little better for everyone. Except, I guess, the sea lice.

This is what I think about as I steer the boat toward the shore. Reflecting, too, that a day's work is a day's work. That there are other things to do in life as well. Which is something else I need to know if I want to be a fish farmer.

Acknowledgments

We are grateful to the anonymized "Sjølaks AS" for their kind agreement to let us locate our study within the firm, and for its generous practical support, including lunches. We would like to thank all those who work for Sjølaks (they too are anonymized) for their warm welcome, their help, and their willingness to let us watch them at work and participate when possible. In many cases their kindness has vastly exceeded any reasonable expectation or need. The project, "Newcomers to the Farm," was funded by the Norwegian Research Council (project number 183352/S30), with additional research leave and financial support from Lancaster University, the Open University, and the University of Oslo, and we are grateful to all of these institutions.

Suggested Readings

John Law and Marianne E. Lien, "Slippery: Field Notes on Empirical Ontology." *Social Studies of Science* 4, no. 3 (2013): 363–78.

John Law and Marianne E. Lien, "Animal Architextures." In *Objects and Materials: A Routledge Companion,* ed. Penelope Harvey et al., 329–37. New York: Routledge, 2013.

John Law and Marianne E. Lien, "The Practices of Fishy Sentience." In *Transforming Politics and Life Matters,* ed. Kristin Asdal, Tone Druglitrø, and Steve Hinchliffe. Farnham, U.K.: Ashgate, 2015.

Marianne E. Lien, "Domestication 'Downunder': Atlantic Salmon Farming in Tasmania." In *Where the Wild Things Are Now: Domestication Reconsidered,* ed. Rebecca Cassidy and Molly Mullin, 205–29. Oxford, U.K.: Berg, 2007.

Marianne E. Lien, "Feeding Fish Efficiently: Mobilising Knowledge in Tasmanian Salmon Farming." *Social Anthropology* 15, no. 2 (2007): 169–85.

Marianne E. Lien, *Becoming Salmon: Aquaculture and the Domestication of a Fish.* Oakland: University of California Press, 2015.

Marianne E. Lien and John Law, "'Emergent Aliens': On Salmon, Nature, and Their Enactment." *Ethnos* 76, no. 1 (2011): 65–87.

3

How to Be a Magician in Paris

Graham M. Jones with Loïc Marquet

Magicians are in many ways bellwethers of the French economy. Like an ever-increasing number of workers in France and throughout the postindustrial Western world, they are freelancers, cultural producers surviving by their wits without the security of a stable job. Yet, like most French workers, they also benefit from an extensive social safety net that provides for healthcare, vacation time, retirement benefits and—very importantly, as we shall see—unemployment insurance. Not surprisingly, they often find themselves on the front lines with millions of other French workers in defending this singular welfare state against winds of austerity blowing from Brussels, seat of the European Union.

Almost every magician's repertoire features tricks involving money—plucking endless silver coins from out of thin air or transforming a spectator's small banknote into one of a much larger denomination (and, of course, back again). "You've got to tap into the audience's primal instincts," a magician once told me, whether that means fear, lust, or—in this case—greed. Onstage, magicians may well incarnate the capitalistic fantasy of commanding incalculable riches, but behind the scenes, their livelihoods irrevocably depend on clients' disposable income, making them particularly vulnerable to capitalism's vicissitudes. Like significant sectors of the French economy, they specialize in a luxury service—entertainment—though some of them describe it as a basic human right.

You are embarking on this perilous career in an auspicious setting. Paris is renowned as the birthplace of magic as we know it today. It was here that Jean-Eugène Robert-Houdin (1805–1871) pioneered some of the nineteenth century's most fantastical illusions—like the first human levitation—and secured a prestigious place for magic in respectable high society theaters, far from its roots in more disreputable settings like the fairground, the marketplace, or the gambling parlor. Perhaps his greatest trick was establishing himself as modern magic's sole progenitor, a feat accomplished in and through his momentous 1858 memoir, *A Conjuror's Confessions,* the book that inspired American Ehrich Weiss to take the stage name "Houdini" in homage.

Your first task is to acquire a cheap used copy of this book. It will constitute your breviary (as it has for generations aspiring magicians) as you go on what amounts to a pilgrimage of sorts. In Paris, you can visit the memorial marking the site of Robert-Houdin's theater, the Théâtre des Soirées Fantastiques, at 11 rue de Valois and admire some of his exquisitely preserved props at the Museum of Magic at 11 rue Saint-Paul. . . . But enough sightseeing! It's time to get to work.

For you, "work" may mean a stint in the world of Parisian cabarets, where you will rub elbows with exotic dancers and can-can girls, and a cavalcade of variety artists (perhaps jugglers, comedians, mimes, ventriloquists, or singers) who ply these storied—and sometimes sordid—stages. It may mean paid gigs in a restaurant or bar, or unpaid gigs, in which you work for tips from customers who might snub you before you can even open your mouth. You might specialize in private events like weddings, birthdays, or office parties—even in product promotion at trade fairs. You may end up working on *en plein air,* busking on a street corner for passersby, like some of Paris's best performers. "Work" may be all a little bit of all these things, and maybe it will add up to something like a living wage.

Insofar as becoming a magician in Paris goes, I have some knowledge to draw upon, but it isn't exactly *practical* knowledge. As an anthropologist, I conducted over eighteen months of participant observation research within the secretive world of entertainment magicians in contemporary Paris, analyzing the social, cultural, and economic conditions in which they work. Along the way, I became an apprentice magician, but came nowhere near turning pro.

To prepare this professional primer, then, I turned to someone who does have practical knowledge: Loïc Marquet, a professional magician, born and raised in Paris, with fifteen years of experience performing and teaching magic. Loïc and I devised a few easy steps to help you get started as a Parisian magician—although by the time you finish reading, you may change your mind about this career path.

Hone Your Craft . . . or Don't

"For starters, you'll need to know how to do a bit of magic," writes Loïc. "But don't worry, it isn't really necessary. It's much more important to know how to sell your skills than to actually have them. This may apply to other professions, but it is especially true for magicians because our craft depends on skills that are *secret*. Therefore, by definition, mere mortals must be totally ignorant and will fall for practically anything—meaning we're not that different from your local auto mechanic."

Loïc is being slightly facetious, of course—most magicians, like him, strive tirelessly to perfect their craft. Still, you're entering a profession based on a very peculiar relationship with technical skill. Other professions have "trade secrets," but magicians make a trade of secrecy itself. Their performances provoke fascination through the display of technical secrets. Spectators will hold you in awe when you find the card that they chose, marked with their signature, and shuffled back into the deck. And if you happen to find it rolled up inside a lemon, all the better. They'll pepper you with questions about tricks you perform and some you don't ("How do they saw the lady in half?" comes up a lot). Some may resent the feeling of inferiority that comes from both being fooled and denied access to knowing how it was done. You give spectators illusions (which they sometimes remember for a lifetime), but you keep the secrets.

As Loïc suggests, in many professional settings, making a convincing display of skill is an essential element of doing one's job. When professionals serve a public, they often face what the sociologist Erving Goffman famously called "the problem of dramatizing one's work" so that people appreciate what a good job you're doing. In magic this problem is particularly pronounced: After all, when a trick is performed well, the skills involved are inherently mystifying. This creates a potentially confounding situation if you gravitate to magic because you long to master the miniaturist virtuosity of imperceptible gestures and the ingenious mechanical gimmicks you'll secretly use. While you may care about perfecting demanding manipulations, non-magicians (referred to in the business as "laymen" or *profanes* in French) may be equally impressed with "automatic" tricks that require little or no skill.

Loïc, himself a technical virtuoso who prides himself on the skillful practice of his craft, once recounted that, when he performs in restaurants, especially receptive spectators sometimes invite him to sit down for a drink. With their rapt attention, he likes to announce that he will perform his most difficult card trick, which is normally reserved only for other magicians. He then proceeds to dazzle them with an automatic trick that an eight-year-old could learn in minutes from any crummy magic book. There is an element of perverse humor in this ploy, but it beautifully illustrates Loïc's message that the level of skill tricks require often pales in comparison to the importance of what magicians call *presentation*: the theatrical embellishment necessary to "sell" a trick. In this sense, telling your audience that a rudimentary trick is some piece of rarified professional arcana can blind them to its almost laughable technical simplicity.

As a magician, you'll come to have an unusual relationship with laymen. To create an illusion, you must have an audience. You cannot fool yourself: Your illusions need other minds to inhabit. Yet when you practice a trick for hours on end, day after day, you can become so fully engrossed in the *method* that you entirely forget about the *effect* it is intended to create. Seeing the impact of that effect reflected in a spectator's astonished gaze can reawaken you to the sense of wonder you may have once felt toward magic but which you can now only experience vicariously.

Although laymen experience wonder and reflect it back to you, they aren't cognoscenti. They don't understand the subtle technical nuances that you are passionate about, and their ability to discern aesthetic qualities you care about may be limited. To entertain them, you may have to compromise your high artistic standards. Having a better sense of the conditions you'll be working in will help explain why this might be so.

Many people immediately associate the word *magician* with glittery boxes, sequined assistants, and man-eating felines. You can certainly go that route, but it's an uncommon career trajectory. Most magicians today specialize in "close-up" magic—sleight-of-hand effects performed with small paraphernalia (cards, coins, banknotes) in situations where the magician interacts directly with a small number of spectators. Typically, this takes the form of "tablehopping" or "strolling" magic, in which the magician moves from table to table in a restaurant or mingles among people at a bar or cocktail reception.

These conditions are intrinsically unfavorable for your art: People generally aren't expecting to see a magician performing, and you may be interrupting them while they're in the middle of a private conversation (or worse, a nasty break-up). Moreover, you may not have a surface to put things down on or a comfortable place to stand, the lighting may be poor, and the background noise can be overpowering. For restaurant work, Loïc recommends mastering a variety of ancillary skills. "Being a contortionist helps. When you show up to a gig, you often find that your 'dressing room' is literally a cramped broom closet. Training in hospitality services also helps: the only thing people will really want from you when you show up at their table isn't performing a card trick, but rather opening their bottle of wine or refilling their breadbasket."

To cover a full room, you have to work fast, spending only several minutes with each group, and moving quickly among them. As you can imagine, these conditions will severely restrict your repertoire: You need effects that are portable, high-impact, and visual and that "reset" immediately. And you only need a few of them. A close-up routine may have three or four effects, and you can base an entire career on that—another reason why Loïc says you really only need to know "a bit" of magic. Still, some magicians incorporate an unusual array of effects into their close-up repertoires: Guilhem Julia actually produces live goldfish from his fingertips while table-hopping, plopping them into a glass of water. (He tells me that only once did an overly intoxicated spectator gulp down the glass, fish and all.)

In Loïc's estimation, the art of conversation is at least as important as the art of magic: "Because you'll have to interact with people from all kinds of backgrounds, you need to have a good storehouse of conversational topics, a charming personality, and the ability to engage in friendly banter with virtually anyone. I have no idea where you can learn all this. There must be some kind of book out there. But you'll have to know this if you ever want the chance to partake in the tasty hors-d'oeuvres normally reserved for guests."

A big part of presentation is your persona. Robert-Houdin pioneered the persona of the "modern magician" as a sophisticated man-about-town. He dressed stylishly in formal attire, instead of wearing an esoteric robe and pointy hat. He also spoke with refinement, rather than telling crass jokes at spectators' expense like his fairground counterparts. Many magicians emulate this ideal in one form or another—though esoteric robes are still out there, and many still make off-color jokes. While you want to *fit in* with your spectators, you also want to *stand out*: a magician is fundamentally a trickster figure. Tricksters in many cultures tend to be liminal beings, with uncontrollable appetites and a love of transgressive mischief. This helps explain some magicians' incurable penchant for outlandish outfits and outré sexual remarks.

"Appropriate attire is necessary to either complement your personality or to compensate for your total lack thereof," writes Loïc. "For close-up, a dark suit often suffices. The dark background will provide optimal visibility for your effects. Black is best, except people mistake you for a waiter. Some solve this problem with a neon tie, others a bolo tie (like Grandpa in *The Simpsons*). If you work in southern France, I recommend leaving the top three or four buttons of your shirt open to reveal a maximum of chest hair. Whatever you wear, it needs to be clean, though working in a restaurant, it won't stay clean for long."

These recommendations of course apply particularly to men. In the image of Robert-Houdin, magic in France (and elsewhere in the Western world) remains a profession dominated overwhelmingly by white men. Women and people of color may face additional difficulties establishing rapport, particularly given that magic involves a potential threat to spectators' intelligence. Marie-Odile Langloÿs, one of the few successful female close-up magicians in France, told me that her elegant evening gowns often led to sexually charged interactions, until she also began to wear a

Figure 3.1 Professional Parisian magician and coauthor Loïc Marquet performs an impromptu card trick for a *profane* at an after-hours gathering of fellow magicos. Photograph by Graham M. Jones

stereotypical magician's top hat to clarify her role as an entertainer. Filaos, an Afro-Antillean magician, told me that he begins his performances with jokes about "African voodoo" to ease potential racial tensions with white audiences.

Magic tricks can be pretty awesome, and wielding secrets can confer an exhilarating sense of power. You may even begin to feel like you're a demigod condescending to mingle among "mere mortals," as Loïc cheekily put it. Resist the temptation. Don't forget that you're *tricking* people, and this can be threatening on a variety of levels. This is particularly true in France, where magicians believe the public to be "too Cartesian" (that is, hyperrational) to enjoy being fooled, and where magic itself is widely viewed as kitschy (*ringard*) and culturally trivial kids' stuff in respect to the serious domain of fine arts. To make your performances as entertaining as possible for audiences like this, a healthy dose of self-deprecation always helps.

That being said, there are also factors that give magic—particularly close-up magic—distinctive cultural appeal. In an era dominated by mass media and computer-generated special effects, the kinds of feats you perform with your two hands and familiar everyday objects can take on the same kind of allure that artisanal crafts now enjoy in the context of mass-market capitalism. What's more, in an age when people in a restaurant are as likely to be surfing the internet as talking to each other, you provide exciting face-to-face contact and give them a memorable experience to discuss among themselves. Insofar as this is *meaningful* work, the importance of this embodied interaction can't be underestimated.

Make Frenemies

It would be difficult to get very far in this line of work without cultivating relationships with other magicians. Although magicians typically work alone, having an active network of colleagues is crucial. Other magicians will provide you with vital technical knowledge and artistic input. They will help you find work. They may become your primary social outlet. At the same time, they will also be your competition for prestige and for work. The magic world is full of strong personalities vying for attention—and harboring bitter animosities toward rivals.

You can meet magicians online, through the Francophone magicians' forum VirtualMagie.com. You can also begin learning from the masters by joining one or more of Paris's half-dozen magic clubs. The largest of these is the local branch of the Fédération Française des Artistes Prestidigitateurs (The French Federation of Prestidigitatory Artists, FFAP). This club meets several times a month, allowing members an opportunity to perform for each other and talk about their craft. To become a member, you must pass an exam before a panel of expert judges in which you perform your own magic act and answer questions about magic history and theory. The FFAP has a two-year introductory course for novices. Other clubs have no entrance requirements at all, allowing even beginners to join.

When I became a member of the FFAP in 2005, one magician friend joked, "Congratulations. You're now officially an amateur magician." Among professionals, magic clubs are regarded as primarily venues for amateurs, but the reality is more complex. While it's true that professional magicians generally don't frequent clubs as much as amateurs, they almost always begin their careers as amateurs. Moreover, amateurs are among professionals' most loyal fans—and clients. Clubs often pay professional magicians to give lectures, with the added incentive of selling whatever trademark props, gimmicks, or instructional materials the lecturer may have to offer.

From a strictly demographic standpoint, magic is largely a hobby. There are scores of amateurs for every professional. It is also a kind of technical subculture, comparable to other arenas of "geek" expertise from ham radio to computer programming. Participants are drawn together by a shared interest in technical challenges, and they rank each other according to various, sometimes contested, measures of technical proficiency. (Loïc once told me that he can tell how good other magicians are before they even do a trick by the way they take their cards out of the box.) Members of a magic club can spend hours on end arguing about the relative merits or historical origins of variants on a particular technique. This is an atmosphere that rewards virtuosity and promotes the display of technical prowess. It is also the setting in which most serious magicians refine their craft.

You don't have to be a professional magician to be an expert on magic—far from it. According to stereotypes within the magic subculture, amateurs freely indulge in the limitless pursuit of gratuitous technical complexity while professionals, facing the practical dilemmas of, say, tablehopping in a hectic restaurant, choose tricks based on entirely different criteria, opting for technically simple solutions wherever possible. Among themselves, magicians perform what they call "magic for magicians," which is often more about showcasing technical novelty rather than producing effects that will impress laymen. Some amateurs are among its most innovative exponents.

It is sometimes vexing for magicians that their own standards of excellence are so different from their audience's. They resent the seemingly unmerited successes of other professionals—particularly those who achieve stardom on television without having either paid their dues or achieved the level of skill of a proficient journeyman magician. "If you're a celebrity," complains Loïc, "you don't have to do much other than just being on TV. Being on TV in the company of other celebrities is its own consecration."

All relationships among magicians are based on reciprocity and a shared moral code. Other magicians will reveal secrets to you, but with an expectation that you will immediately do the same, or at least share a secret sometime down the road. To maintain these collegial relationships, you need to be able to offer secrets in exchange. In this sense, the more you give, the more you receive. But the impulse to give is offset by the desire to keep:

By withholding knowledge, you make that knowledge more exclusive—and everyone wants to possess original, distinctive material.

Magicians value technical innovations that few others possess, and they hold technical innovators in high esteem. When individual magicians publish a new secret in a magic magazine or book, they can be said to "own" it, because it will forever circulate with their name attached to it. When they discreetly reveal unpublished secrets in private settings, these secrets are more valuable because of their exclusivity, but they are also more fragile as a form of intellectual property. Without a published provenance, they could be stolen or lapse into unattributed circulation. If someone authorizes you to use and circulate an unpublished secret, you must always mention the innovator's name. You should never make unauthorized use of the unpublished inventions of others. Violation of these more or less tacit protocols can destroy friendships and spoil your reputation among magicians forever.

Maintaining a good reputation will help you participate in the reciprocal exchange of trade secrets *and* get access to work. Many employment opportunities pass through professional networks. For instance, if you have multiple job offers on the same day (as often happens during the winter holidays or the summer wedding season), you might give one to a colleague. If a colleague has a job that requires multiple performers (such as tablehopping at a large wedding reception), she might call you. Again, reciprocity is key. If someone gets you a gig, it is with the expectation that you'll eventually return the favor. Loïc jokes that constituting a professional network is difficult for magicians "since they are so often antisocial people who get into magic precisely because they don't have any other way to make friends." Because magicians are also professional rivals, egoism may limit generosity: information about lucrative engagements and regular clients is jealously guarded.

To become a member of the magic world, you have to master both a technical activity and a way of talking about it. For starters, professional magicians in France refer to each other not as *magiciens* but as *magicos*. The *-os* ending is a kind of diminutive. In the mouth of an outsider, calling someone a "magicos" would derogatively connote the lowly status of a hack—the unspecified drudge picked haphazardly from the phone book for a children's birthday party. Among insiders, it is a term of endearment. "Using it means you're part of the tribe," Loïc once told me. Other verbal mannerisms also reflect this sense of camaraderie. While in most parts of French society you should address people you don't know or people with higher social status using the formal pronoun *vous,* magicos almost always address each other with the familiar *tu* to mark trade solidarity.

Because magicos primarily work alone, swapping stories with each other about experiences on the job is a favorite social activity. These stories fit into familiar patterns, in which the teller is either a victim of the stupidity of clients or spectators (like the drunk who swallowed Guilhem's fish) or a hero displaying particular virtuosity or cunning in the course of performance (like Loïc's story about presenting a simple automatic trick as advanced magicians-only magic). In addition to their sheer entertainment value, these stories also inevitably reflect the moral universe that you'll inhabit as a professional magician, the foibles of the various categories of people you have to deal with, and the personal attributes that magicians themselves value.

Get on the Dole

One of the most surprising things you'll discover about being a magician in France is that you are eligible for state subsidies. Perhaps more than any other Western nation, France makes culture an affair of the state, with decidedly mixed consequences. On the one hand, the government, viewing cultural industries as a key to national vitality, makes itself a powerful patron of cultural institutions and culture-makers. On the other hand, its patronage creates expectations that are hard to meet and serves to establish implicit standards for what counts as *legitimate* culture.

For magicians, the most important form of patronage comes from a program called Intermittence du Spectacle. Doing magic is freelance work: You'll probably never have stable employment, and you'll always need to be hustling for gigs. Through Intermittence, as it is called, the French state provides an indirect subsidy to people in the performing arts by guaranteeing a regular minimum salary, effectively offering unemployment insurance for the days between gigs.

"Just imagine," Loïc muses,

> You set aside money for unemployment when you work, and when you're not working, the unemployment office pays for your days kicking back. Sounds like the realm of fairy tales, right? Well it's not. It's Europe.
>
> It seems nice, but it gets complicated quick. Very complicated. So complicated, in fact, that in the unemployment office, you'll go out of your way to

find the one caseworker who knows something about the system. And there might not be anyone in your local office. Even when you do find knowledgeable people, they might not know the rules well enough to help you out.

To qualify for this program, you have to work 43 times in 319 days. That's 507 hours of work, since each gig is considered the equivalent of 12 hours. Unless of course you work five consecutive days, in which case each gig counts as eight hours. For your 319 days of work, you'll receive a daily benefit for 243 days. The benefit is a function of the average amount you earn for each gig (which we call a *cachet*), and will fall somewhere in the range of 30 to 130 Euros. To get the maximum, you'd need to be a worldwide star, in which case you probably don't need the money anyway . . . but who's counting?

On the days you work, you won't get Intermittence benefits. But even then, there's a catch. . . . When you've got a gig, it doesn't count as a day of work, but roughly 1.4 days. So, if in a month of 30 days you actually have five gigs, the unemployment office counts those five gigs as seven days of work, and gives you 23 days of benefits. Once you qualify for benefits, you'll have 319 days to re-qualify, by accumulating 43 more cachets.

You can probably begin to imagine that a situation in which you've got multiple employers, clueless bureaucrats, and complicated paperwork—to which you add contractual errors, uncompromising deadlines, and clerical delays—results in a giant mess.

A giant mess indeed, but one that is vital to the livelihood of most professional magicians. As in other performing arts, qualifying for Intermittence benefits has now become for magicians the de facto credential of professionalization. It signals that you have moved from the status of amateur to professional. Many established and aspiring professionals alike think of work less as a series of performances and more like a "scramble for cachets." (In French, a "cachet" is both the sum an artist earns for a performance and an official stamp of the sort applied to government paperwork.)

To attain the objective of 43 cachets in 319 days, there are plenty of clever tricks you can use. For instance, you can persuade an employer to pay you in two installments for one performance, creating the illusion of two cachets. The drawback of course is that this lowers your average income, reducing your overall benefit. We're not revealing anything particularly secret by telling you this: The intense scrutiny Intermittence received during a recent period of reform led to the embarrassing public disclosure of many similar forms of subterfuge.

In addition to its practical advantages, Intermittence provides a framework for thinking about stereotypically "popular" genres in connection with forms of "high" culture. After all, it accords the same professional status to magicians as it does to ballet dancers or classical musicians: All of these performers characterize themselves as "Intermittents." In this sense, it provides magicos a measure of cultural distinction as makers of "art" and a modicum of insulation from the punishing marketplace of "entertainment."

Intermittence has the potential to confer the cultural luster of the munificent state, encouraging the French to see magic as an art. Magicians interpret the symbolism of the benefits accordingly. The program originated as a form of employment insurance to protect workers in industries that the French government viewed as particularly precarious (admittedly, this is a difficult argument to maintain today, given the increasing precariousness in all sectors of the neoliberal economy). Magicians, however, tend to view the benefits in terms of what they signify about the art-like nature of their work. Thus Loïc writes that the government created Intermittence "based on the belief that professional artists need time to write, rehearse, and refine a show that they only have an opportunity to perform periodically." It's all a matter of perspective.

In recent years, there has been a highly publicized "crisis" of Intermittence. Fiscal conservatives have argued that these "unofficial" cultural subsidies have created huge deficits in the state unemployment budget. The left has contested these figures and also argued that supporting the living arts is an intrinsic public good and national duty. Beneficiaries of Intermittence have staged high-profile strikes and protests. This crisis puts performers in a different kind of spotlight: French audiences may ask— themselves and you—whether the "tricks" you do merit state sponsorship, interpreting your cultural legitimacy against the backdrop of an ongoing national dialogue about the public value of cultural industries.

"In spite of the taxes you pay every time you perform (roughly 45% of what you charge your client), all the other taxpayers in France (your spectator pool) view you as a parasite," Loïc cautions. "They don't understand that for the fleeting moment of pleasure you try to offer them, you had to practice in monk-like solitude for hours a day, for years on end, without pay."

Conclusion

Being a magician has a singular mystique. You embody mystery, personify cunning, and incarnate illusion. At the tips of your dexterous fingers, reality and fantasy collide, as a coin or a card appears, transforms, and then vanishes from sight. You inspire awe, challenging spectators' easy assurances about the certainties of the everyday world. Your connection to secret knowledge confers a special aura of power. Your role as a trickster gives you license to deceive others and flout social conventions of dress and speech. The figure of the modern magician, while sanitized by Robert-Houdin, maintains subtle symbolic associations with occult and criminal activity, imbuing your every move with a titillating frisson of danger.

Yet the day-to-day reality of being a magician in Paris is mundane and unglamorous. Yes, you get to make a living using dexterity and wit to create wonderful illusions and playfully interact with people in an unconventional manner. You can even get public assistance to make this precarious career choice viable. But the social pressures of an insular subculture divided by rivalries and squabbles can be stifling. And it's very difficult to escape the nagging feeling common in so many professions that, beyond the bounds of that subculture, your work is poorly understood and fundamentally undervalued.

Suggested Readings

For a complete account of the French magic scene, see:
Graham M. Jones, *Trade of the Tricks: Inside the Magician's Craft*. Berkeley: University of California Press, 2011.

For further practical advice about becoming a professional close-up magician:
David Stone, *Close Up: The Real Secrets of Magic*. Graham Jones, translator. Paris: Pamadana Editions, 2008.

For classic treatments of relationships between professionals and their publics, see:
Erving Goffman, *The Presentation of Self in Everyday Life*. New York: Anchor, 1959.

With particular reference to performing artists, see:
Howard S. Becker, *Outsiders: Studies in the Sociology of Deviance*. New York: Free Press, 1966.

For a definitive statement on the politics of culture in modern France, see:
Pierre Bourdieu, *Distinction: A Social Critique of the Judgement of Taste*. Cambridge, MA: Harvard University Press, 1984.

To learn more about Intermittence du spectacle and the crisis of reform, see:
Jérémy Sinigaglia, "The Mobilization of Intermittents in the Entertainment Sector in France." *French Politics* 7 (2009): 294–315.

Being a Village Court Magistrate in Papua New Guinea

Melissa Demian

The fictional magistrate speaking in this chapter is imagined to be from lowland Papua New Guinea. The eulogy he gives is in keeping with the style of funeral speeches on the Papuan (southern) coast, where presenting actual details of a deceased person's life would be the height of disrespect, but it is considered entirely appropriate to use a recent death as an opportunity for moral instruction.

Papua New Guinea is a country of some eight hundred distinct languages. The greatest cultural divide in the country is between lowlanders from the coasts and highlanders from the mountainous interior. Papua New Guinea is made up of two former colonies, one British and one German, both governed by Australia under slightly different legal regimes from the end of World War I until the country's independence in 1975. Port Moresby is the national capital. At the time of writing, one Papua New Guinea kina equaled 0.37 U.S. dollars.

All of you listen now; I am going to talk about our magistrate so that we remember him properly. Listen, his widow and his children are crying in

the house there. But we people must stay awake and remember him properly. God saw who killed him, and if we are virtuous, we will find those
people too and bring them to court. But for tonight, you must listen and
I will talk. Especially all of you who have come here from Australia—I
know you are here to give respect to your uncle and cry for him, but you
must also listen to me. You have not lived in the village for a long time;
your children have never lived here at all! And I think perhaps you have
forgotten what our lives are like here.

All of you people, you look at us magistrates, you see the badge and you
think we have a good job, a big job. I am telling you, it is a big job truly,
and it is very heavy with us. When I became magistrate many years ago,
I felt how heavy it was. I went to Port Moresby for my training. I got the
badge and the uniform—and that uniform is gone now, it was spoiled by
some people who were jealous. They didn't give me a new uniform. I am
paid only 288 kina per year. What can I buy with that, some rice, some
tinned fish? I cannot even cover my children's school fees with 288 kina.
And sometimes the government doesn't even pay it on time: I might wait
for months to receive the allowance. But it's enough, I know the work is
important so all right, I do it. It's the law, the government's law. I have had

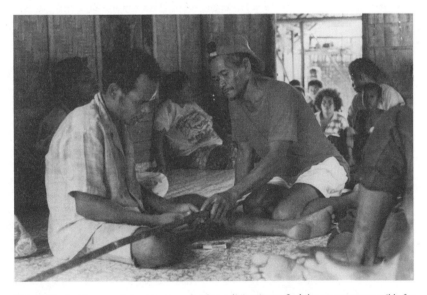

Figure 4.1 A village court magistrate conducting a divination to find the sorcerer responsible for a woman's death, 1997. Photograph by Melissa Demian.

no other training, they just give us the handbook and say enough, you are a magistrate now.

Yes, people will be jealous. They think we magistrates just give out fines so we can buy tobacco and beer; I know there is this kind of talk, don't deny it. People were jealous, and that is why our friend died. They were jealous or they were angry. And we have no protection against this kind of jealousy, only our own resourcefulness. If we behave with integrity and people respect us, all right, we might be lucky, and we will live our lives in peace. But watch out! If I make someone really angry, if he doesn't like the decision he gets in court, then there may be trouble and complications, yes. Maybe he will talk to his relatives. Maybe he will pay someone to make some bad medicine for him. And then I have to worry about my own children, my wife, my brothers and sisters. Myself I don't worry about, but I have to think of all my relatives. If someone is jealous or angry then I have no protection, and neither do they.

Because people are not always respectful like we are, sitting down here tonight. All of you, you know why we have the courts. Suppose you have some problem with your in-laws. Most of the time you can sit down with them, talk to each other, come to an agreement, and then you're of one mind, and that's good. That is our proper way of living, as Christian people. If it's a serious problem then maybe you can get the pastor here to help you, or the local government councilor. They can help you straighten out your problem, and then it's finished and your lives are good again.

But we magistrates have to do the work when people can't straighten out their own problems. The government decided this back in 1975. In 1975, at independence, they said: We will have these courts for all the grassroots people in Papua New Guinea, all the people in the villages. They made the handbook and the uniform then, and they taught us magistrates how to run the court.

Now, I have heard about those courts up in the Highlands. Those magistrates there, they think they are judges like in Port Moresby. They make everyone bow, they say prayers to the flag, things like that. What rubbish! We are not judges, we can't send you to Bomana jail. All right, we in the court here can make an imprisonment order, but if the police run out of fuel, they'll say forget it, we're not coming, and then nobody goes to jail, not even in the provincial lock-up.

You know how our courts are. When there are enough cases, enough problems, we will come together and have a court. Three magistrates will come together, otherwise it's not enough, we can't have a court. We will just sit down under this casuarina tree here, like we are doing tonight. The pastor will help us to pray together, so that our feelings are not too angry. And the peace officer will call up the cases. And listen, at a court we see the same kinds of cases again and again. Some woman has committed adultery against her husband. Some man has let his pigs spoil somebody else's garden. There is a soccer game, and after the game there is a fight and someone's house gets spoiled. And all the debts! "You bought on credit at my trade store for a year and now you have to pay me." Or, "I gave you a pig for so-and-so's funeral feast three years ago, and you never gave me any pig back, so now you have to give me a pig *and* compensation." We magistrates get very tired of this. These are problems you can sort out for yourselves, but you love to bring them to the court, so all right, we try to help.

I remember the time when you could borrow a pig from your brother-in-law for ten years, twenty years, and you never heard about it. Finally you would pay that pig back. But these days! We are greedy people. One year, two years, and it's "Pay that pig back or I will take you to court." You lot from Australia, that's how it is there, yes? I know white people live like this. "You have to pay me back right away or I will take you to court, I will have the police come and arrest you." They are the people who eat money, they have to work for money all the time. We didn't used to be like that, no, you could leave a debt to your in-law standing for years. Now we are becoming like white people, and all we think about is money too. Money is our new magic. Show your friend a fifty-kina note and he will do anything you ask him to, even wrong things.

But this is all right, this is why we have courts and magistrates. This is why our friend did his job, because people can't solve these problems for themselves—they're too angry, or too greedy, their thinking is not straight. And if you have problems, you don't ask the government to help you. Forget about them. We older people, we remember the time of the Australians. That was a good time. The patrol officers were strong men. If you behaved badly, starting fights or using bad language or those sorts of things, you'd get hard labor, maybe you would build a road. If you stole something or committed adultery, you'd go to jail. If you killed someone, they would hang you! Yes, truly! There was none of this bighead behavior like we see nowadays. But then the Australians went away, the patrol officers who came from the government, that finished. Yes, remember Mr. B.? He was our last patrol officer, when, 1962, 1963, I don't remember.

The Australians went away for good, and there was independence, and then the new PNG government started the village courts. They chose the first magistrates. But we are not patrol officers, we don't have any great power. I can order fines, yes, and I can order compensation. I can give an imprisonment order, or a community service order, but the police don't care. If the police don't feel like it, they won't come, and people who do wrong things won't go to jail, and they won't do community service. We are not patrol officers, and we are not judges. I will tell you the reason why. If you go to the court in Port Moresby, that judge is somebody you have never seen before. He will probably speak a completely different language from our language! He could come from Gulf Province, or New Ireland, or Simbu: anywhere. But you know they don't use real language in the National Court, only English. And that judge only thinks about the law. He doesn't live in the same place as you, he doesn't go to church with you, his children don't go to school with your children, no, they go to school in Australia. So he comes in, and you stand up, you bow, you sit down. There are lawyers. The lawyers speak for you, not like in our village courts where we can all speak. The lawyers speak for you and maybe you get to talk a little bit, but you won't want to talk, no, because you are just a person from the village and you'll be ashamed. Maybe you're not wearing shoes. Maybe you don't speak English very well. Maybe you don't understand properly what is going on because you didn't go to school. Never mind, you're there in the court and the judge is just thinking about the law. He makes his decision and that's it, it's finished. Somebody has won and somebody has lost, like a soccer game. If you are the one who lost? My friends, then you are sorry for sure! You gave all your money to those lawyers, and you walk out of that courtroom with nothing. And the judge goes home, he doesn't care, he goes to the country club and drinks beer. You will never see him again.

In our village court it is different. All of you know me, you know our good friend who died, you know the magistrate up at E_____ and the other one across the river there at P_____. We are the same people, we speak the same language, we go to the same churches. If I make a bad decision, can I just go back to my house and forget about it? Nonsense! I will see all of you every day. You will not let me forget about it. Maybe you'll bring the same case next year to try to get a different decision. Yes, this happens, you know it. Or else, if I made a decision you like but your neighbor doesn't like it, they will bring another case. When you are a magistrate, you know that you carry the weight of keeping everyone's feelings good. Because we all live here together, one village, all of us together. I can't do like the judge in Moresby, where one person gets everything and another person gets nothing. No, it's not good enough. Suppose somebody's pig spoils your garden. You come to the court and you say, "My neighbor's pig wrecked my garden!" and that person over there says, "It wasn't my pig, it was a wild pig, you're lying." And everyone will have something to say about it. We magistrates, we must just be patient and listen while everyone talks. Some people will talk about how we should all fence our pigs so they don't go around eating people's gardens. Some people will talk about how it's your own fault if pigs got in, because you didn't make the garden fence properly. Some people will say that pigs got into your garden because you made some mistake, you didn't take care of your grandparents' graves, and there are ghosts angry at you. Some people will talk about how you shouldn't have a garden in that part of the forest anyway, because it's their land. Then you will talk about how long ago, some of your ancestors were given that land by those other people's ancestors, and you will tell the story of how you got that land. All right, we magistrates will listen to all this talk. We people, we all really like to talk! But when it's finished, finally the court can say, "Look here, your friend's garden got spoiled, and you say your pig didn't do it, but you must make his feelings better. Give him a chicken and some garden food and some money, fifty kina maybe." Then in church we can have a basket-to-basket and collect more garden food so the family isn't hungry. And maybe the ladies will bring sweet potato runners, taro crowns, and banana suckers so that a new garden can be planted. It's all right. We hear problems like this all the time, but it's all right, because our work is to make sure that nobody is so angry that really bad things happen.

And we do this outside of the court too. If you can't get three magistrates together you can't even have a court, then we can only mediate, try to get people to talk to each other and solve their problem on their own. Three magistrates can be difficult—you have to provide food, transportation, and maybe some of those magistrates are not able to come—they have a funeral like us here tonight, or they have gone to visit relatives in town. Getting three magistrates for a full court can be a lot of work, that's why it takes so long, people wait and wait to get the food and money together, and when we finally have the court, oh please! We will go for a day, two days. We won't sleep, we'll just keep going. I told you already, we people like to talk. People will bring up problems from before, their grandparents' problems. We have to hear them all, think about all those old problems when we come up with a solution. And I warn you, if you bring up old problems, we will find old solutions. If you tell me you got that land because people from that lineage stole a woman from your lineage back in the grandparents' time, and they want that land back, all right, maybe a woman has to go back to your lineage, or a child. Maybe they can give you a child to raise. People get upset about those kinds of resolutions these days, but they are from the old time, the time of custom. If you don't want us to suggest those kinds of remedies, then don't bring us your old disputes.

And if you want to have a land dispute, you're making a mistake if you bring it to the village court, we can't even hear those. Everyone knows this—maybe you people living in Australia don't, maybe you forgot, but that's the way, you can't take just any kind of dispute to any court you like. No. You want to fight over land, you have to go to the land mediators for your solution. But listen, people bring land disputes to us anyway. They say, "I am having a problem with someone putting medicine on my garden so everything is dying" or "I am having a problem with my in-laws who haven't paid any bride price," but really they are fighting over land. Yes, I know this. I have seen it happen many times. And if we make someone unhappy with our decision, there could be more trouble later.

If the government gave us real power, we could stop these silly problems. I know they are trying some new things in Port Moresby. I hear we will have new uniforms soon, and badges, so that people see we are doing the government's work. I hear there are magistrates in Port Moresby who are women! This is a good thing, but you know, the Highlanders won't do it. They don't respect their women the way we do. But you look at the towns, and there are women teaching in the schools, working for the government. There are women magistrates in the District Court—yes, I have seen it, with my own eyes. We could try this here in our village courts, but you won't see any women magistrates in the Highlands. Now, all you ladies, don't laugh! As long as you are knowledgeable, and have integrity, and people listen to you, you can do this work. You just have to understand the law. I am an old man, one fine day I will die too and you will need a new magistrate. It could be a man or a woman. Yes, truly.

We could try having women as magistrates, but it won't make any difference if people don't understand how serious this work is. We have the court under a tree, on the beach, at a magistrate's house, and people get stupid ideas about what we are doing. The government should build us a proper courthouse, where the local government council meets. They should give us proper police, not these rubbish men who use up all their fuel on their kinsmen and friends. And when someone does something really bad, we need to have the power to make them feel it. Send them to jail. Make them do hard labor, like in the time of the Australians. Then you wouldn't see all these bighead young men going around for nothing, getting drunk, getting high, smashing up people's houses, stealing things and raping women.

But the government doesn't care, no. You see these big politicians come around during an election and they say the same thing: "Give me your vote and I will give you roads, schools, aid posts, and health centers. I will build a guest house so tourists will come. I will bring development here." They say all these sweet words, like sugar. They give you a T-shirt and they go away, and you say, "All right, I will vote for that one." And you vote and what happens? Nothing! Forget it! That politician is going to sit in Parliament and do nothing. He is going to go around Port Moresby in his big truck and wear his smart clothes and have lots of wives. I am not lying to you: I have been to Moresby and I have heard about this. Those Members of Parliament, they have eight, ten wives. They have to pay bride price for all those wives, and it's not like our village bride price, just a few pigs and some garden food, no, they have to pay ten thousand kina, twenty thousand. So when we grassroots people go to them and ask for a road or a guest house, they say, "Oh, sorry my friend, there is no money left." There is no money left because they spent it all!

But we magistrates, we are doing the real work of the government. The government doesn't see us, but we do the work of the government's law. Those Members should come here and see us. They should see how our friend died because he was trying to straighten out the problems here in the village, and someone got angry at him for it. People are angry because they are jealous. They see someone else has something good, a trade store, a truck, a dinghy. They see someone else eating rice, tinned fish, bully beef, noodles. They see someone else's child go to high school, go to university, find work in town. They think, "I should have those things instead of staying here in the village, working in my garden," and that's what causes problems. If we had development, we wouldn't have these problems because everyone would have those things, and nobody would be jealous. When people are jealous, their minds start thinking about doing bad work, sinful work.

Sometimes it's just talk. Suppose it's a lady who says, "My husband keeps leaving me for this other woman, I think she practices bad ways, I think she's putting some medicine in his food." Well, we can get her husband and the other woman up in front of the court and ask them to explain what's going on. And I tell you, it's almost never about the husband going with the woman, no, not really. That would be bad enough, because adultery is a sin. But when we talk to them we find out it's about land, or a debt, or some fight between their families many years ago. And then we have to say to the woman who brought the case, "Look, you can't go around talking like this. This is very dangerous talk. You know witchcraft is against the law? It's against God's law and the government's law. Do you know anyone who truly does those things? You saw her do it with your own eyes, did you? You saw what she put in his food or his tea? Think, what kind of person behaves like that?" And even accusing someone of witchcraft can get you in very big trouble! My friends, it's right there in the magistrates' handbook. You can get fined for talking like that. If you have a problem with this other lady, say what the true problem is. If she's really been going with your husband, then all right, we'll fine her and your husband must pay compensation to your brothers. If he really wants to do it right, then he should kill a pig for you, or at least a chicken, and say sorry properly. But if he hasn't been going with that other lady, and you're angry at her for some other reason, then you have to say the true reason so that we can straighten things out. Look, cases of that kind, nobody likes them, it makes everyone's hearts bad, but we can find the solution. Sometimes it's enough for one person to make another person cry, then we can all shake hands, pray, and go home. It's finished.

And then other times, it is not just talk. You remember that one we had after Christmas. You visitors, you don't know about this, this is what our lives are like sometimes, and you need to know. You think the witches and sorcerers can't find you in Australia, but they can! And if they can't find you, all right, they'll get one of your relatives here in PNG. I'm telling you, that court, it went on for two days. Everyone was afraid, everyone was angry. But we got the old man up there at S_____ to confess to his bad ways. We knew why the wife of Mr. R. died, because of that problem between her family and the other family. It was terrible, yes, but think about what would have happened if we hadn't forced him to confess and pay compensation. Somebody might get hurt, some more people could die, and you know it was hard enough for us to keep that lady's brothers from killing him on the spot. My friends, we must put a stop to this sorcery rubbish now. It's no good, it belongs to the time before, to those old-time people. Maybe those bush people up there in the mountains are still doing it, who knows, but when we Christian people practice sorcery, please, what is the matter with us! If you have a disagreement with someone, you can talk to them about it, or give them some money or a pig to make their feelings better. If you can't solve the problem then all right, you bring them to court and we magistrates will find out what to do. But if you go to a sorcerer, or those other bad ways, then your problems will go on for five years, ten years, twenty years. All right, so the sorcerer kills your enemy, and you think, "My problem is finished." It is not finished. Because then someone from their side will get a sorcerer to kill your spouse or your children or your brother or sister. And it will go on like that. The sorcerer will be brought to court, and he'll tell us who hired him. That sorcerer is doing terrible things, yes, but who told you to go hire him in the first place? It is our own bad hearts causing these problems! You make things terribly complicated, and then you come to the village court and you say, "Magistrate, my neighbor hired a sorcerer, my sister-in-law is a witch, my husband used love magic on me and now he's going around with other women, I don't want to be married to him any more. . . ." Forget about all that! This sorcery and witchcraft is with us because our hearts turn away from God and we don't pay any mind to the proper way of living.

We are not all proper Christians, you see. Certainly you see everyone go into church on the Sabbath. But not all of us are Christians in our hearts. Everyone knows this. There are plenty of backsliders. And if someone is properly angry, they will find some medicine or some other sinful ways to make you sick or kill you. Yes, that is why our friend died! I am not afraid to say it! Those bloody witches, those bloody sorcerers, they are spoiling this whole place! Forgive me, my language is bad, but I know these people are listening, they killed our friend, maybe they are even here with us tonight, and we will find them out. If they hear me, that's fine. I am not afraid.

But tonight it is our friend who is gone, and we must think about him, all the good things he did for us. He was magistrate here for how long? Twenty years, thirty years? He did all the hard work for this place for all that time. He kept this place peaceful. If there were small problems, no worries, he would listen to those small problems and mediate, find the straight way for us to solve those problems. If there were big problems, he wasn't afraid, he would gather us magistrates together and we would have a full court for those big problems. Two days, three days, never mind, we would keep the court going until all the cases were finished. But as I have told you, we have no protection when someone's heart becomes bad against us. We are not sophisticated men. Myself, I only have a Grade 3 education! I became a magistrate not because I wanted to, no, but there was pressure on me to do it. I was reluctant, but I was asked many times, and at last I allowed the local-level government to appoint me. Because this is heavy work. It is heavy work, and some sinful person finally caught our friend and killed him for the work he did. Soon we will have to find a new magistrate to replace him. This is no small thing. Who can replace him? Who among you thinks you can do this work? There are some who will want to right away, but they are the wrong people. They have confused notions about what we magistrates do, they think it is easy, that they will get prestige for this work, maybe they think they will get money, but now I have told you the truth about the work that we do. We do not get money; the government does not support us; some people respect us but others will just come looking for trouble. We do this work because it is the work of the law, and because we do our best to help people live good lives, Christian lives. That is the only reason. All right, enough, I've finished now.

Acknowledgments

This chapter is dedicated to Elia Seromai of Leileiyafa Village in Milne Bay Province, Papua New Guinea, who was the first to call my attention to the difficulty of a village court magistrate's life and the skill involved in doing his job. He is pictured near the start of this chapter, conducting a divination to find the sorcerer responsible for a woman's death.

Suggested Readings

For a general overview of Papua New Guinea's political history and its connection to more recent social issues, see:

Sean Dorney, *Papua New Guinea: People, Politics, and History since 1975*. 3rd ed. Sydney: Random House Australia, 2000.

Paul Sillitoe, *Social Change in Melanesia: Development and History*. Cambridge: Cambridge University Press, 2000.

On Papua New Guinea's village courts, see:

Michael Goddard, *Substantial Justice: An Anthropology of Village Courts in Papua New Guinea*. New York: Berghahn Books, 2009.

On the history of Papua New Guinea's legal system more generally, see:

Peter Fitzpatrick, *Law and State in Papua New Guinea*. London: Academic Press, 1980.

On one version of Papua New Guinean Christianity, see:

Joel Robbins, *Becoming Sinners: Christianity and Moral Torment in a Papua New Guinea Society*. Berkeley: University of California Press, 2004.

On Papua New Guinean expectations of the government and what it ought to deliver, see:

Paige West, *Conservation Is Our Government Now: The Politics of Ecology in Papua New Guinea*. Durham, NC: Duke University Press, 2006.

On incarceration experiences in Papua New Guinea, see:

Adam Reed, *Papua New Guinea's Last Place: Experiences of Constraint in a Postcolonial Prison*. New York: Berghahn Books, 2004.

On ideas about magical violence throughout Papua New Guinea, see:

Michele Stephen, ed., *Sorcerer and Witch in Melanesia*. New Brunswick, NJ: Rutgers University Press, 1987.

The Chaplain: Being a Physician of the Soul in a Secular Age

Winnifred Fallers Sullivan and Christopher Swift

Chaplain Wanted: Increasing openings but limited opportunity for career development. Frequently asked questions to which there are no answers. Daily work ranges from mundane religious duties to attendance at the traumatic and most intense experiences of someone's life. Often marginalized, may on occasion perform key public role, such as leading memorial service for senior colleague. International pay range: $25,000–$80,000

Chaplains are both an old-fashioned, mostly Christian profession that has been around for hundreds of years and a brand new profession that is at the forefront of providing spiritual care for people around the world in many different contexts, whether or not they have a formal religious affiliation. The chaplain's role remains embedded in local histories and cultures even while it responds to growing religious diversity and mobility. In this chapter, we explore the practices of chaplains in the United States and the United Kingdom to provide insight into their little-understood and fascinating world of work—in hospitals, in prisons, in the military, in schools, and workplaces. This chapter is presented as a discussion between the two contexts and draws out the rewards and challenges faced by chaplains as they work with people to co-create sustainable meaning in the face of personal adversity and suffering.

The authors of this chapter are Christopher Swift, a Church of England priest employed by the National Health Service (NHS) in Great

Britain, and a research fellow of Leeds Metropolitan University, and Winnifred Sullivan, a professor of religious studies and a lawyer who teaches at Indiana University in the United States. Each has written a book on chaplaincy. Swift speaks from his twenty years of experience as a hospital chaplain but also from his experience as a leader in and researcher about health care chaplaincy in the United Kingdom. Sullivan speaks out of her interest in the nature of religion more generally under the modern rule of law. Both study the ways in which religion is being transformed today and focus on how these changes can be seen in the remarkably adaptable role of the chaplain. Together they offer some background and some advice to someone thinking of becoming a chaplain, taking turns and comparing this job in these two countries that share a lot and yet are also very different in ways that affect how chaplains do their work.

Prof. Sullivan: Let me begin by asking you to look around your public spaces a little more closely. If you pay careful attention, you will see small, inconspicuous signs for interfaith or multi-faith chapels in an amazingly diverse number of public spaces today, some permanent, some temporary, some marked by simple arrows, some by the international symbols for such spaces, a kneeling stick figure or praying hands, fitted in between other necessaries, toilets and ATMs and broom closets. There are interfaith chapels in hospitals, prisons, military installations, airports, schools, businesses, police stations, disaster relief camps, and national parks. The design of these chapels ranges from the deliberately nondescript, even brutally bare, to elaborate efforts to accommodate the ritual needs of different religions. The chaplains who preside over these spaces represent a range of religious and spiritual options from priests and rabbis to self-described humanists or universalists of various kinds. The work they do is important and demanding—honoring the dignity of ordinary lives—but it is work that is often barely recognized by most of the public. Kate Braestrup, who is chaplain to the Maine Warden Service, explains why she is a chaplain:

> If you prefer applied and practical theology to the more abstract and vaporous varieties, it is difficult to find a more interesting and challenging

ministry than a law enforcement chaplaincy. Law enforcement officers, like all human beings, are presented with grand questions about life's meaning and purpose. They consider the problem of evil, the suffering of innocents, the relationships between justice and mercy, power and responsibility, spirit and flesh. They ponder the impenetrable mystery of death. I was sure that working with cops would take me right up to where the theological rubber meets the road.

Braestrup explains why someone might want to be a chaplain. But what does a chaplain do every day? And how does someone get a job as a chaplain?

Rev. Swift: What do I do? There are so many ways to answer that question. Because I work in a hospital, sometimes I recite millennia-old Middle Eastern poetry to people as they die. On other occasions I listen to the emerging story of someone trying to make sense of their life after a major heart attack. Between these episodes of pastoral care are management meetings and budget negotiations; the chaplain also ministers to hospital staff, bearing witness to the pressures and rewards of their efforts to do their best in the fraught world of patient expectation and horrendous cost

Figure 5.1 A chaplain chatting with hospital staff. Photograph courtesy of University of Leeds.

pressures. These pressures exist in most economic activity, but it's important to be mindful of the unique experiences of health care. Somehow we need to factor in the human cost of caring for those facing life's biggest challenges—and the tiny reminders of aging and mortality that are part and parcel of almost every contact with a hospital. In their own way hospitals are sacred places—set aside for life-defining experiences. They have to be looked at differently.

Prof. Sullivan: Chaplains are employed by hospitals in the United States too, public hospitals and private, big and small. Urban and rural. American hospital chaplains see hospitals, as you do, as sacred places with people in particular need of spiritual care. The Joint Commission that accredits U.S. hospitals requires that the patient be provided spiritual care alongside traditional biomedicine. Some U.S. chaplains work for the hospital. Some are paid for by their religious communities, and some are volunteers. Many have special training and certificates that testify to their special expertise in hospital settings. They often do the work that others will not or cannot do. But chaplains struggle with how to minister to an increasingly unchurched and diverse patient population. Wendy Cadge, author of a book on hospital chaplains in the United States, *Paging God,* suggests that hospital chaplains in large hospitals in the United States increasingly practice an almost invisible religion, as they are trained to sit with a patient without imposing on him or her any particular religious perspective or ritual tradition. They are trained to wait for cues from the patient. The people they serve come from such different backgrounds that they work hard to accommodate a wide range of practices and positions. More visible traditional religion is left to the patients themselves as well as doctors and nurses and visiting clergy.

In the United Kingdom, you work in a setting with a longer sense of history than do chaplains in the United States, given its comparatively short history. Your book describes a history of chaplaincy in the United Kingdom going back at least as far as Tudor times—to Henry VIII!—and perhaps much further. You tell a history of the parallel and interwoven development of the Church of England and the welfare state. Is that right?

Rev. Swift: Yes, I'm the twelfth person to do my job since 1861, and that sense of history and continuity is an implicit part of my context. In one of our main buildings, at the back, there's a list of us all on a metal plaque.

Some of the chaplains stayed just a few years, but many worked at the hospital for over a decade, in a couple of cases more than thirty years. Has the job changed? Perhaps less than you might think. From time to time I'll get called to baptize a dying baby or say final prayers and offer pastoral support to a family. The content of what I say would be familiar to a chaplain 150 years ago and even further back than that. But the balance of what I do has shifted between the recognizable rituals and a more open and creative kind of spiritual care. There is a lot of interest in spirituality in the nursing and chaplaincy literature as well as a growing body of research and evidence on the importance of spiritual health to overall wellness. Today a chaplain has to be highly skilled in hearing the patient's concerns, and working with them to create a response that dignifies and expresses their spirituality.

Prof. Sullivan: As you say, one interesting aspect of chaplaincy today is the way in which diversity is partly addressed through the language of spiritual care. While many U.S. chaplains continue to come out of particular religious communities, as you do, if you are a young person in the United States choosing to train as a chaplain, it is actually increasingly the case that you will not be trained by your church or other religious community. Instead, you will be trained, as for other occupations, by qualifying yourself through university degrees and certificates for this specialized work. The religious/spiritual work you will be learning to do is intended for all. Everyone is understood to be in need of such care from time to time whether or not they consider themselves religious.

One sign of the increased homogenization and standardization of spiritual care in the United States is that many chaplains there increasingly describe their work as a "ministry of presence." The ministry of presence can be traced back to the religious practices of French monks, but today it is a ministry that describes itself as a simple "being with," sometimes "suffering with," whomever you are ministering to, whether that person is a patient, soldier, prisoner, or anonymous member of the public who has found his or her way to your chapel. The presence can be understood very specifically to be the presence of the divine, or the presence can be understood more humanistically as a solidarity between two people, without overt religious identification or content.

Rev. Swift: Presence has been important in U.K. chaplaincy for a long time, partly due to an influential book entitled *Being There,* which came out in 1988. Written by an Anglican priest, a focus on presence runs through the work, perhaps reflecting the Established Church's presence across society in England. That idea is being interpreted in new ways today because the relationship between Church and State is evolving. Nowadays the Church of England is seen increasingly as one faith group among many. There are still significant elements of privilege for the Church, such as in the presence of bishops in the House of Lords (upper house of U.K. parliament), but the approach of the National Health Service (NHS) is to make as many chaplaincy positions as possible open to all qualified applicants, whether from a particular tradition or not. In many ways this reflects the shift in society to less defined religious identification, a change apparent in people's answer to the question about their religion in the 2011 national census for England.

Prof. Sullivan: You might wonder why people choose to become a chaplain today when religious affiliation is declining. Becoming a chaplain is increasingly attractive to many people today, both as a first and as a second career choice. Chaplaincy positions often offer greater job security and benefits than many congregational positions. Chaplains serve a ready-made clientele; they aren't required to do as much entrepreneurial marketing and fundraising as the leaders of local congregations. But more important, perhaps, than these practical considerations, working chaplains talk about the exhilarating challenge of working with strangers in periodic high-risk encounters rather than the sometimes tedious everyday dullness of parish life; they also mention the opportunity for service outside what they see as the rigid dogma and discipline of particular religious communities. There is an indispensable quality to the role; the chaplain occupies a place between the sacred and the secular, between the private and the public; his or her work is witness to the broken and ambiguous nature of religious lives today. It is a job that traces its origins to the medieval church and yet is at the very forefront of a rapidly changing and diverse religious scene in the twenty-first century. Chaplains, helpful and heroic, sometimes foolish or sinister, populate world literature and are the stuff of cinematic myth-making; yet they are largely invisible in the world today, in spite of their ubiquity and their importance.

Chaplaincy is difficult work, demanding much of the chaplain with limited recompense, financial or otherwise. The chaplain is often asked to do what others consider the dirty work: attending to dying patients, sitting with anxious relatives, acting as go-between, trying to maintain a sense of decency in the face of the demands of authority, and being present to the value of the persons he or she ministers to while being obligated as well to the purposes of the secular institution that employs him or her. And this all takes place in a context made tense by the pressure of politics, data-driven metrics, and the economic bottom line.

In much of the world today it is chaplains, rather than congregational clergy, who are doing the necessary work of delivering spiritual care. That is because people are moving more and changing religious practice and affiliation more. They are also intermarrying more. All religious communities are undergoing changes in understanding their own traditions and those of others. Many people are finding ways to combine prayers, practices, and traditions from a variety of sources. They are less settled in home religious congregations. Chaplains are expert in meeting the person where he or she is in his or her spiritual journey. They mix or swap out age-old liturgies and other rituals with new forms of pastoral care, combining contemporary spiritualities and psychologies, that may or may not look like traditional religion but that serve a similar need.

Rev. Swift: It is important to remember that chaplaincy always has a lot to do with the needs of a particular time and place. The patients in our beds are changing. For one thing they are sicker. In the past, patients stayed longer, weeks at a time, whereas now patients are discharged as soon as possible to transitional care or back home. That's not a bad thing: Hospitals are dangerous places as well as centers of healing. In the United Kingdom, as in many other countries, there is a move to treat more people at home and in the community. It means that the trend toward hospitals treating only the most urgent and dependent cases will continue. Patients and staff are less likely to practice an orthodox faith than in previous years. Patients' beliefs are more eclectic and, on the whole, more open to reflection and transformation. Of course there are notable exceptions to this. With greater pluralism in society there are patients and staff whose beliefs were formed in parts of Africa and Eastern Europe, places where the certainties of faith are more often taken for granted than in the United Kingdom.

Prof. Sullivan: While chaplaincy is an internationally recognized occupation and religious/spiritual practices are converging in some ways, different national laws and political systems still matter. In the United States, chaplaincy, whether in government or private institutions, is deeply influenced by the often controversial law and politics of the First Amendment to the U.S. Constitution. The First Amendment to the Constitution points in two directions. On the one hand, it prohibits the government from sponsoring or supporting religion; on the other, it requires government to protect the free exercise of religion. The ending of state-supported religion such as the Church of England—at the time of independence—means that religious life in the United States has gradually been intentionally deregulated. Deregulation means that there are no official churches for the government to partner with to provide spiritual care to soldiers and other workers, as there often are in other countries. Deregulation presents a particular problem for chaplaincies. Many people are understood to have a right to the free exercise of religion provided by the government: prisoners and soldiers, principally, but also patients in public hospitals and various other institutions. But it is also understood that the government should not engage in proselytizing. The services provided should be voluntary. A solution to this problem is being found through officially redefining the work that chaplains do as being spiritual rather than religious. Because U.S. judges and others are starting to accept studies showing the value of spiritual care to overall health and wellness, chaplaincy is coming to have a more broadly accepted role in American public life. Judges and others believe that public provision of spiritual care is not sectarian or divisive the way traditional religion is and that it should therefore not be considered an unconstitutional establishment of religion. All the same, most Americans would see a major contrast between the United States and the United Kingdom in the continued existence of an established church in the United Kingdom. How important do you see the Church of England's privileged position to be in the way chaplaincy works in the United Kingdom?

Rev. Swift: The Church of England is no longer as significant as the established partner of the state, and as a result, that partnership is less and less understood as basic to the provision of spiritual care. Other political priorities have become more important, not least the drive for greater equality. The 2010 Equality Act places a duty on public bodies to secure and promote a number of "protected characteristics." This includes religion. It's hard to see how large hospitals can do that effectively and consistently without an in-house chaplaincy service. No other member of a hospital staff has the particular job of supporting the religious and spiritual needs of patients the way the chaplain does. In recent years some other professionals in the NHS, people who weren't trained to be chaplains, have been formally investigated for using prayer with patients or for introducing religious topics too assertively. The chaplain is specially trained and skilled in holding spiritual conversations with many different kinds of patients. While other staff may well be able to pray with a patient, they may not be equipped to deal with the aftermath when the thing prayed for hasn't happened (for example, when the patient doesn't recover). That kind of conversation is the bread and butter work of a chaplain. Handled well, it can open up new spiritual possibilities, deep honesty, and a recognition of our physical limits.

Prof. Sullivan: Providing spiritual care to a diverse population at times of great suffering raises similar challenges in the United States. For some religious folks, a right to religious freedom is understood to be a right for all to express their own religious convictions at all times and places. That can result in an unwanted imposition on the recipient of such communications. Professional chaplains in the United States also pride themselves on their ability to provide care at times of great pain without imposing their own religious views on their clients. Equality is important to Americans, too, who find that value also in the Constitution—in the Fourteenth Amendment. A drive for equality creates pressure to provide a ministry to all, without discrimination, people of any faith or no faith. There is a sense that all patients are equal, and, indeed, so are the other recipients of spiritual care. But there is also a sense of equality among workers.

But we haven't yet addressed one of the questions asked at the beginning—how do you get this job? If you are interested in becoming a chaplain in the United States, the required credentials are becoming more shared, no matter what your religious background. The three credentials required for many, perhaps increasingly most, chaplaincy positions in the United States are the master's of divinity degree, clinical pastoral education certification, and ecclesiastical endorsement. These credentials are required in hospitals but also in the military, in prisons, and in other social service and public service settings as well as in the private sector. All of these credentials focus on a ministry to all, not just to those who share your religious beliefs and background.

The MDiv degree, a three-year professional master's degree qualifying students for public ministry, is offered by many U.S. colleges and universities. The training is a combination of traditional academic courses, field education, and internships, similar to the JD or other professional master's degrees in business, art, architecture, and so on. The student is required to take courses in history, scripture, and theology as well as to prepare for professional work in personal counseling, worship, and management. For many of these programs the student does not have to be a member of a religious community or even have specific religious commitments to qualify for admission. While the MDiv originated in the mid-twentieth century as a preparation for ordained ministry in the mainstream protestant denominations, today the degree has been adopted across the Christian denominational and nondenominational landscape and by non-Christians as well. In many of these programs, your fellow students would often not share your own religious background or beliefs. The training and discipline of the MDiv is understood to prepare the student to minister to all and to qualify the student for a job with benefits from the government.

Clinical Pastoral Education, or CPE, began in Massachusetts in the 1920s in a collaboration between a Harvard doctor and a Protestant pastor. Together they instituted internships to provide an opportunity for Protestant ministers to train in hospitals, in one-on-one encounters with patients. Chaplains learn in CPE to understand themselves and their vocations better and to develop best practices for a ministry understood to be focused on "sitting with" the patient. CPE-like practices are now common in hospice as well as in many forms of social service ministry. Certification is managed by the Association for Clinical Pastoral Education.

An ecclesiastical endorsement is usually also required as a condition of employment. In government chaplaincies, applicants must have a document from their religious organization stating that they are in good standing in that community, whether it is Presbyterian or Greek Orthodox or Buddhist or Muslim. There is a list of all approved endorsing organizations posted on the Armed Services Chaplaincy website. In the military the chaplain can be terminated either by the endorsing agency or by the armed services. While there are hundreds of approved endorsing agencies, this requirement continues to allow the government to claim that it is not the government that is making decisions about religious orthodoxy.

Rev. Swift: I wish it was so clear how to be accredited to become a chaplain in the United Kingdom! For reasons no one has fully explained, clinical pastoral education didn't take off as a common requirement in Britain.

As a result there are chaplains with a wide range of qualifications. Faith community endorsement is certainly one of these qualifications, and the way things are going, that is likely to include endorsement by a "community of belief." In Europe *belief* does not necessarily mean a religious conviction. This is reflected in the 2010 Equality Act, which defines belief as follows: "any religious or philosophical belief or reference to belief, including a reference to a lack of belief." For example, a vegetarian may hold the belief that human beings do not have the right to kill animals for food. This would not need to be a religious conviction in order to be a protected belief from a legal perspective. Quite what this means in the practice of chaplaincy is yet to be seen, but I can imagine a time in the not too distant future when a humanist organization will endorse someone to practice as a chaplain.

As in many Western countries, there are a growing number of patients registered as "not known" and "none" when asked about religion by the hospital staff. Some of these patients will request chaplaincy services, either because they've been recorded incorrectly or because they decide that the chaplain's listening and accompanying skills have something to offer them even though they have no fixed religious commitments. In the early twentieth century, in the Army and elsewhere, people who stated "none" on their paperwork would have been classified as Church of England. Now there is a new risk that those saying "none" may be inappropriately categorized as humanists or atheists. Most people's views about faith and belief are more tentative. They might reject identification with religious authority but be very happy to speak freely with a chaplain. In the future I can see chaplains being appointed on an entirely open basis, from all kinds of faith and belief groups, to meet the needs of these patients. Some chaplains may be worried about this, perceiving it as loosening the link with traditional religions, but I think it will only enrich and strengthen the chaplaincy profession. We talk about patient-centered care, and chaplaincy needs to evolve if it is to reflect and engage the diversification of beliefs in our communities.

Apart from faith/belief community endorsement, a chaplain in the United Kingdom must be educated to degree level, normally at a master's level for the main category of chaplaincy appointments. This can be in theology and, increasingly, in chaplain-specific master's programs. Suitable experience is also a key requirement, and many clergy now have this as a mandatory part of their religious training. I envy the clarity given around the world by CPE, and there are promising signs that a form of central profession-specific accreditation will emerge from work being done by the U.K. Board of Health Care Chaplaincy. However, a local U.K. solution will still present some difficulties for chaplains wanting to leave the United Kingdom and work in CPE settings where their accreditation is unlikely to be recognized.

Prof. Sullivan: As Chris's work, focused as it is on hospital chaplaincy in particular, shows, people usually think of and study chaplains within a particular sector, and chaplains themselves often think of themselves as trained and qualified for particular settings—the hospital, the prison, the military, or the university, and so on. But looking across the various secular institutions in which chaplains do their work, one can see a similar transformation. Religious and spiritual lives are less tied to traditional religious bodies. As you suggest, the spiritual care delivered by governmental and quasi-governmental chaplaincies in the United States—as well as by chaplaincies within private but regulated industries such as hospitals and schools—reflects a religious practice that responds to the uncertainties inherent in imagining religion today, given increased diversity and fragmentation.

All chaplaincies today seem to make religion more like other kinds of work and, at the same time, to set it apart. In some ways the chaplain looks like any other worker who has hours and benefits and conditions of nondiscrimination set by the government, but the chaplain also has other authorities to answer to, authorities within their religious communities as well as transcendent authorities. The chaplain's work is justified because he or she is doing something that most Americans think is important and necessary. Yet many also think that it is work that should not be regulated by the government. This is a delicate balancing act.

Chaplains work in many settings in the United States that would be familiar to Britons. But I do think the National Health Service is a special case, don't you?

Rev. Swift: We like to say the NHS is special. If you remember, the 2012 Olympic Games opening ceremony in London made a big fuss about the health service. It involved six hundred nurses and health care workers who volunteered to take part in a performance that celebrated the role of the NHS in Britain's national life. For many people, although perhaps a declining number, the NHS represents what government can achieve at its best. Victory in World War II had been brought about by a command economy that marshalled the resources of society to defeat a terrible evil in Europe. During and immediately following that war, people believed that the same success could be used to defeat the worst effects of illness—for everyone. It was a noble vision. The reality has always been a struggle, and the catalogue of failures is long and ongoing. Yet the British people hold the NHS to be an almost sacred institution of society. In fact an NHS chief bemoaned this quasi-religious status as a barrier to change. Clearly, the sense of public ownership and pride in the NHS remains resilient.

It might sound an odd way of putting it, but when the NHS came into being in 1948, the chaplains serving in hospitals at the time were nationalized. Their employment was taken over by the state. In practical terms this drew chaplains together and the first conferences and a fledgling literature began to emerge at the same time. But the way forward for chaplaincy has always been fraught and contested. I think the reason for that lies in the dual identity of most chaplains. Chaplains are first selected and trained for ministry in a religious community context, and then they are taken into NHS employment. Once they occupied a semi-detached place in hospitals, more like tenured post-holders than employees, but that situation has changed in recent years. A major overhaul of terms and conditions took place in 2004, and that change embedded chaplains more clearly along-side other NHS staff. This has many benefits. Before 2004, few chaplains were paid anything for being on call or attending the hospital for emergencies. The most they got was compensatory time off at some point after the call-out—but with many demands on their time this was often notional rather than actual. Now on-call is remunerated for chaplains. However, most members of the public, seeing a chaplain, would still associate our role as religious community-based rather than as a health care professional.

Prof. Sullivan: Nationalization of the chaplaincy would be politically and legally unacceptable as an idea in the United States! Nationalization sounds to Americans like socialism or religious establishment. Yet the extensive regulation and universalization of spiritual care that is coming into being in the United States through the regulation of academic degrees, for example, or the constitutional guarantees to the free exercise of religion—which is regulation intended to provide care fairly to all—may have some parallel effects. Standardization also results from the secularization or spiritualization of religious ministry caused by clinical and sociological studies of the effectiveness of spiritual care. In the United States an entire industry of spiritual assessment has grown up, allowing chaplains and others to measure spiritual health. Such assessments justify the work that chaplains do, but they also make the work look less religious.

But for a researcher like myself who looks at this job from the outside, it is sometimes difficult to understand the attraction of this work. What would you say to someone considering being a chaplain? What are the best and the worst things about your job?

Rev. Swift: It's hard to answer that question in the abstract. Perhaps it would help if I told you about what happened to me one Christmas Eve. It was 11:30 p.m., and my pager went off. I often take this day for on-call, partly because I'm involved with a visiting choir in one of the hospitals in the early evening. But when my pager went off, I was at home wrapping presents while my wife—also a Church of England minister—was taking her Midnight Mass service.

By 12:10 I was baptizing a one-day-old baby in our neonatal unit. It's the last place any of us wanted to be. Some problems were indicated during pregnancy, but mum and dad had focused on the element of hope that all would be well. Who wouldn't, in their position? But it was not to be. When I walked into the room, the baby was in an incubator. The parents were present along with a few relatives. Most of the time there was silence, sniffing, and sobs. I explained who I was, that I understood they would like their baby baptized, and outlined the content of the simple service. I asked if they had any particular preferences, but no one said anything. It's too difficult for everyone. I conducted the baptism, and as we were getting to the final "Amen" the hospital staff stepped forward and said that the baby was starting to go. Now would be the time for her parents to hold her if they wished. Which of course they did. I looked at the clock, and it was 12:15 on Christmas Day, and their baby had died.

There are things that are very difficult to face, situations no one would choose to be in. When a call comes to visit the Emergency Department for a family when there's been a crib death, you know that for those people their world has been turned upside down. You stand on one side of the door and know that as soon as it opens, you will enter a world of pain and sorrow. Perhaps some of those present will be angry with God about what's happened. Somehow, in the middle of it all, you have to establish a rapport quickly and effectively. That's not just done with words but by body language, stillness, and a careful attention to those present. I can recall going into one room, and the mother was just sitting on the floor cradling her child and weeping. So I just got on the floor myself and waited a long time until it seemed the right moment to speak. People in these situations are usually so bruised and devastated by what's going on that you need to be very gentle. Their world has just ground to a halt, and sometimes I need to take a breath and slow myself down enough to come alongside them. Remarkably, however hard these situations are, I have a sense that it's right—fitting—for me to be there. So while these kind of things may be the worst part of my job, they're also the things that affirm my sense of vocation and value in the whole process of caring for people.

What do you need to believe in order to do this? Well, as a religious chaplain, I'm attached to the idea of a god who doesn't look away. There's no magic wand to resolve the often terrible experiences of being human, and the least we can do is to keep on the same side of the street. When I'm in these situations it seems important to me to embody that sense of God being with us and choosing, gently and yet with resolution, to be present within our suffering. If we're not offering a god who changes things to how we'd like them to be, the least we can do is represent a sense of the sacred alongside and even within our personal tragedies.

Suggested Readings

Kate Braestrup, *Here If You Need Me*. Boston: Little Brown, 2007.

Wendy Cadge, *Paging God: Religion in the Halls of Medicine*. Chicago: University of Chicago Press, 2012.

Mark Cobb, Christina M. Puchalski, and Bruce Rumbold, eds., *Oxford Textbook of Spirituality in Healthcare*. Oxford, U.K.: Oxford University Press, 2012.

Sophie Gilliatt-Ray, "Being There: Shadowing a British Muslim Hospital Chaplain." *Culture and Religion* 11, no. 4 (2010): 413–32.

Kim Philip Hansen, *Military Chaplains and Religious Diversity*. New York: Palgrave, 2012.

Van McNair Jr., *Chaplain on the Waterfront: The Story of Father Saunders*. New York: Seabury Press, 1963.

Daniel O'Connor, *The Chaplains of the East India Company, 1601–1858*. New York: Continuum, 2012.

Peter W. Speck, *Being There: Pastoral Care in Time of Illness*. London: SPCK, 1988.

Winnifred Fallers Sullivan, *A Ministry of Presence: Chaplaincy, Spiritual Care, and the Law*. Chicago: University of Chicago Press, 2014.

Christopher Swift, *Hospital Chaplaincy in the Twenty-First Century*. 2nd ed. Farnham, U.K.: Ashgate, 2014.

Being a Crime Scene Technician in Sweden

Corinna Kruse

Police and crime scene work can differ considerably depending on where in Sweden one is employed: it is a small country in terms of population, with about nine million inhabitants, most of which live in the cities in the southern part of the country—the largest cities being Stockholm, Gothenburg, and Malmö. In the south of Sweden, there are more crimes related to border traffic with Central and Eastern Europe. Police in Skåne, the southernmost county, claim that they have to deal with the highest murder rate in the country. In the urban centers there are crimes related to high population density and large sporting events. In the sparsely populated rural areas in the north, where there is more hunting, conditions are favorable for poachers.

Traditionally, the Swedish public sector is obliged to serve the citizenry's best interests, and trust in the state is quite high in Sweden (although due to political changes, this trust seems to be declining lately). Because of this trust, the police's impartiality is rarely questioned (even if the police are criticized for other things), and generally the public can be expected to cooperate with the law, for example, by reporting crimes and giving information to the police.

The fictional crime scene technician speaking in this chapter is giving advice to someone inquiring about the job; the advice is colored by the assumption that people are interested in forensics because of popular TV shows, such as the popular U.S. show *Crime Scene Investigation*, which has been on the air in Sweden for more than a decade. These shows make an otherwise rather invisible job look dashing and glamorous.

So you want to become a crime scene technician. Perhaps you think that it is a job that you could do well and that would allow you to serve your community in a productive way, or perhaps you are attracted to the glamorous portrayals of the job on television or in crime fiction. Not that one excludes the other, of course.

Whatever your motivation, there are a few things you should think about beforehand. Are you prepared to be part of such a large bureaucratic organization as the Swedish judicial system? Do you enjoy working carefully and systematically? Do you enjoy doing so even when wearing uncomfortable protective coveralls, gloves, booties, and a mask in cramped conditions or perhaps being outdoors in the freezing cold? How do you feel about other people's clothes or body fluids—will it gross you out to see blood or to touch a stranger's underwear? And are you a people person? Would you enjoy working as part of an investigation or would it make you impatient to have to explain things that are self-evident to you but a police investigator or a prosecutor doesn't seem to understand? Can you talk to the upset residents of a burgled house, both calming them and finding out what has been moved in their home?

Do you think you will be fine with that?

Then you might want to know a little more about the work itself. What does a crime scene technician do, and what is important in his or her work?

Examining Crime Scenes

One of the most important things you will need for working crime scenes, apart from training in forensics and crime scene work, is a good imagination. In order to recover traces, you have to find them, and in order to find them, you need an idea about where they might be.

A burglar, for example, may leave traces while walking through the rooms of a house or an apartment looking for valuables; perhaps shoe prints on the floor or fingerprints on drawers and cabinets. But, of course, the person living in the house or apartment also leaves traces, and a lot of them: fingerprints on cabinet doors and kitchen surfaces, DNA traces on cups and bottles, shoe prints in the hallway. And while it theoretically is possible to collect all of the traces from a burgled house and send them for analysis, in practice this consumes too many resources. Besides, it is unnecessary.

Finding and recovering the burglar's traces instead of those of the resident(s) will be part of your professional skill. You will use your imagination and your experience to find places where you have a good chance of recovering the burglar's traces and hopefully only their traces. You will, for example, become good at finding possible points of entry and concluding where an intruder might have gripped a window frame in order to heave him- or herself into the room—which makes it possible to dust for fingerprints and handprints in a more efficient and directed way.

Finding these traces may take some time, so another thing you will need is patience. If you storm in and rush through, you may overlook traces or, worse, trample them and make them unrecoverable. So, however much there is to do or however boring the crime scene might seem, you have to work calmly and methodically.

If this goes for regular crime scenes, it goes doubly for serious crimes. You might want to make a habit of bringing a thermos of coffee to such a crime scene and start your work with a coffee break. While this may seem heartless to you right now, you will appreciate a slow start to your examination, discussing the scene and some strategies with your colleague. You will also notice that the cup of coffee in your hands will prevent you from touching things before you have planned out what you want to do.

You will also need to be familiar with forensic technologies and their strengths and weaknesses. You will need to know how to operate different devices such as cameras or light sources. You will also need to be familiar with forensic methods, both understanding how and why they work and acquiring the dexterity to use them. In order to make a cast of a tool mark, for example, you need to know on which surfaces the plaster works

Figure 6.1 Crime scene technician dusting for fingerprints during a course at the Swedish National Laboratory for Forensic Science. Photograph by Marcus Andrae, Swedish National Laboratory for Forensic Science.

and does not work (according to chemical composition) and which color plaster is easy or difficult to examine later. But you also need the hands-on experience and skill that enables you to make a good, clear cast. And the same goes for other methods of recovering traces.

Thus, you will also need to be careful and thorough. You need to be thorough enough to make a good cast every time, to take photographs from every angle, and to make sure that you do not contaminate the traces you recover. You do not want to smudge the fingerprint you are recovering, and you do not want to contaminate a possible DNA trace with your own. So you cannot take shortcuts, neither with methods nor with protective clothing.

You will need to get used to the protective clothes. In winter, the extra clothes may be quite pleasant, but in summer—even if it is only the Swedish summer—protective coveralls, a hairnet, a facemask, surgical gloves, and plastic booties can be stifling. You will still need to work as patiently and carefully and thoroughly.

You will also need to get used to getting close to and touching things that most people find disgusting. There are the obvious things—dead bodies and bodily fluids—but there are also less obvious ones: used condoms, shower drains, trash cans, vacuum cleaner bags, clothes. And when you examine clothing and bedclothes for damage or traces, you will come in close contact with fabric that has rubbed against someone else's skin and perhaps their intimate body parts. You may, of course, still find these things disgusting, even after years of examining crime scenes, but you do not want that to affect your work.

You will also need an open and analytical mind. You will have to draw conclusions from the traces you find—is there evidence of a crime? Which courses of action do the traces suggest? Are there any clues as to when it happened?

Unless you work with a colleague, you will be the only person in the investigation to see the crime scene, so you are in a unique and important position. No one else will have a similar firsthand understanding of the crime scene.

But traces can be ambiguous. A broken window may be the point of entry or of exit, or it may have been broken independently of a suspected burglary. It is your job to look at the crime scene as a whole and to develop and examine different hypotheses. Just like everyone else in the Swedish judicial system, you are obligated to be impartial, so you will have to consider different alternatives with equal seriousness. What at first glance looks like a murder may have been an accident, or vice versa; in both cases, sticking to that first impression might lead to overlooking traces, which would impact the evidence and the case as a whole. Thus, your willingness to question and test your own conclusions is a crucial part of examining crime scenes.

What can make this part of your work tricky, and perhaps even uncomfortable at first, is that there is no yardstick against which you can measure how well you did. There may be a verdict at the end of the criminal justice process, but after all, there is a risk, hopefully a very small risk, that this verdict is based on erroneous evidence. The lack of a verdict, on the other hand, doesn't mean that you failed to do your job properly. An investigation that is closed due to lack of evidence does not necessarily mean that you could have done more or better; you cannot find traces that are not there. But of course you have no way of knowing. Were there no traces (or no other traces), or did you just overlook them? Your work does have consequences for people's lives, contributing to finding someone guilty or exonerating them. You will never know whether you did enough or perhaps made a mistake. Living with this uncertainty may take some getting used to.

The final thing you will need for crime scene examinations is what in a doctor would be called a good bedside manner. Of course, you will not be sitting beside a patient's bed and discussing their ailments with them. However, you will sometimes meet victims of a crime or an accident in your work: You will go to burgled houses and meet the residents; you will talk to people whose house has burned down; you will call people and ask for directions or clarifications. A few of these people may have tried to commit insurance fraud by reporting a burglary or robbery or may— intentionally or accidentally—have caused a fire, but you cannot know that from the outset. Most will be victims of crime and will be genuinely upset and perhaps frightened or angry. Nonetheless, you will need to talk to them about the crime. In burglary cases, for example, you may want to know what the house usually looks like, so that you can focus your attention on places where the burglar may have left traces. Thus, you will want the residents to point out irregularities to you—people who in all probability already are very upset about having had their home and their privacy violated and must now tolerate you going through their personal space all over again.

You may also have to explain to victims of crime what they can expect from the police investigation. While they may be unfamiliar with the details of police work, many people read or watch crime fiction in Sweden, and they often shape their expectations from what they see there. They may be very disappointed when you do things differently or have to tell them that you have not been able to find anything very useful.

But examining crime scenes is not all a Swedish crime scene technician does. Their work is also shaped by being part of the judicial system—a crime scene examination is only one part of a pre-trial investigation.

Being Part of an Investigation

In Sweden, pre-trial investigations are conducted by the police but led by a prosecutor as soon as there is a suspect. For very severe crimes without a suspect (so far), the investigation is conducted in contact with a prosecutor. Both the police and the prosecutor are obligated to be impartial, that is, not to take sides and to focus as much on exonerating evidence as on incriminating evidence.

The prosecutor is focused on the case as a whole. She or he will relate pieces of evidence to each other and to the law with an eye toward a possible future trial. Some questions are always on the prosecutor's mind: Which criminal acts can be proved? And can the evidence be expected to hold up in court?

The police investigators assemble the evidence that the prosecutor assesses. They interrogate plaintiffs, witnesses, and suspects, so they must be good at relating to people from very different walks of life. They also collect other types of evidence and information—surveillance films, telephone records, register data.[1]

Crime scene technicians are part of the police. They do not investigate crime scenes on their own initiative; they are always responding to orders from the pre-trial investigation leader. The traces they recover

---

1. Data recorded in various governmental databases, for example with the tax agency, national registration, or in the police's criminal and suspicion records.

from a crime scene usually are sent to the Swedish National Laboratory of Forensic Science (Statens kriminaltekniska laboratorium; SKL) for analysis. Crime scene technicians perform only some forensic analyses, but they do conduct preliminary examinations on the traces they recover and other materials that are brought in—for example a plaintiff's or suspect's clothes—in order to decide whether to send them on to SKL. What looked like a bloodstain at first may not be one, for example, and such an examination is more efficiently done at the crime scene division.

When you come back from a crime scene and have perhaps had a look at the traces you collected in order to see how promising they are, you will give the leader of the pre-trial investigation a call or you might drop by their office. You will explain what you saw at the crime scene and what your conclusions are, and you will discuss with them how to proceed. If, for example, you have found a forced window in a burgled house as well as a handprint on the inside of the window frame, your conclusion will probably be that someone (or several someones) broke into the house that way, and you will recommend having the handprint analyzed. If you have not been able to find any traces of a break-in, the conversation might revolve around your doubts that the reported burglary in fact happened.

The investigation leader will probably have questions of her or his own. They have an understanding of the case as a whole, and during the time you have spent at the crime scene, the police investigators may have worked on the case in other ways. They might have talked to witnesses or the plaintiff; they might have looked at financial or telephone records; they might have obtained surveillance films. All that other evidence generates a context for the crime scene. For example, a plaintiff may have told the police about having tried to fight off an intruder at the door, and the investigation leader will want to know whether there were signs of a struggle in the hallway. Conversely, you might have been unable to find traces of violence in an apartment. Meanwhile, perhaps other police investigators have discovered that the plaintiff felt so violated and upset by the crime that they cleaned before calling the police.

The investigation leader will have an overview of the whole case and thus will know which issues need to be resolved in order to identify a suspect and either exonerate them or prove their guilt. But you will bring the expertise on forensics that can help them decide which traces (and which potential evidence to be produced from these traces) are relevant and important to the case. You may also have to explain to the investigation leader which analyses SKL can perform and what kinds of questions these analyses can contribute to answering.

In many cases, investigators and prosecutors will of course have quite a thorough understanding and experience of these matters themselves, but when it comes to unusual analyses or complicated cases, they may require your help. You may, for example, have to remind them that a fiber analysis will not be very useful in a case where the victim and the suspect share a home. Or you might alert them to the possibility of having a watch tested for DNA in order to determine its owner (whose DNA may have accumulated between the links of the wristband).

You are also expected to act as a kind of filter between the investigation and the forensic laboratory. An eager investigation leader might want SKL to do every conceivable analysis, especially in a violent crime. But while SKL's capacity is large, it is not unlimited, so its forensic scientists cannot run every possible analysis in every case. Choices must be made. Which materials should be sent for analysis? And which analysis? When you find a trail of blood drops at a crime scene, for example, you might have taken a sample of each and every one of them, just to be on the safe side. But it might never become important to the investigation to determine whether all the drops come from the same person, so it might be enough to send only one of the swabs for DNA analysis.

You will also need to help the investigation leader set priorities in cases in which there is a lot of material, or there are traces for which different possible analyses are mutually exclusive. A bloody fingerprint, for example, forces a choice: Is it more important to try to find out whose fingerprint it is or whose blood it is? One analysis will make the other impossible; having a bloody fingerprint analyzed as a fingerprint makes it impossible to extract a DNA profile from the blood later on, should the question arise. The investigation leader may need help assessing the quality of the bloody fingerprint and the circumstances of where and how it was found in order to decide whether the fingerprint or the DNA profile is more important or which analysis has more chance of success. After consulting with you, the leader may decide to hold the analysis until later, in case the evidence that is being assembled fundamentally changes the case.

But you will not only communicate and discuss your findings in person. You will also write crime scene reports that will make it possible for the investigation leader to understand the crime scene and thus the forensic evidence. If the case leads to an indictment, the defense and the court will also be reading your report. The crime scene report explains not only the place itself but, more importantly, your observations, the traces you have found, how you recovered them, the results of SKL's analysis, and your conclusions. Your reports must convey both an overall picture of the crime scene and how every trace is connected to it—without bogging down the reader in details. Still, a lot of these details may be important or become so later, so you must be able to communicate them in a structured way.

All of the readers of your report will approach your writing with different expertise, different from each other's as well as from yours. Thus, you will need to develop your skills in writing accessibly without compromising on accuracy, and you will have to write in a way that is clear and concise for different types of non-experts. To do this, you must be aware of your expertise and where it differs from the expertise of other members of the judicial system. You will have to avoid jargon and you will have to spell out things that are self-evident to you and your colleagues but will not be to your readers. (However, if and when the case goes to court, the report will become a public document. So clarity will not be your only concern. You will also have to consider issues such as privacy protection and what any criminals or potential criminals might learn from your report.)

Your role in the criminal justice process will be twofold. First, you will contribute expertise in crime scene examinations, but second, and at least as importantly, you will liaise and mediate between different members of the investigation and judicial system. You will convey the results of your work to others, you will make the laboratory's work understandable and accessible to the police and prosecution and, on occasion, the defense, and you will help the police and prosecution sort through the traces and decide which ones to send for analysis. Part of your job is to contribute to conserving resources in the judicial system and keeping the laboratory's workload reasonable. Thus, being a crime scene technician is just as much about working with people—and very different people at that—as it is about working with forensics and technology.

In this way, crime scene technicians are very much members of a large organization. They are experts who cooperate with other experts (each of whom has a very different expertise). As you cooperate, you will constantly be reminded that although the members of the judicial system share the goal of solving crimes, they work in different ways toward that goal. They also see different parts of the process. The prosecutor—as well as the court—sees the whole of a case, including the outcome, whereas crime scene technicians see only a part. And the part that technicians see belongs typically to the beginning of the process, when there is a lot of uncertainty about what may have happened and how the investigation will proceed. Unless the case is very notable or they take a special interest, crime scene technicians do not always learn the outcome of a case.

This is exactly what you want? Well, then this is how you go about it.

Becoming a Crime Scene Technician

Swedish crime scene technicians start out as regular police officers and specialize in crime scene investigation later on—civilian crime scene technicians are extremely rare—so your first step (if you already are a Swedish citizen) is to apply to the Swedish National Police Academy. Competition is stiff: In the latest of the semiannual admissions, around 4 to 6 percent of applicants have been admitted.

To become a police officer, it certainly helps to be in good shape; one part of the admission test is physical. Other parts are psychological and medical. Passing all the tests does not guarantee you one of the three to four hundred places, though. You may have to re-apply, perhaps several times.

If you are admitted, you will undergo a two-year training course at one of the Police Academy's three locations. There, you will learn about police work both in theory and in practice. You will, for example, learn about the law, you will be trained in driving police cars, especially in stressful situations, and in using communications equipment as well as in conflict management. After that, you will spend an additional half a year as a trainee, an *aspirant,* before becoming a regular police officer.

Your first years will be spent in uniform, on the street. But the Swedish police needs all kinds of people for all kinds of different jobs. You might want to spend a couple of years as an investigator, for example, contributing to solving crimes by interviewing plaintiffs and witnesses and, of course, suspects. No? You want to become a crime scene technician as soon as possible?

Well, then your next step is to wait for a position to become available at a crime scene division and to apply for a transfer. This may take some time—staff turnover is not very high at most crime scene divisions, so there are few open positions, and there may be many applicants.

When (if) you succeed, you will work alongside your colleagues for a while, typically a year or maybe two. Then, you will go to the Swedish National Laboratory of Forensic Science for a training course. The course is spread out over a year, and you will spend about half a year there, two or three weeks at a time, alternating the coursework with your regular work.

There, you will meet forensic scientists, and you will learn both how the traces you and your colleagues recover and send to the laboratory are analyzed and what that means for your own work as a crime scene technician. You and your classmates will practice under these scientists' supervision how to recover traces and how to screen and prioritize—which traces should be sent off for analysis, which can be held until later, and which traces are the most important ones. While training, you will also devote quite some work and effort to some aspect of forensics that interests you.

You will, of course, already have learned some of what is being taught while working at the crime scene division, but perhaps not in a systematic manner. And before this training course, you will not have had a lot of chances to try out different methods and technologies. During the course, you will be working several practice cases, which allow you to do exactly that. When you examine these practice crime scenes, there will be teachers there who will be able to give advice or discuss your questions with you. And this won't be as stressful as investigating an actual crime scene, as a mistake here will not affect real investigations or people.

From your work at the crime scene division, you already know how important your work at the crime scene is for the whole of the criminal justice process. You know that the traces you recover are the basis for the forensic evidence that the laboratory will produce and that will become part of the investigation and thus contribute to the verdict in court. You probably already are aware that the quality of your work will affect the quality of the forensic evidence.

The course will help you see more clearly in which way your work ties into that of others. You will meet prosecutors, who will discuss crime scene reports with you. They will talk about what they need to read or hear and what about forensics is tricky for them. You will also hear the forensic scientists talk about what is important in their work and what frustrates them. They will explain exactly how you should recover and package different traces and why, and you will learn why analyses take the time they do, even though a quicker turnaround would be better for you and the police investigators and, of course, the victims of crime.

You may find some of their requirements hard to meet in everyday practice. Standardized methods of recovering traces may not be workable in exactly every situation and crime scene—after all, crime scenes do not come as standardized as laboratories. Still, you will probably appreciate the opportunity to talk and think about your work in relation to the judicial system as a whole. And understanding why forensic scientists make these requirements will help you come up with good solutions for those crime scenes and situations when you come across a case where the standard method will not work.

Occupational Hazards

A word of caution. Some occupational hazards you may be aware of already: Working as a crime scene technician does expose you to chemicals, some of which may not be beneficial to your health. There is also the risk associated with being a police officer—although being a crime scene technician will keep you away from most of the conflict that other police officers are exposed to on a regular basis.

What you also might want to think about is that being a crime scene technician will change your perception of the world.

The first change will come when you become a police officer and you learn to think about people in categories such as troublemakers versus the public. You may look back on your old self as having been a bit naive, or perhaps sheltered, especially when you look at a crowd and notice signs of criminal activity that would not have registered as suspicious before.

The second change comes with working crime scenes. For one, you will encounter the effects of people's violence against each other or against children. You will not go to murder or assault scenes every day of your working life, but probably you will go often enough to be affected. Others can choose to look at photographs only cursorily or not at all, but you will not be able to turn away. You will have to look, and look closely. And you will probably get used to it, although some cases will still be harder than others, even after lots of experience.

Secondly, your work will take you to a lot of homes. You will see how people in all parts of society live, and, as crime—particularly violent crime—tends more often to affect those who already are vulnerable, you will probably see quite a number of depressing homes. What is more, you will always come unexpectedly, so the residents will not have prepared their home to be seen by strangers. Perhaps you will find it even harder to see human beings living in destitution than you will find dealing with the aftermath of violence.

Finally, you will also probably see landscapes and cityscapes differently. Places that may have been familiar before will become overlaid with the cases in which you have been involved. A high-rise may no longer primarily be a building that disfigures the city or gives it a metropolitan flair, but the site of a family tragedy or a suspicious accident you investigated. An underpass may no longer only be trouble waiting to happen—be it because of slippery ice or because of local thugs—but the place where you searched for traces of what turned out to be a murder, working at three o'clock in the morning, with local news crews filming.

Summing Up: Being a Crime Scene Technician

So, being a crime scene technician, at least in Sweden, is not the glamorous high-speed and fast-returns job that you come across in books or on television. You will not be the one to reach a breakthrough in an interrogation—that is someone else's job. And sadly, unlike in the television shows, the Swedish police force does not provide flashy cars. You will perform a sometimes sweaty, disgusting, or tedious job, and you will always have to be thorough. You will talk to and write for a lot of people with very different types of expertise and different communication styles. You will write reports rather than participate in car chases, and you will certainly not solve violent crimes singlehandedly. But you will be able to make an important contribution to criminal justice and thus to society—which is what many crime scene technicians find rewarding with their job.

Acknowledgments

I am deeply indebted and immensely grateful to all of the crime scene technicians who so generously opened their world to me. I am also very grateful to Ilana Gershon for inviting me to contribute to this book. Special thanks to Marcus Andrae and Torbjörn Liwång for the wonderful photograph!

Suggested Readings

On forensic science, see:
Jim Fraser and Robin Williams, eds., *Handbook of Forensic Science*. Portland, OR: Willan Publishing, 2009.

On epistemic cultures, see:
Karin Knorr Cetina, *Epistemic Cultures: How the Sciences Make Knowledge*. Cambridge, MA: Harvard University Press, 1999.

On professions, see:
Andrew Abbot, *The System of Professions: An Essay on the Division of Expert Labor*. Chicago: University of Chicago Press, 1988.

On police investigations, see:
Camilla Hald, *Web Without a Weaver: On the Becoming of Knowledge: A Study of Criminal Investigation in the Danish Police*. Boca Raton, FL: Dissertation.com, 2011.
Martin Innes, *Investigating Murder: Detective Work and the Police Response to Criminal Homicide*. Oxford, U.K.: Oxford University Press, 2003.
Robin Williams and Jason Weetman, "Enacting Forensics in Homicide Investigations." *Policing and Society* 23, no. 3 (2013): 376–89.

On forensic evidence in the Swedish judicial system, see:
Corinna Kruse, "Legal Storytelling in Pre-Trial Investigation: Arguing for a Wider Perspective on Forensic Evidence." *New Genetics and Society* 31, no. 3 (2012): 299–309.
Corinna Kruse, "The Bayesian Approach to Forensic Evidence: Evaluating, Communicating, and Distributing Responsibility." *Social Studies of Science* 43, no. 5 (2013): 657–80.

On the history of some kinds of forensic evidence in the United States, see:
Michael Lynch, Simon A. Cole, Ruth McNally, and Kathleen Jordan, *Truth Machine: The Contentious History of DNA Fingerprinting*. Chicago: University of Chicago Press 2008.
Simon A. Cole, *Suspect Identities: A History of Fingerprinting and Criminal Identification*. Cambridge, MA: Harvard University Press, 2001.

On the complexities of forensic evidence in practice, see:

Amade M'charek, Rob Hagendijk, and Wiebe de Vries, "Equal before the Law: On the Machinery of Sameness in Forensic DNA Practice." *Science, Technology, and Human Values* 38, no. 4 (2013): 542–65.

On forensic evidence and the law, in particular its (perceived) credibility, see:

David S. Caudill and Lewis H. LaRue, *No Magic Wand: The Idealization of Science in Law.* Lanham, MD: Rowman and Littlefield, 2006.

Roland Bal, "How to Kill with a Ballpoint: Credibility in Dutch Forensic Science." *Science, Technology, and Human Values* 30, no. 1 (2005): 52–75.

On understandings of forensic evidence outside of the judicial system, see:

Helena Machado and Barbara Prainsack, *Tracing Technologies: Prisoners' Views in the Era of CSI.* Farnham, U.K.: Ashgate, 2012.

Johanne Yttri Dahl, "Another Side of the Story: Defence Lawyers' Views on DNA Evidence." In *Technologies of Security: The Surveillance of Everyday Life,* ed. Katja Franco Aas, Helene Oppen Gundhus, and Heidi Mork Lomell, 219–37. Abingdon, U.K.: Routledge, 2009.

Playing Piano without a Piano in Bolivia

Michelle Bigenho

The following narrative is an imagined scenario of a father giving advice to his son about working as a Bolivian musician. Urban working-class mestizos (non-indigenous Bolivians) often are those who play the indigenous inspired sounds that have come to represent this nation's music at home and abroad since at least as far back as the 1950s. Mestizos perform music that has roots in the indigenous Aymara and Quechua traditions of Bolivia's highlands as well as in the multiple lowland indigenous traditions. The music of these "popular" musicians often puts them at odds with those of the country's elite "classical" music scene, those trained in a conservatory and showcased in a national symphony orchestra. Even though many musicians cross these musical boundaries in their work, the greater prestige remains with the classical musician who has graduated from the conservatory. Popular musicians who play indigenous music as national folklore are keenly aware of these differences in status and power. In their careers, they have to learn how to navigate these complex social divisions.

The classically trained musician, however, usually does not tour the world under the label of "Bolivian" musician. Folklore musicians take up this niche in the world music machine, which has been built on the fame of Simon and Garfunkel's cover of the Andean song "El cóndor pasa" and global fascinations with leftist solidarity politics and indigenous sounds. Bolivian musicians try to push back against the market expectations that have been narrowly fixed by the typical sounds of the four-person Andean bands that have been far too ubiquitous in cosmopolitan cities. Because musicians now consider the European market to be saturated when it comes to Andean music, many Bolivian musicians consider themselves fortunate to have entered touring circuits in Japan, where they are more likely to perform as part of a school's multicultural curriculum than to give a concert in a major theater. Performance venues hold different values for Bolivian musicians—ascending from the street, to the school, to the theater. However, performing in these Japanese tours has brought relatively significant economic benefits for the Bolivian musicians lucky enough to secure such contracts.

You ask me, son, how did I get started as a musician? Well, I began as a dancer, not a musician. As a child, I was taking folklore dancing and ballet with Miss U. She used to teach only ballet, but by the 1950s and '60s, she had discovered the potential of "folkloric" ballet. A friend at the dance studio gave me my first *quena*.[1] When Miss U. found me practicing it in the bathroom at the studio, instead of rehearsing the dances with the other students she became enraged and snapped the instrument in two. That could have ended it all, but I was determined to learn music.

No one ever gave me lessons on the quena, son. I taught myself. If my family had more money, maybe I would have gone to the conservatory. But you know how that is. They didn't even teach folklore instruments then. Too far beneath them! Sure, conservatory training would have really helped, particularly now, as I am doing so much composing and arranging for my ensemble. I end up paying others to do the arrangements for our repertoire. Oh, I can arrange things. But others who have studied, they can come up with something prettier. There is nothing like someone who has

---

1. A *quena* is a notched flute played in Andean music.

studied! If you can get some conservatory training, son, it would help, as long as you keep in mind that "their way" is not the be-all and end-all of music, particularly in our country.

Son, see that piano in the corner of our living room? You have no idea yet how lucky you are. As a boy, I dreamed of playing the piano. I once took some lessons with Mr. E. What an amazing pianist! The problem was, we had no piano at home. In my desperation to practice for my lessons, I made a paper keyboard at home, drawing the black and white keys, running my fingers over them, and trying to imagine their sounds. When I went to my piano lesson, Mr. E. would scold me for not practicing. But how can you practice piano without a piano? Son, that's what it's like to work as a musician in Bolivia. You have to do everything with nothing. You have to learn to play piano without a piano. Needless to say, my piano lessons didn't last long. If you get the chance, son, get some conservatory training and learn the piano, especially for harmony and arrangements. Not having to pay others for arrangements would be a big perk, and you might even get some arranging contracts of your own.

I know you already have your heart set on putting up your own recording studio to make money. It's true. You can make money recording musicians and making advertising jingles. Everyone needs to record *something*. But that's not always so easy either. Keep your options open. Yes, son, to work as a musician in Bolivia, you always have to keep several things going at once. You never know which contact will bring you your next job, and you can't do all that late-night gigging forever. It wears on the body and the soul. Back in the '90s, that's what I was doing. I was playing with the groups Wara, Bolivian Jazz, and Música de Maestros as well as working in the back-up band for singers like la Q., el J., la Z. and la J. In those days, the clubs in Sopocachi, that upper middle-class neighborhood, still prominently featured Bolivian music—traditional, fusion, and all. Not today. It's all rock and heavy metal stuff in those places now. But in the '90s, we would be hired for the three-night weekend gig—Thursday, Friday, Saturday. Starting time was 10:30 p.m., but nothing ever happened before 11:15. I usually wouldn't make it home before 5:00 a.m.; sometimes the sun of the new day was already up. Every night my clothes reeked of cigarettes. And of course, I often had a few too many. Even if I didn't want to drink, a friend would show up to listen, and when we finished playing, he would insist on drinking with me. Each night brought a new encounter with a different long-lost friend who would feel greatly miffed if I didn't drink with him. The next day, after receiving the silent treatment from your mother and suffering the usual hangover, I'd be back in the same place again, longing for Sunday and four days of recovery before the next engagement.

Smoke and drink. Those are the big hazards of working as a musician in Bolivia. They'll try to get you hooked on other stuff as well. Lots of providers populate the scene. I managed to avoid them, unlike some of my fellow musicians. I've been in the United States and Europe, and there, they hardly allow smoking anymore. Can you imagine if they tried to keep people from smoking in Bolivian clubs?

Once you get involved in playing with so many different groups, you have to really watch out for the double bookings. I used to have simultaneous weekend gigs, say, at the nightclubs Equinoccio and Thelonious. We would play three sets at each venue, but I would be running back and forth between the clubs. The other band members, in both venues, were always pissed off at me. They would be marking time, impatiently awaiting my return from playing a set with the other group at the other club. When you have double bookings, you end up pleasing no one. You should be careful about playing with too many groups. You'll spend yourself, and people will think you'll just play with anyone. A musical prostitute. Of course, it's hard to say "no" if you have no other source of income. Today, most of that work in traditional Bolivian music has moved out of Sopocachi, up above the Plaza San Francisco, in those dance and music venues like the Eye of Water. In those places, by two in the morning, you really have to watch out for the drunken brawls. Do you want to see your children grow up? Do you want to meet your grandchildren? Son, look for work beyond the clubs.

Working in *prestes* carries even greater risks, when it comes to alcohol.[2] That's the problem when you play with a popular Bolivian group these days. You get sucked into the preste circuit. Everyone wants your group to play for their major ritual feast. Then it's rivers of drink. Straight through the weekend. No break. Remember Mr. T? He had to quit playing with

---

2. *Prestes* refer to large ritual feasts or fiestas that are held for patron saints of neighborhoods or villages.

the A's because his health couldn't take all the drinking that came with their preste contracts. People come to me, begging to hire my group for a preste. I always refuse. It's not worth it. Anyway, that's not what we're about.

We sound best in the theater performance. The problem is we don't have enough theaters in La Paz. It's really hard to secure dates for the theater, even when we have a friend working in that department. Too many performers and too few venues, even though the city has recently been turning some of the old cinemas into music venues.

No, son. We don't make money in the theater either. We are lucky if we cover our expenses and if the musicians get enough pocket money to cover their transportation costs for rehearsals. We are *really* lucky if we make enough so that musicians might buy new strings for their instruments. We have to pay so many fees just to perform at the theater—to the city, to the theater, and also to SOBODAYCOM.[3] Now that's a racket! You know that SOBODAYCOM charges me to perform my own compositions? And I never see anything significant from them in terms of payment to me as the composer. I think they just pay their own salaries. Such bureaucrats! They are supposed to protect us from piracy, but they don't seem successful in that department either. I have threatened to leave the association completely, but they have all my songs and works registered. I'm not sure what would happen if I tried to leave. So when we play in theaters, we barely cover all the fees we have to pay.

And that's to say nothing of advertising and publicity for the performances. That's when we really work the *ayni*.[4] Why do you think we do all those little performances they want us to play as "collaborations"? Not everyone from the group wants to play those, and as the director, I can't require it. But when it comes time to place an ad or print a concert program or get an interview about our concert on a television show, I call in favors. But even so, when we perform in the theater, we are lucky if we don't end up losing money.

Playing for tourists? Well, son, that too has its own challenges. Night after night, you have to play the same thing. And it's not just weekends,

---

3. SOBODAYCOM (Sociedad Boliviana de Autores y Compositores de Música) is Bolivia's music royalty collection society.

4. *Ayni* refers to reciprocal exchanges of labor, favors, or goods.

either. Remember Mr. A.? He often had to juggle our rehearsals and performances so he could make it to the *peña* Los Escudos.[5] Every night he had to be there for the tourists. The same time, night after night. It brought him a trickle of income, but it was something he could depend on—as long as he never missed a night.

Some tourists, mostly Europeans and Japanese, come looking for another generation of peña music, what they used to do up on Sagárnaga Street in the Peña Naira. That's all gone now. There's a restaurant there. It has the same name, and they might have some music now and again. But it's not the Peña Naira! In the '60s, the Naira used to be such a Mecca of artistic and cultural creativity. Such great musicians played there! Ernesto Cavour, Alfredo Domínguez, and the Swiss Gilbert Favre. The Peña Naira ended up being an important connection for some of our international touring contracts. Favre connected some Bolivian musicians to Europe. Cavour, who went to Europe with Favre in the group Los Jairas, quickly returned to Bolivia. He said he never could get used to living in Europe. I couldn't either. Things never have gone very well for me in Europe, at least financially. We never make money in those two-month folklore tours in France. We stay with families, play in the streets, and play at local fairs. But tour participants go into debt to pay their airfare for the trip. We drink a lot of good wine and eat some amazing food, but economically, it's a loss. We take artisan crafts and CDs to sell on the tour, but we hardly cover our out-of-pocket expenses. Why do we do it? Well, son, not all work as a musician has a direct payoff. It's about long-term commitments to the dance troupe that travels with us. It's also about showing the world something different about Bolivian music, to surprise them. They're all expecting some four-person Andean band in ponchos, something they hear on the street corner or in the subway on their daily commute. We show them something totally different.

I've toured Europe with musicians only, but these experiences have been pretty dicey. Granted, we have had some fabulous professional experiences, like teaming up with orchestras in Germany. Sometimes I have come home with all of one hundred dollars in my pocket after three months of touring. In those cases, we have to measure our success by the

---

5. A *peña* is a music club that usually features folklore and/or politically motivated songs.

tremendous applause we received. I was also proud to be representing my country. Over there, the ensemble's name becomes secondary to the fact we are a *Bolivian* band.

Some of these tours, though, have been a little too improvised for my taste. One tour was organized by Mr. C., a Bolivian living in Germany. We spent endless hours in a van, as Mr. C. drove us to different gigs. Once, I caught him falling asleep at the wheel. From then on, I never slept in the van while he was driving. Mr. C. never communicated to us about any schedule of events. Once, we were all sleeping at a friend's house. When we woke up and asked, "What are we doing today?" Mr. C. said, "You can go back to sleep. I'll let you know later what we're going to do." Daily meals were improvised as well. Sometimes we wouldn't eat all day. Then after a performance, our hosts would provide us with a huge meal. It's horrible to eat like that just before you sleep. One day, we hadn't eaten anything. From the back of the van, E. said, "I'm hungry. When are we going to eat?" Mr. C. responded, "What? Are you hungry again? You just ate yesterday. Go back to sleep." Yes, son. That has been a running joke in the family when we are all back home. "Oh, you're hungry again? But you ate yesterday. Go back to sleep." Yeah, it's funny now, but it wasn't so funny at the time. Son, there just isn't much of an audience now for Andean music in Europe. Besides, Europeans are going now for that New Age Native American look, not Andean music. I see the musicians losing their ponchos for the feather headdresses, fringed suits, and moccasins. And who knows what they are playing! But that's what the Europeans are going for now.

Japan is a different story altogether. You can still make relatively good money on a tour of Japan, and those tours are anything but improvised! The Japan connection began in the Naira too. It started with Cavour, who played at the Naira and who was contracted to tour Japan as a soloist on *charango*.[6] He turned on many Japanese to Bolivian music, putting Bolivia on their Andean map. Before Cavour, they only had sounds and images of Argentine folklore musicians who accompanied touring tango groups, along with some vague ideas about the Incas and Machu Picchu. Of course, they also were listening to Simon and Garfunkel's "El cóndor pasa" on

---

6. The *charango* is a small stringed instrument played in Andean music.

the radio. You know Takaatsu Kinoshita? His journey to Bolivia, which lasted ten years and eventually launched his Latin American music career, began with hearing Cavour play in Japan. Takaatsu's eventual return home marked the beginning of our touring contracts in his country. Those contracts, son, are definitely worthwhile, even though they too come with their own personal costs of being away from family.

Our work in Japan starts at home, when the company sends us the contracts. No, son! The contracts are never in Spanish. We ask Takaatsu to help us out. We have to trust them. The Japanese company always takes care of everything to get us there—airfare, visas, the works. But of course, if we are leaving our families for extended periods, we often have to leave financial obligations paid, and then some. One time, before leaving on tour, I had to leave a whole mountain of disposable diapers for you, all bought and paid for. A mountain of diapers, like the snow-capped Illimani you see on the horizon of the city. I hated leaving you. That is always the absolute worst part about these tours.

When we arrive in Japan, we have a few days to catch up to the jet lag and to hold a few rehearsals. Sure, we've all played together at different times in Bolivia, but at home, all the musicians are so busy with their own work. Sometimes, it's not until we arrive in Japan that we finally get to rehearse with *everyone*. The Japanese company also takes this time to observe us and to make suggestions about what will work best for Japanese audiences. The Japanese sound engineer uses these rehearsals to study how each musician plays and on what instruments. We have had really fabulous sound engineers, even if they were often frustrated with the company's lack of investment in decent sound equipment for the tour. The sound engineer did top-notch work in spite of the bad equipment.

Once the tour begins, the pace can be relentless. We might play over eighty performances in ninety days of touring. We play very few concerts in theaters. The company we toured with had us playing for school children in gymnasiums that have a stage at one end. Ideally, we arrive a couple hours before the show, with plenty of time to unload the bus, set up, do a sound check, put on our performance clothes, and practice a few passages before the concert. But we aren't always that lucky. Sometimes the company books multiple concerts in multiple schools on the same day, and we find ourselves doing all our preparations in a mere thirty minutes. Once we had three concerts in three separate schools, all in the same day!

Our shows for the kids run between forty and fifty minutes. Koji always has the repertoire timed to the minute, and when we're in Japan, he usually sets the program. He knows what the different Japanese audiences will like. For the schools, it's like a show on cultural diversity. We try to teach the kids about the different kinds of music we have in Bolivia. But they don't often see us beyond the categories of "Latin American" or "native." We always open with "El cóndor pasa" and an Aymara set to show the kids indigenous music from the highlands.

I know, son. "El cóndor pasa" is not Bolivian. But out there in the rest of the world, people equate that tune with the Andes. So we always have to play it. Later in the performance, we change to mestizo costumes and music. At the end of the show, though, some of the kids still don't know where we come from. Or they might even think we are Brazilian!

After the show, we have to break the set, load the bus, and sign autographs. Yes, the kids usually line up to get our autographs. Some of them come up to you with the tiniest piece of paper, asking: "Sign, please?"

After we finish the last show for the day, the bus driver takes us to a supermarket center where we break for lunch before the long drive to the

Figure 7.1 The Bolivian ensemble Música de Maestros performs an indigenous festival in Japan. Photograph from the collection of Michelle Bigenho.

next day's jobs. They used to drop us off at expensive restaurants where we were supposed to spend our per diem. But we saw the Japanese go elsewhere, to less expensive places, and we began to follow them.

Everyone tries to save money during the tour. The company pays for our hotel, and they give us the per diem for food. This is in addition to what they pay us as part of our contract. But our contract pay only comes at the very end of the tour. The company now pays us less, in the contract and in the per diem, than they did when we first started touring. They say the demand for our performances has gone down. Some musicians have complained, but what are we going to do? It's not like there is an abundance of these touring contracts.

Some people don't like these school tours. They prefer to stay at home and wait for the call to tour as a headlining musician. They say they want to be treated "like artists," play in theaters, stay in five-star hotels, and travel by airplane and bullet train. It's true. Playing in theaters is a whole different experience. When you arrive, the stagehands do everything for you! You don't lift a finger until sound check. You play with amazing sound systems that take your performances to a whole different level. People come hear you play, not because you represent a lesson in cultural diversity, but because they know and like you and your band. But that touring invitation doesn't come to just anybody. Not everyone is an Ernesto Cavour.

In Bolivia, we all work just as hard, but without ever seeing anything like the sums we make in Japan. With the money they earn on these tours, some people set up home recording studios, buying the equipment over several years of touring. You can get excellent systems there at good prices, sometimes used items that are just like new. You have to be careful, though, about how much you buy at once. One time Mr. E. had bought so much that it wouldn't fit in his luggage. He ended up having to leave part of the equipment in Japan until the next tour. Others use the earnings to build a home, buy a car and put it to work as a taxi, or pay studio fees for their next recording sessions. Ernesto Cavour spent much of his Japanese earnings setting up his museum of musical instruments on Jaén Street. Yes, son. These tours of Japan end up subsidizing the personal dreams and cultural projects of many Bolivian musicians. Otherwise, we just keep on playing piano without pianos! The work in Japan is still some of the best you can get as a Bolivian musician today. But it is so hard to leave your family for two or three months. That, son, is the very steep price of working as a Bolivian musician.

Acknowledgments

The details of this piece emerge from ethnographic fieldwork conducted over twenty years (1993–2013) with Bolivian musicians in La Paz, France, and Japan. Different musicians have told me their stories. Those who are fully named are actual individual musicians. All others are presented in ways that protect their privacy. This piece would not have been possible without many long conversations with several Bolivian musicians, primary among them being Rolando Encinas, Yuliano Encinas, René Alinas, Victor Hugo Gironda, Waldo Trujillo, Ernesto Cavour, Koji Hishimoto, Takaatsu Kinoshita, and Edwing Pantoja. I greatly appreciate their generosity in talking with me about their lives and in sharing their music with me.

Suggested Readings

On working as a Bolivian musician in La Paz during the 1990s, see:
Michelle Bigenho, *Sounding Indigenous: Authenticity in Bolivian Music Performance.* New York: Palgrave Macmillan, 2002.

On *prestes,* see:
Sian Lazar, *El Alto, Rebel City: Self and Citizenship in Andean Bolivia.* Durham, NC: Duke University Press, 2008.

On media piracy in Bolivia, see:
Henry Stobart, "Rampant Reproduction and Digital Democracy: Shifting Landscapes of Music Production and 'Piracy' in Bolivia." *Ethnomusicology Forum* 19, no. 1 (2010): 27–56.

On *ayni* and reciprocity in the Andes, see:
Catherine Allen, *The Hold Life Has: Coca and Cultural Identity in an Andean Community.* Washington, DC: Smithsonian Institution Press, 1988.
Rudi Colloredo-Mansfeld, *The Native Leisure Class: Consumption and Cultural Creativity in the Andes.* Chicago: University of Chicago Press, 1999.
Sian Lazar, *El Alto, Rebel City: Self and Citizenship in Andean Bolivia.* Durham, NC: Duke University Press, 2008.

On the Peña Naira, see:

Gilka Wara Céspedes, "New Currents in 'Música Folklórica' in La Paz, Bolivia." *Latin American Music Review* 5, no. 2 (1984): 217–42.

Giovanni Enrique Bello Gomez and Tomás Augusto Fernández Tejerina, "Peña Naira: Ruptura o continuidad en el folklore boliviano." *Anales de la Reunión Anual de Etnología* n. 24. La Paz: MUSEF, 2012.

On Los Jairas, see:

María Antonieta Arauco, *Los Jairas y el Trío Domínguez, Favre, Cavour: Creadores del neofolklore en Bolivia (1966–1974)*. La Paz: All Press, 2011.

On the history of the Andean flute connection with Europe, see:

Fernando Rios, "*La Flûte Indienne:* The Early History of Andean Folkloric-Popular Music in France and its Impact on *Nueva Canción*." *Latin American Music Review* 29, no. 2 (2008): 145–89.

On Bolivian music in Japan, see:

Michelle Bigenho, *Intimate Distance: Andean Music in Japan*. Durham, NC: Duke University Press, 2012.

Making Do in Perpetual Crisis: How to Be a Journalist in Buryatia

Kathryn E. Graber

Buryatia is a semi-autonomous republic of the Russian Federation, just north of Mongolia and about a five-day journey east of Moscow by train. With rugged mountains, sweeping steppe, dense taiga, and beautiful Lake Baikal, Buryatia's landscape resembles that of Montana, but some parts of it are also very urban. It is often called an "ethnic republic" because it is largely inhabited by ethnic Buryats, a Mongolic people who were incorporated into the Russian Empire in the seventeenth and eighteenth centuries. Today, however, two-thirds of the population is ethnically Russian, and only one-third Buryat. Both Russian and Buryat, an indigenous language closely related to Mongolian, are widely spoken, and ethnic Russians and Buryats work together in most offices and industries.

Workplaces in Buryatia are structured according to very different principles than those in the United States. Some of these differences proceed from the fact that Buryat culture differs from American culture—and from the Russian culture surrounding it. Buryats, for instance, place a great deal of emphasis on traditional kin networks and on personal relationships with people from the same ancestral villages and counties, people called your *zemlyak*s.[1] Whether you get a job or not may depend on who you know or on whether you are from the same district as the person doing the hiring. This is not in itself so different from hiring in the United States; we often call it "having connections." But while in the United States it is generally considered legally and morally wrong to engage explicitly in nepotism or to consider place of origin in hiring decisions, in Buryatia this is not necessarily so. Taking care of one's family and friends is considered honorable and proper, and some employers see prioritizing Buryats over Russians in hiring decisions as balancing out other structural inequalities.

Many other unique aspects of work life in Buryatia arose because this region, like the rest of the current Russian Federation, had a socialist economy for several decades before the Soviet Union disintegrated in 1991. In state socialism, the means of production were owned by the state, not by private individuals or corporations. Workplaces like farms that had previously been managed by single families were collectivized and managed by centralized government authorities that gave directives to local workers in a top-down fashion. The amount of macaroni to be produced in Buryatia, for instance, was determined in Moscow, as was the number of minutes of radio programming to be produced and aired. Production and consumption were carefully monitored. While this might sound very strict and authoritarian, in practice people came up with many decentralized ways of managing life and work that had nothing to do with what their bosses in far-off Moscow told them to do.

Journalists in Buryatia work all over the republic, but they are mostly based in the capital city, Ulan-Ude. In size and population density and in its relationship to the centers of power, Ulan-Ude is similar to Wichita, Kansas. And in many daily activities, being a journalist in Buryatia is not so different from being a journalist in Kansas. Journalists hold editorial meetings, go out on assignment to collect material for stories, conduct interviews, write and edit stories, and work together in office buildings. Around noon or 1 p.m. on weekdays in

---

1. *Zemlyak* literally means "a person from the same land or soil (*zemlya*)" and can be roughly translated as "fellow countryman" or "compatriot."

Figure 8.1 A popular *poznaya* in the center of Ulan-Ude, 2009. Photograph by the author.

Ulan-Ude, offices empty out so that everyone can have lunch. Some of the most popular places to eat lunch are *poznaya*s.

Poznayas are cafes that serve hot, milky tea and steamed meat dumplings called *pozy* in Russian or *buuza* in Buryat.[2] You might also order a garlicky, "Korean-style" carrot salad and a couple of slices of black bread to sop up the salty juices of your dumplings.

In the imagined interaction that follows, Bulat and Ayuuna go to lunch at a poznaya while Bulat is on break from his work at the newspaper office where Ayuuna will soon start an internship. Bulat, Ayuuna, and the people they discuss are all composite characters, containing bits and pieces of many different people I have known. Although in this imagined dialogue they are speaking English, in reality such people would likely be speaking a mix of Buryat and Russian. When Bulat

---

2. Steamed meat dumplings are widely loved across Turkic Central Asia, the Caucasus, Russia, Mongolia, China, and Tibet. The traditional Buryat version is round and usually filled with onion, salt, pepper, and chopped mutton, sometimes mixed with beef, pork, or horsemeat.

and Ayuuna talk about people being "Russian," they mean ethnically Russian, not that they live in Russia or are Russian citizens (there are separate words for this). Ayuuna follows Russian politeness norms in calling her elder "Bulat Dambaevich," with both his first name and his patronymic, whereas he may call her simply "Ayuuna" as his junior. "Uragsha!" is a popular Buryat exclamation meaning "Forward!"

Bulat: Waitress! I'll have two buuza for this girl. Four for me. Two teas with milk. Ayuuna, this is my treat—I invite you. Students never have any money. You must learn to survive like a student! Anyway, you want to be a journalist, as far as I understand, and you'll never make any money at that, I can assure you. . . . But remember, I'm an old man, almost retired. Don't let me dampen your youthful optimism. I'm very happy that you'll be joining us at the newspaper for your internship. We could use some new faces, some fresh blood, and I know you are a talented young writer. Your father has been our respected zemlyak, and of course, we are happy to help a young journalist from Yeravna spread her wings. . . . We saw you in the dance ensemble last year. Very beautiful. My, my, but you look very young. How old are you, anyway?

Ayuuna: I'm seventeen. I just started at Buryat State University, on scholarship.

Bulat: Good, good. It's good that young people want to practice journalism. I mean real journalism. Stories that illuminate the problems of real life and give people the tools to change them. Inspiring stories that show a person—the common man—his place in the world. Not advertising and gossip, like the crap that some of our colleagues peddle down the road. You know, journalism is of paramount importance to society. You don't remember the Soviet slogans, of course. You probably think Lenin was some kind of cartoon character. Ha! In my day, journalists were revered, and it was an honorable career. We were on the front lines, building state socialism and monitoring its progress. We had a *goal*. True, there was ideology, but there was honor, too. When there were problems, real problems—I'm talking about *glasnost* and the 1980s, you don't remember it, but you should know the history of your trade. When there were real problems—people abusing narcotics, Baikal being pumped full of industrial pollution, Russian ethnocentrism at the highest levels—it was journalists who illuminated them.[3] Yes, journalists in the Soviet period could be proud. Today everyone wants to major in psychology or management, everything is about money, and journalists don't get the respect they deserve. But Russia . . . ah, Russia. . . . You know, Russia needs you. Your *people* need you!

Ayuuna: I can only hope to have as honorable and celebrated a career as you, Bulat Dambaevich. We always read your articles in the village. And we watched you on television. My father always wanted me to get a good education, and he would say, "Look at our zemlyak, Bulat Dambaevich, and imagine what you could accomplish!"

Bulat: Well, understand, Ayuuna. Journalism is not work. Journalism is a calling, a lifestyle—a *career,* as you say. You won't be paid much. But this might be a good career path for you if you have literary aspirations. Or . . . you're a beautiful young lady, of course. And a beautiful, talented dancer. Maybe you want a career on the stage. But maybe you are wondering what you will do with your dance performance career after you break your ankle. They just hired a former dancer at the television station, you know. She looks a little like you. You might go into the performing arts, finish at the arts academy, and become a television reporter. But understand that if you do this—if you do this *as a woman*—you will be washed up by the age of forty.

Ayuuna: Why?

Bulat: Because, my dear Ayuuna, no one wants to see an old woman on camera. Age suits a man, it gives him greater authority. It does not suit a woman. But! But . . . some of our nation's best writers are women of a dignified age. A television reporter who can write

---

3. In the late 1980s, Mikhail Gorbachev attempted to make Soviet government processes more transparent and open to the public, a reform he called *glasnost* (meaning "openness"). Censorship of the press eased, and there was much greater freedom of information. Journalists exposed political corruption, environmental degradation, social ills, and systemic flaws in Soviet government that had previously been carefully hidden.

can move to a radio station or a newspaper. So work on your writing skills, while you are at our newspaper. Work hard.

Ayuuna: I don't think I want to be a television journalist anyway.

Bulat: No? What kind of journalist do you want to be?

Ayuuna: I want to travel! I want to write stories that are important to my relatives, that my grandmother in Yeravna will want to read.

Bulat: Hmm. Your grandmother in Yeravna might just want to read about the neighborhood cows. It is important to identify topics that people will want to read, but you must think a little bigger. Your grandmother—what do you think she wants to read?

Ayuuna: Um, well . . . maybe about our history? She always cuts out articles about the history of our family, relatives, about how they got separated during the war . . . about boys who became well-known Buddhist monks and scholars . . . about you.

Bulat: So you want to write stories just about Yeravna?

Ayuuna: Well, no . . . I mean, not really. I don't know. . . . How do you choose what to write about?

Bulat: Ha ha, don't worry! You won't have very much choice at first anyway. You know, being a rookie journalist is like being an apprentice. You have to start by doing what other people tell you to do. And seize every opportunity! When I was your age, I was studying to be a schoolteacher. Then one day, my uncle called me on the dormitory phone. He called all the way from our village to the city, and he sounded excited. He said that at the collective farm that morning, a man had come in to trade ledger books. It seems that in his office in Ulan-Ude, they had run out of paper—notebooks and typewriter paper and so on. Paper was always in short supply back then. There was always a "paper crisis" or a "press crisis" or some such thing. It was very difficult to even get enough newsprint to print the newspaper—editors had to work very hard at that—so there was nothing left to write on or use in typewriters. We saved cardboard boxes and posters and wrote on the backs of them. This man had heard that there was a box of ledger books at our village farm. So while he was visiting the village for some other reason, he came to see about those ledger books.

Ayuuna: To buy them?

Bulat: Of course not! To "buy them," geez. . . . With what money?! No, not to buy them; he wanted to trade for them. You know, we did a lot of trading in the Soviet period, even more than now, because stores would not always have what a person wanted or needed. Paper, steel, shoes . . . it was all part of the "shadow economy." We were all going about our daily business, moving things from here to there and getting things done, outside of what was written down in the official numbers of economists. You had to trade to survive. Because if you waited for paper to arrive from Irkutsk or Moscow, ha! You'd wait a long time. So this guy, he wanted to trade for these ledger books. Only, he said, he had nothing to trade. He was rich in words and spirit, he said, but he had nothing that would improve the weight of sheep or wheat.

Ayuuna: This is like a riddle. Are you teasing me, Bulat Dambaevich?

Bulat: No, no. But he did have a way with words, and he invented many a great riddle in his day. He could speak Buryat in verse, just make up poetry like he was having a regular conversation with you! And he knew all of the great Russian classics, of course—Pushkin and Tolstoy, Dostoevsky and so on. Who do you think that man was?

Ayuuna: Rich in words and spirit . . . doesn't help animals. . . . Well, I guess he was . . . a journalist?

Bulat: Of course, my dear. He was the senior editor of our venerable newspaper. So when he said he had nothing to trade, my uncle—my uncle was a very smart man, very quick on his feet—my uncle said, "Ah! We have this bright young nephew in the city who's studying to be a schoolteacher but is a talented writer!" He gave the editor all of the farm's ledger books, and the editor told him that I should show up to begin work at the newspaper.

Ayuuna: So that is how you launched your career!

Bulat: Well no, not exactly. Like I said, to be a journalist is to be an apprentice, and you do not begin by writing important stories for the front page. First I helped the typographer set the daily newspaper to be produced, every night, very late. Only one day, finally, one of the regular reporters was sick—I say "sick" but in truth he was very drunk, on some bad vodka, and his wife couldn't find him for three days—but we didn't say so because he might have been fired—and because I was there, working hard at the printing press, the assistant editor came down to ask me to go report the story.

Ayuuna: Was it terribly exciting?

Bulat: No, it was a story about milk. You know, Ayuuna, you say a journalist doesn't help animals, but that's not true. One of the first stories that I wrote was about this dairy worker. She was the top milker in Buryatia three years in a row, with all kinds of Soviet orders and medals from Moscow. A very important lady, important for the development of the nation. But I wasn't so interested in this. I wanted more . . . philosophical stories, on literary topics, culture and so on.

Ayuuna: You like big ideas.

Bulat: Yes, that's right. I like big ideas. Later I could write more of the stories that I wanted to write. And later on I moved to radio and television to develop new formats and kinds of material. It's important to keep the creative energy alive. It's practical, too. Our Buryatia is not large—you know, you can have a varied career here, in radio and television and whatever internet things become possible, if you have writing skills—that's what's paramount, writing skills—and it pays to be flexible. . . . Eat, eat. Eat your buuza while they're hot. If you're going to be a journalist, you need to know how to eat quickly when you can. Journalism isn't like other careers. It's not like you'll be an accountant or a government official, looking slowly over books. Not like your uncles in Yeravna, tending sheep. It's a fast-paced career. There's always a deadline, always an appointment, always someone to see.

Ayuuna: Do you have any advice . . . like, general advice . . . for what I should do to become a good reporter?

Bulat: Sure. Well, your teachers in the journalism program at the university will have some ideas about this. When I was your age, we didn't have a journalism program or even Buryat language and literature departments in Buryatia—you had to go west, to Irkutsk. It's good there's a local program now. You will be a real professional.

Ayuuna: I'm sure it will be a good program. But . . . what do *you* think I should do?

Bulat: OK. Waitress! Another two cups of tea with milk. OK. "Advice for the Young Journalist"—that's how we'll title it. I can see it on page four, above the fold, in the "youth" section. "Advice for Our Young Journalist Ayuuna, of Yeravna."

Ayuuna: ". . . of the Republic of Buryatia, Russian Federation, . . . Planet Earth."

Bulat: Good, you're already thinking bigger! First, read and watch. . . . Do you have a pen? You should always have a pen and notebook. Ah, good, I see you brought something. That's good. Write this down.

Number one. You should READ AND WATCH THE NEWS EVERY DAY. I know young people like the internet, and they say that there's a "crisis in journalism" and so on and that there's not going to be print newspaper for very much longer. There is always some kind of crisis going on. This so-called "digital age" is not going to change the fact that someone has to write a good story! Anyway this is Siberia, not New York. Your grandmother in the village probably doesn't use the internet anyway. Maybe on her cell phone, I guess. So you need to read the print newspapers and listen to the radio too. Remember that most of our local newspapers and television and radio stations don't have the technical expertise or the computer . . . what do they call it? "Server?" Well, whatever it is, there's not space or money to put a lot of broadcasts and stuff online.

Come to think of it, that is something that I wanted to ask you about. We have started a new project to publish some of our stories online, for young people and for some of our Buryat friends and relatives living in the diaspora, in Moscow and St. Petersburg, the United States, Germany, and so on. Could you help with that project?

Ayuuna: Well I don't know very much about the internet. But . . . my brother does. He's really good at computers, and he lives here in Ulan-Ude. He could help. He doesn't have a job right now; he just helps our cousin with his business. . . . Could you hire him?

Bulat: Ayuuna, with what *money* could I hire him? Have you been listening at all?

Ayuuna: Oh . . . right.

Bulat: This brings me to Number two. This is connected to how I got my own job. LEARN TO BARTER. No one has money, so you've got to learn to trade what you *do* have. We, for example, want your brother's help with our internet project. Now, what might your brother need?

Ayuuna: I don't know. . . .

Bulat: You said he helps your cousin with his business. What kinds of things does he do?

Ayuuna: They call it "tech support"—they fix cell phones, print out documents. . . . They get old, broken computers and fix them to resell.

Bulat: So what do you think we could provide your brother?

Ayuuna: Maybe . . . maybe he could use the office to run the business? Like, use the printers and computers after hours?

Bulat: Good thinking! That is how you barter. We also have advertising space. We could see about running an advertisement for your cousin's business. Or perhaps we would do a news story on the business, "Young Tech Support Professionals of Ulan-Ude" or something to that effect. That could be a good human interest story.

Ayuuna: But, Bulat Dambaevich, isn't that hidden advertising?

Bulat: Oy, that "hidden advertising" nonsense! Where did you hear that?

Ayuuna: I read about it in my journalism textbook.

Bulat: Ayuuna, ignore what those naive westernizing journalism textbooks tell you about the distinction between advertising and reporting. As a reporter, your duty is to provide information. That includes covering sales at local grocery stores, because the people deserve to know where they can find the best products for the best prices. It includes covering new businesses when they open so that your readers know where to find new services. And it certainly includes covering the accomplishments of your brother and cousin so that the residents of our city know whom to call to get their computers and cell phones fixed. And so that your relatives in Yeravna can be proud, of course. Don't *you* trust your brother to fix your cell phone? Wouldn't you agree that people in Ulan-Ude should know that they can call him to get their cell phones fixed, rather than some other random guy?

Ayuuna: Yes, I guess so. I never thought of it that way. It just seems like it would be hard to be an objective reporter, if I'm reporting on my brother's business. American journalists have a professional creed, and they say you are supposed to provide objective reporting and analysis.

Bulat: Nonsense! Of course the American newspapers will tell you there is such a thing as "objectivity," but they are owned by huge corporations, and they are corrupted by money. They are even more dependent on advertising revenue than we are, because at least some of our operating budget comes from the state. Do you think they can be "objective" when their salaries come from private businesses and enormous corporations? Everyone has bias!

Ayuuna: So how can I be objective?

Bulat: Don't worry about it so much. In the Soviet period, we had to report on certain things, using certain language. But readers knew that, and they knew how to look past the surface to the depths of a story. It's the same today. Your readers aren't idiots. They can read between the lines.

Ayuuna: Do you think American readers can read between the lines?

Bulat: No. I'm afraid they suffer from a different type of ideology—the expectation of objective reporting! Our poor comrades.

OK now, Number three. USE YOUR CONNECTIONS. We journalists can only do our jobs because we have *access.* Access to people, access to events, access to the secrets inside of organizations. . . . To get access to the institutions you'll be reporting on, you'll need to work your connections through friends and family.

Ayuuna: I don't have any connections, Bulat Dambaevich.

Bulat: Nonsense again! You have some very powerful connections. How did your brother get his driver's license? How does your cousin find business associates? How do your girlfriends find their husbands?

Ayuuna: Well, I guess they're mostly people we know . . . people from Yeravna. Our zemlyaks.

Bulat: Exactly! You are connected to many, many people by being from Yeravna. Many of your zemlyaks live right here in Ulan-Ude, and all over Russia. And even all over the world. We have many events for people from Yeravna. So go to those events to keep up networks in your ancestral district. And LEARN TO DRINK! That, probably, should be Number four. Journalists love to drink, and Russians love to drink, and Buryats love to drink. If you were a man, I'd tell you that most of your professional connections will be made and maintained through alcohol. As a woman, you won't have to drink as much. But the most respected women in journalism, they can sling it back like the men! So you better develop a high alcohol tolerance and learn all the appropriate toasting and drinking rituals. Now where were we?

Ayuuna: Using connections.

Bulat: Right, use your connections. Now, *blat* is something different.[4] You are very young. Have you heard of blat? Do you really know what it means?

Ayuuna: I think so. When you say you got something "by blat," it means that you had a friend or relative on the inside of an organization, or maybe that you paid someone a bribe. When Medvedev, the last president of Russia, said he was trying to combat "corruption," that's what he meant, right? Isn't blat just corruption?

Bulat: Well, sort of. Blat is grease for the wheels. Sometimes you could call that corruption, but most of the time if you give someone a little gift or do him a little favor, and he does something for you in return, how is that corrupt? That is being a reasonable person and knowing how to get things done. You need a document processed faster, so you bring in some nice cognac. Fine. Now if you don't know the person, or he asks you for something when he should be doing it for you anyway as part of his paid job, that's more like a bribe. Recently bribes have become more . . . delicate. After Medvedev's campaign against corruption . . . well, a guy will still ask you for a bribe, but it won't be straightforward like it used to be. He won't just ask for it. He'll beat around the bush. It's very important to understand when a person is asking you for a bribe and what exactly he expects. Most of the time we can't pay

---

4. *Blat* is sometimes translated as "pulling strings."

money for information or paperwork, because we don't have any way for the accountant to list the expense. But sometimes we can barter something. Many years ago, when I worked at a television station in another city, we had to reapply for our broadcasting license—the media laws are always changing, you know—and a local bureaucrat denied our registration. He said a form was missing. Well, of course a form wasn't missing. He just wanted a bribe.

Ayuuna: That's definitely corruption!

Bulat: A journalist has got to consider a story from all sides. Now, Ayuuna, this was during one of our many economic crises, the collapse of the ruble in 1998. This bureaucrat hadn't been paid in four months. His children were hungry, the public health care system had completely fallen apart, and his grandmother needed medicine. This was the only way he knew to take care of them. What would *you* have done?

Ayuuna: I guess . . . I guess I would do the same thing.

Bulat: Of course you would. This bureaucrat's problem was that you can't get blood from a stone. The station didn't have any money for blat! But at least we could pay our employees. The bureaucrat's eldest son was very good with a video camera, it turned out, so we hired him as a cameraman. The registration problem went away.

Ayuuna: I think I see. It's like how I got this internship, except the cameraman wasn't the relative or zemlyak of anyone at the station, so he had to use some other kind of leverage. So . . . if you had been the director and it had been your relative, you would have hired him, even if it hadn't been to get rid of the registration problem or solve any of your own problems?

Bulat: Naturally.

Ayuuna: Is there a difference between that and nepotism, Bulat Dambaevich? My friend Natasha has a brother, I think his name is Ivan. He wanted to get a job at a factory as an engineer. They said he was the smartest in his class at school, that he graduated from the vocational-technical school with the highest grades. But the factory didn't hire Ivan. Instead they hired someone who was related to the assistant director. Natasha and her parents were very upset about it. They said that it wasn't fair—that it was nepotism.

Bulat: Let me guess. The guy they hired was Buryat.

Ayuuna: Yeah, that's what they said. They said he was Buryat, and that they always hire Buryats at that factory.

Bulat: And is your friend Natasha Russian?

Ayuuna: Um. . . . Yes, she's Russian.

Bulat: Then she doesn't know. Russians . . . I won't say Russians are bad people. We all—all nationalities—we all have our pluses and minuses. But Russians have a different outlook, a different worldview. You must remember first and foremost that you're a Buryat and help your friends and family. Sure, Russians complain all the time about how Buryats keep jobs for their own kin and friends, but they don't understand the system. This is Buryatia. If your cousin comes to you and needs a job, and you do not help, where will he go? What will his father say to you, when you have disrespected them?

Ayuuna: You're right, of course. We depend on each other a lot. This is all really good advice.

Bulat: Let me tell you, Ayuuna, we survived socialism, we survived capitalism and the crazy privatization that followed. There is always one "crisis" or another. In the most recent global financial crisis, you saw how America fared. They thought it was a catastrophe, like a second Great Depression! But here we weathered it fine and kept our good humor, even though the economy took a much larger hit. Why do you think we're so good at it? How do people survive? I'll tell you. Every person knows his place in the world. We know how to get things done without money and when to rely on our relatives. Everything I have told you today is about making do—making do in a state of perpetual crisis. You will be a great journalist in Buryatia. Uragsha!

Acknowledgments

The field research informing this chapter was generously supported by the National Science Foundation, the Social Science Research Council, the U.S. Department of Education Fulbright-Hays program, and the University of Michigan. For comments on drafts, I thank Ilana Gershon, Emily

McKee, Richard F. Nance, Mikaela Rogozen-Soltar, and Tristra Newyear Yeager. Most of all, I thank the journalists of Buryatia who invited me into their world.

Suggested Readings

On the shadow economy and blat, see:
Alena V. Ledeneva, *Russia's Economy of Favours: Blat, Networking, and Informal Exchange.* Cambridge, U.K.: Cambridge University Press, 1998.
Alena V. Ledeneva, *How Russia Really Works: The Informal Practices That Shaped Post-Soviet Politics and Business.* Ithaca: Cornell University Press, 2006.

On crisis, see:
Olga Shevchenko, *Crisis and the Everyday in Postsocialist Moscow.* Bloomington: Indiana University Press, 2009.

On risk in postsocialist contexts, see:
Katherine Verdery, *What Was Socialism, and What Comes Next?* Princeton, NJ: Princeton University Press, 1996.

On Soviet language and cynicism toward it, see:
Alexei Yurchak, *Everything Was Forever, Until It Was No More: The Last Soviet Generation.* Princeton, NJ: Princeton University Press, 2006.

On reading between the lines, see:
A. Sinyavsky, *Soviet Civilization: A Cultural History.* J. Turnbull, translator. New York: Arcade Publishing, 1988.

On Russians' expectations of journalistic bias, see:
Ellen Mickiewicz, *Television, Power, and the Public in Russia.* Cambridge, U.K.: Cambridge University Press, 2008.

How to Be a Professional Organizer in the United States

Carrie M. Lane

As secure, well-paid jobs become increasingly scarce in the twenty-first-century United States, many Americans are scrambling to find work that is both profitable and personally fulfilling. Self-employment can seem an alluring alternative for those who have endured repeated layoffs and prolonged job searches. Running your own business might offer both autonomy and some semblance of job security. But what should this business be? As the gap between the wealthy and the poor grows ever larger in the United States, the expanding high-end service sector offers new opportunities for those with the right skills and connections. Many of these occupations are explicitly gendered, as women tend to be perceived, and often perceive themselves, as the most skilled and appropriate providers of intimate physical and emotional services. Professional organizing, in which organizers are hired to design and implement systems to organize clients' spaces, belongings, and schedules, is one such overwhelmingly female service occupation.

Most organizers are women, usually white, middle- and upper-class, educated women. So are their clients, those in the United States who are willing and able to pay the fees that organizers charge—between $25 and $150 per hour. That so many organizers and clients are white, well-off, educated women plays a key role in shaping both the structure and culture of this occupation as well as the outside perceptions of this work and its value. In addition, the field has struggled to establish occupational legitimacy because the profession involves physical and emotional labor that has traditionally been performed for little or no pay by low-status women such as domestic workers, homemakers, and secretaries.

Professional organizing is still a relatively small field—the largest professional association for organizers has around four thousand members, most in the United States. But the industry's impressive growth since its start in the 1970s testifies to the rising allure of this young occupation as well as the growing demand for such services across the United States, especially in urban and suburban areas. Overwhelmed by their own prosperity, Americans find themselves in the position, absurd by global standards, of having too many possessions. One in ten American households now rent a storage unit to house excess belongings. The culture's rampant materialism, combined with nearly unlimited access to cheap, disposable goods, has fostered a situation in which many people find themselves unable to cope with the cluttered, disorganized spaces in which they live and work. Those with the resources to do so can now hire organizational experts to help them sort, store, and even discard their belongings, reflecting the tendency of privileged Americans to outsource even the most intimate aspects of their homes and lives.

In the imagined email that follows, an experienced professional organizer explains to a newly unemployed acquaintance the delicate balance it takes to succeed in this distinctive profession. Although the email's author and recipient are both imaginary, its content reflects what I have learned from interviewing, observing, and working alongside more than fifty professional organizers in Los Angeles, New York, and other large and small U.S. cities.

Dear Sarah,

I'm sorry to hear of your recent job loss. That's a hard thing to go through at the best of times, and the current economy certainly doesn't help matters. I can understand why you've decided to take your career in a new direction, and I'm so glad you reached out to me about professional organizing. I love my work and I'm always happy to chat with folks interested in starting their own organizing businesses. Of course I have to keep a few trade secrets for myself—I can't be handing my whole business model over to the competition!—but I'll be happy to tell you about the field and what I see as the most important "tricks of the trade."

First, I should explain exactly what a professional organizer is, as there are plenty of misconceptions out there. Yes, organizers are sometimes hired to alphabetize a celebrity's shoe collection by designer or make a living room resemble a page from the Pottery Barn catalogue. But more often than not, we're hired by real people to help create and maintain organizing systems that work for their real, everyday lives, whether at home or in the office. Some clients are a bit disorganized and just need a helping hand and a gentle nudge in the right direction. Perhaps a busy holiday season has led to a daunting stack of unopened mail and unfiled paperwork—we've all been there!—or the arrival of a new baby demands repurposing a home office into a nursery. Some of our clients face more serious challenges. I once worked with a family who needed to sort through decades of accumulated belongings in just two weeks before they moved out of state. That was a rough one, but I brought in a few of my organizer friends as assistants and we got the job done in time! Mind you, I don't always work in people's houses. Just last week a doctor decided to adopt an online filing system and brought me in to completely re-imagine her office's layout and workflow.

Because organizing can involve such a wide range of tasks, most of us choose to focus on specific types of jobs or clients. Some of us specialize in closets, others work only in garages. (It's mostly the few men among us who do the garage work—I guess it feels less "girly" to them than organizing kitchen cabinets!) With the Baby Boomers getting older, lots of organizers are catering to senior citizens who are in the process of downsizing. On the other end of the spectrum, I know an organizer with seven children who works almost exclusively with big families. And when you have been doing this for long enough, you get to say no to doing some things that you can't stand. I personally hate working with paper—sorting it goes so slowly!—but I don't mind getting my hands dirty, so closets, attics, and storage units are just my style. I'm not all that tech-savvy, so I leave the digital organizing (cleaning up those desktop icons, organizing digital photos, moving documents to the "cloud," whatever that is) to the younger generation. But in the beginning you probably won't choose at all—you'll just take whatever job comes and figure out later, like I did, where your special talents and interests lie.

Even though we all specialize in our own little areas, some parts of the job are the same regardless of exactly where or with whom you choose to work. As I see it, there are three basic principles all organizers should follow, and please forgive me if I sound a bit preachy at times. We organizers, especially those like me who have been at this since the early days in the 1970s, tend to be protective of our profession. We welcome new people to the field (there's enough work for everyone, I always say), but we also want to make sure new organizers don't tarnish our reputation. You've got to understand, we've worked really hard to be taken seriously as a profession. As you can imagine, a bunch of women trying to get paid for helping people get organized didn't always go over well back in the 1970s. I still remember the man at a cocktail party who, when I described what I did, said, "So you basically want to get paid for being a housewife?" Well, you can imagine how mad that made me, especially since the whole reason I started this business was because I needed to make my own money after my divorce!

I don't really think of myself as a feminist (although some of my organizer friends do), but I think it's fair to say that when a job is done by women, and about 95 percent of us organizers are women, especially when it's often done in the home, people tend to look down on it and think the work is unimportant and not worth much. It's true that clutter is what people sometimes call a "first-world problem," and yes, we know organizing can seem trivial when you think about the people living in dire poverty and hunger around the world. But that doesn't mean disorganization doesn't create real problems for people, and not just for the ultra-wealthy. That said, most of the time I am working for people who, in one way or another, are pretty privileged. I tend to be okay with that, because I think I provide a useful service to the folks who hire me, but that doesn't mean it doesn't sting a little when people turn their nose up at what I do because I'm not curing cancer or righting the wrongs of the world.

Despite these criticisms, demand for organizing services is higher than it's ever been, and not just in the United States—I know of organizers in at least twenty-three other countries! With so many dual-career couples out there working longer hours, lots of the tasks that used to be handled by homemakers are left undone. And I think it's fair to say that Americans today are asked to do more and more with less and less—work more for less pay, parent more intensively with less time, keep up better appearances with less money—and they're feeling overwhelmed by it all. It's no surprise so many people have started turning to others for help managing their busy, crazy lives.

With all that demand out there, it's a wonderful thing that people like you are interested in becoming organizers. But it's important, for you and for the profession, that you understand what this job really involves before you leap into a new career. So here goes—the first rule of being a professional organizer is. . . .

Be Organized, But Not Too Organized

You mentioned that you watch a lot of organizing TV shows. I've seen those, too, and I'll warn you, most of them aren't very realistic. Sure, if I had an unlimited budget and a team of twenty people I could reorganize an entire home in a weekend, but for us mere mortals the process usually takes much, much longer. And I'm not sure the people on those shows get served all that well, really, if after the camera crew departs they just go back to their old habits.

Still, when you watch those shows it can seem like becoming an organizer takes nothing more than buying a label maker and setting up a website featuring before-and-after photos of the great job you did on your mom's garage. Voilà—a business is born! And it's true there's a low cost of entry to the profession, which is one reason it's so appealing to people looking for a new career that won't take too much time or money to get started. With secure jobs so hard to come by these days—and even harder to keep!—working for yourself, even if it means working longer hours for less money, has become an alluring option for a lot of people. Plus, this is one of the few jobs these days that can't be outsourced to another country. On top of all that, when I was first starting out, running a business out of my own home meant that I could schedule my work around my kids' school days, at least when my clients were willing. If there were more affordable child care situations out there I might have gone the more traditional route of working for someone else. But as it was, my options were pretty limited, and I think lots of women with kids today find themselves in a similar situation.

So I can see lots of reasons why a single mom like you might want to be a professional organizer. And as you said in your email, you've always been a very organized person. Me, too! I even alphabetized my bookshelves when I was a kid! And that's important—having a good head for organization is a big part of what we do. We need to be able to visualize how objects fit in space, re-imagine how crowded rooms will look once piles of belongings are moved out, and know how best to approach thorny organizational challenges.

That said, being organized and helping other people get organized are two very different things. I once got a call from a nice young woman who, like you, wanted to start her own organizing business. She told me she was so organized it drove her crazy to see her coworkers' cluttered desks. I'll tell you what I told her: Being an organizer means voluntarily surrounding yourself, day after day, with disorganized people and cluttered spaces. If you can't tolerate messy spaces or the people who create them, then organizing isn't the job for you! And that's why I say you need to be organized but not *too* organized.

Being too organized means you aren't able to empathize with people who, unlike you, have trouble getting organized, or you will try to impose your own standards for order on your clients. If you want everything to look perfect, you might be better off sticking with organizing your own things. One person's standard of tolerable clutter can differ widely from another's, and if you're too rigid about what being

Figure 9.1 Most goods in the pantry are transferred from their original packaging to clear, labeled bins to keep things organized and see they are running low. Photograph by the author.

organized looks like, you might end up creating a system your clients won't be able to keep up.

For example, I like to arrange the clothes in my closet by color. I like how it looks, and it makes it easy for me to find things. And as you can see from the attached photo, I'm a fan of labeled containers for keeping track of items in my pantry. But that doesn't mean my clients want the same systems. Just last weekend I was helping a family unpack the kitchen in their new home. They had forty-seven coffee mugs for a family of four—forty-seven! I suggested they choose the dozen or so mugs they liked the best and donate the rest, but they had no interest in that. They said they use every one of those mugs. I don't believe them, but it isn't my job to tell them how many mugs they need, so I found room for every last one of those darn coffee mugs on their kitchen shelves. I did convince them to pare down their Tupperware collection by at least half, though, so I'll take my victories where I can get them.

As you can see, being a good organizer requires sensitivity to other people's perspectives and proclivities, which leads me to my next guideline. . . .

Be Emotionally Connected, But Not Too Emotionally Connected

Being organized is only half, perhaps even less than half, of what it takes to be a good organizer. We have to work closely with clients to determine what needs to be done and how best to do it, as well as what underlying issues or behaviors might have contributed to the disorganization. That means we have a lot of work to do before the actual work of organizing can even begin.

During our initial phone call I try to establish what the client hopes to accomplish and whether I'm well suited to assist with that goal. For instance, when a job requires financial expertise, I refer the client along to an organizer with more experience in that field. Or when you're starting out you might come across a job that involves a level of hoarding you're not trained to handle. In that case, you could call an experienced organizer like me to take the lead. (I'm certified through the Institute for Challenging Disorganization to work with clients who have conditions, like hoarding disorders, attention deficit disorder, and obsessive-compulsive disorder, that impair their ability to get and stay organized.) Finding another organizer to take the job or work alongside you is rarely a challenge. We organizers refer to ourselves as the most collaborative group of competitors you'll ever see. We pride ourselves on our willingness to support and assist one another. This doesn't mean we never step on one another's toes or compete over clients—it happens!—but it does mean you'll always have a group of experienced organizers to turn to for advice and assistance, especially if you join one of our professional associations such as NAPO (that's the National Association for Professional Organizers) or, as I mentioned above, ICD (the Institute for Challenging Disorganization).

Once I've decided to take a job, the next step is to develop a trusting, honest relationship so that the client feels comfortable discussing what can at times be sensitive or difficult subjects. Most people hire organizers to help deal with "stuff"—too many belongings for a given space, back-logged files, or overstuffed storage units that have become too expensive to maintain. Yet organizing is rarely, if ever, just about stuff. Instead, the problems we're brought in to solve usually have to do with how people feel about their stuff, rather than with the belongings themselves. For example, helping someone sort through a deceased spouse's possessions is never just a physical task, not for the client and not for me. Moving can be a stressful experience in the best of situations; when the move is prompted by a layoff, eviction, or relocation to a retirement facility, more complicated feelings and issues are bound to come up during the organizing process. Handling jobs like these involves sensitivity and sometimes a level of emotional care-taking you might be surprised that your clients expect of you.

When the client is satisfied, though, it is great. I have many repeat clients. I helped one woman move into her new home when she was expecting a baby. That baby is now in college, and I still work with her once a month to keep on top of her filing and bills! Our long relationship helps us work together more efficiently and effectively, but it has its drawbacks, too. I think some of the people who hire me are looking for a friend as much as they are an organizer. Nowadays most of us are more disconnected than ever, even with Facebook—or maybe because of it! It's seems we're more comfortable hiring people to help us, even to help us feel liked and supported, than we are reaching out to friends and family. I don't mind playing that role for clients, but it does muddy the professional waters a bit.

My clients and I may be friendly, we may even both consider ourselves to be friends. But when I'm on the job, I'm there as a paid service provider. No matter how friendly we may be, we organizers believe there are certain lines that should not be crossed, for ethical and practical reasons. That doesn't mean we all agree on exactly where those lines lie, but we do agree that they exist. NAPO provides ethical guidelines for the profession. We must advertise our services in an honest manner, keep all client information confidential, and respect the intellectual property rights of other organizers. In practice, however, each organizer must decide for herself when and how to apply those guidelines in a given situation.

Even experienced organizers sometimes disagree about what constitutes a "problem" during the organizing process. For example, some organizers refuse to accept gifts from clients, while others accept gifts so long as they are inexpensive. Some organizers do not discuss their private lives with clients. One of my organizing friends and I debate this all the time. She believes that the client is best served if she keeps the focus entirely on them, so she refrains talking about herself during organizing sessions. To me, it feels lopsided and artificial to be intimately involved in another person's life—sorting their clothes, hearing about their kids, talking through their problems—but share nothing with them from my own life. Also, just because I'm an organizer doesn't mean that everything in my life falls together perfectly, and it can be a relief to clients to hear that I struggle with a backlog of catalogs and magazines too, or that I had trouble finding a system to get my own kids out the door on time in the morning.

Another topic organizers sometimes disagree about is how to respond when a client becomes emotional during the organizing process. Organizing can tap into all sorts of sensitive subjects. Deciding whether to toss photos of an old boyfriend, for instance, can bring back a flood of memories, good and bad. Even when dealing with everyday objects, making decision after decision for hours on end can be overwhelming, especially for people who aren't great at making those sorts of decisions in the first place (after all, that's how clutter accumulates). When clients get especially emotional, some organizers immediately stop working and recommend rescheduling for a time the client is less upset. And it's true that we're not therapists and we need to know our limits. But I see emotional moments as a natural part of the organizing process, so I try to talk through the problem by asking questions and offering support without judgment. Sometimes I suggest we stop for a soothing cup of tea or switch to a less stressful task (moving from sorting family memorabilia to rearranging a linen closet, for instance).

As an organizer you might be a coach, confidant, and housecleaner all during the course of a single organizing session, so it is not always clear which tasks are appropriate to handle and which are not. Part of that is because this is still a young profession, and many clients just aren't sure what to expect. Most people have a much better sense of what the appropriate relationship would look like between a mechanic and a car owner, for instance, than between organizers and the people who hire them. As you can imagine, this makes figuring out the fuzzy boundary between being emotionally supportive and overly connected even trickier, especially when each new job brings up new sorts of challenges and complications.

This is a challenge not just for individual organizers but for the profession as well, and it always has been. We have been working for decades to get *occupational legitimacy,* to convince people the work we do is legitimate, important, and deserves to be paid well. As I mentioned earlier, part of that is because most of us are women, but it's also because much of what we do involves providing personalized emotional support to clients. You might think of that as a good thing, but I can tell you, the labor market doesn't! Have you noticed how jobs that involve caring for others—such as children, the elderly, or the ill—tend to be low-paid and low-status? And the people who perform them usually come from the most disadvantaged groups in society. If you want to be paid well and treated with respect in America, you need to downplay the caring, emotional nature of your work, no matter how meaningful and necessary that support can be for anyone feeling isolated or anxious and doubting themselves.

This stigma around care work is part of why when a bunch of us organizers here in Los Angeles started meeting regularly back in the 1970s, we felt it was important to make clear why what we did was different from and worth more money than other occupations such as homemaking, housekeeping, and being "office wives," as secretaries were once called. Today, the world is a much different place in lots of ways, especially in terms of attitudes toward working women, but we organizers still struggle to be taken seriously. Sometimes when I look back I wonder if we did the right thing. Rather than distancing ourselves from "women's work" or other jobs that involve the important work of caring for people, what if we'd banded together with people in other occupations like this and demanded that care work and female-dominated occupations be given as much respect as any other job? But that's not what we did. Instead, we ended up emphasizing all the ways in which we were professionals, hence our decision to call ourselves "professional organizers," rather than just "organizers," which leads me to my third and final rule for you. . . .

Be Professional, But Not Too Professional

At our annual conferences, business experts are always telling us that if you want your business to be taken seriously, you need to take yourself seriously. What they mean is that we need to focus less on the touchy-feely part of what we do, the hands-on work with clients, and more on building our businesses. They talk about legal issues for small businesses, how to write an invoice, and what type of insurance we need. They advise us to have our websites professionally designed and, in this tech-crazed world of ours, to have a regular presence on popular social networking platforms (right now that means Facebook, LinkedIn, Twitter, and Instagram, but by the time your business really takes off, there will undoubtedly be a whole new crop to keep track of).

There is also an emphasis in our field on always presenting yourself professionally, but that can be a tricky feat for organizers. Our society has a certain image of what a professional looks like, and that image is usually male! It's hard enough for women to achieve that ideal, but nearly impossible when your job that day might involve moving furniture or crawling through cobwebby attics. Most organizers say the best you can do is to be always clean and presentable. I'll tell you right now, for those of us who started our businesses back in the '70s and '80s, that means no jeans! But that probably sounds absurd these days, so you'll just have to decide that one for yourself.

Being professional isn't just about what you wear, though. As I mentioned, I was initially drawn to organizing because I myself have always been organized, but also because the work can be scheduled around other responsibilities, like raising my kids. Paradoxically, though, I found that coming across professionally often meant downplaying the very aspects of my life I became an organizer to accommodate. For instance, when I was just getting started, another organizer, one of the founders of our profession, called me at home, and my daughter—she was five— answered the landline. When I got on the phone, that organizer let me have it! She told me I needed to get a designated line for my business, because no one would take me seriously if my kids answered the phone when clients called. I felt just terrible, and I got another phone line right away. In the years since, I've heard the same advice given again and again to organizers with kids living at home (although that's less relevant with cell phones now, I guess). But I recently met an organizer who handled that same situation very differently. She has a large family and her clients are mostly other moms. She told me her kids answer her phone all the time. Not only do her clients not mind, but it shows them she's a mom, just like them, and it makes them feel more comfortable with her. I admire her for that. She didn't conform to somebody else's definition of what it meant to be professional, instead she redefined it in a way that suited her life and business. It does seem crazy to pretend I'm not a parent so that I can live up to some professional ideal. And this ideal was established by people whose kids were probably at home being raised by someone else while they were out being appropriately professional!

Now let's talk about what you've probably been waiting for— money. We American women sometimes have trouble asking people to pay us, and pay us well, for what we do. That probably has something to do with being brought up to be humble and nice (as opposed to boys, who are encouraged to be assertive and competitive) and that leads us to undervalue our own skills. Lots of organizers have a hard time making the leap from working for free for friends to actually charging for what they do. When they do charge, they often agree to work for really low rates because they feel awkward asking for more. That might seem like a nice thing to do for clients, but it's bad for the rest of us organizers. If you charge $15 an hour in order to seem nice and not overly demanding, that undercuts the rest of us. That's why most of us aim to keep our fees in the range of $50 to $150 per hour, although of course that depends on where you live, how much experience you have, and what your specialties are. Business organizing tends to pay higher rates than residential organizing. So as you set about pricing your services, you need to think both about how much money you need to live and about how much money you think you can convince clients to pay you. This can be a real challenge, especially since most organizers avoid disclosing our rates to competitors—even friendly competitors—to prevent being underbid. We also want to avoid accusations of price fixing within the industry.

All this talk of money can be misleading, however, because even though we organizers care a lot about the need to be professional, we also all know that if you're just in it for the money, you're in the wrong business. First of all, most of us don't make that much! Fifty dollars an hour sounds like a lot, but professional organizers consider twenty hours of organizing a week to be full-time, because in the other twenty-plus hours of the work week, you need to manage the other aspects of your business—such as billing, marketing, and networking. And many organizers do this as a part-time business. Some have other part-time jobs that, along with organizing, allow them to support themselves (in today's economy I think many people feel more secure having multiple income streams in case any single one dries up). Others are part of two-earner families, and their income supplements that of a primary earner. Occasionally you'll hear a snarky remark or two from full-time organizers about the "dabblers" among us, but I see that as an unfortunate result of our culture's tendency to pit women against one another. What we should be criticizing is the idea that anyone has the right to tell anyone else how, or whether, they should balance paid work with maintaining a household or raising children.

This may surprise you: I've never met a single organizer, not even the ones pulling down more than six figures, who said money was the most important part of the job. Many of us were drawn to this job because it offers us the opportunity to help others—to assist them in making better use of the spaces in which they live and work, to prevent them from feeling overwhelmed by their possessions, and to save them money they'd otherwise be spending on storage units, late fees for lost bills, and the purchase of items they already own but cannot find. As we often say, we help people live the lives they want to live. Lots of us have other reasons for entering this line of work as well. Many want to own their own business, others desire a more flexible schedule, and some are eager to escape the drudgery of our former jobs. And yes, some of us are even hoping for the big bucks, although as women I think we're discouraged from admitting that. Still, when organizers talk about why we do what we do, we like to talk about the helping part, not the other, more tangible benefits of the job, like pay and flexible hours. I've heard so many touching stories over the years from my organizer friends: about the client who invited someone over for coffee for the first time in twenty years after an organizer helped her declutter her home; about the man who said that one day of organizing helped him more than years of therapy; or about the couple whose marriage was saved when their home became more livable and their constant fights over clutter ceased.

In telling these stories, we organizers tend to frame what we do as a *helping profession,* one that involves the same sort of care-taking work as that performed by nurses and nannies and teachers and moms. Ironic, isn't it? The very same sorts of female-dominated occupations I've told you we've always tried to distance ourselves from in our pursuit of occupational legitimacy. If you think this puts us between a rock and a hard place, it does! Emphasizing the intimate, emotional nature of the work we do could end up devaluing our own labor. On the other hand, if we were in it just for the money or didn't actually care about our clients and their well-being, then we'd be going against the very values that led us to this career in the first place. Now that I think about it, this puzzle is built into the nature of organizing itself. Ours is an occupation built around helping others but whose legitimacy depends on ignoring that very fact.

I should wrap up what has become a very long email, so let me say that when it comes down to it, becoming an organizer requires walking a series of crisscrossing tightropes between your professional aspirations and personal values, clients' needs and preferences, and society's ideals and expectations. I can't say that any of us has really mastered that balancing act, not even an old-timer like me. Perhaps that's because the game we're playing in, the American culture of professionalism, has been rigged from the start against certain kinds of work and certain kinds of workers. I hope that doesn't sound too discouraging, because there's no reason that can't change if people decide to make a concerted effort to change it. But for now, I think it's wise to know the perils, along with the pleasures, of this unique profession of ours. Whether you embrace them or rail against them, these tensions will undoubtedly shape your career. They've shaped this profession as long as I have been in it.

I wish you the very best with your career transition. I really hope you manage that rare feat—even rarer still in today's economy—of finding work that pays your bills and feeds your soul.

Warmest regards,
Susan

Acknowledgments

I am grateful to the many professional organizers and clients across the United States who shared their time and opinions with me as part of this research project. My thanks especially to those organizers who brought me along on jobs as an unpaid assistant and allowed me to experience the organizing process from the inside. My thanks also to Ilana Gershon, Fran Benson, and two anonymous reviewers for their comments and suggestions on an earlier draft of this piece.

Suggested Readings

On the sale and impact of clutter on American families, see:
Jeanne Arnold, Anthony Graesch, Enzo Ragazzini, and Elinor Ochs, *Life at Home in the Twenty-First Century: Thirty-Two Families Open Their Doors*. Los Angeles: Cotsen Institute of Archaeology Press, 2012.

On the purchase of intimate services, see:
Arlie Hochschild, *The Outsourced Self: Intimate Life in Market Times*. New York: Metropolitan Books, 2012.
Viviana Zelizer, *The Purchase of Intimacy*. Princeton, NJ: Princeton University Press, 2005.

For an overview of research on care work and the devaluation thereof, see:
Paula England, "Emerging Theories of Care Work." *Annual Review of Sociology* 31 (2005): 381–99.

On occupational legitimacy in related fields, see:
Molly George, "Seeking Legitimacy: The Professionalization of Life Coaching." *Sociological Inquiry* 83 (2013): 179–208.
Rachel Sherman, "'Time Is Our Commodity': Gender and the Struggle for Occupational Legitimacy among Personal Concierges." *Work and Occupations* 37 (2010): 81–114.

On how to become a professional organizer, see:
Dawn Noble, *How to Start a Home-Based Professional Organizing Business*. Guilford, CT: Morris, 2011.
Sara Pedersen, *Born to Organize: Everything You Need to Know about a Career as a Professional Organizer*. Shoreview, MN: Time to Organize, 2008.

For information on professional associations for organizers and how to find an organizer in your area, see the websites of the National Association of Professional Organizers (www.napo.net) and the Institute for Challenging Disorganization (www.challengingdisorganization.org).

THE CHARACTER IN QUESTION: HOW TO DESIGN FILM COSTUMES IN INDIA

Lovleen Bains and Clare Wilkinson

All costume design starts from character, and our character here is a film industry in the South Asian subcontinent. India's film industry in its scale and variety is truly one of the great culture industries of the contemporary world. It boasts several filmmaking centers spread throughout the country, the biggest centered in Chennai and Mumbai, with the Mumbai industry (known popularly as "Bollywood") perhaps the best known around the world. Hindi films made in Mumbai have for many decades enjoyed a remarkable global appeal not simply among Indian émigrés but also in several other parts of the world: the Middle East, Central Asia and the former Soviet Union, East and West Africa, and Eastern Europe. Back in India, film and the culture surrounding it has penetrated Indian life and the Indian psyche to a striking degree. Film music, dialogue, and scenarios serve as models both for how to be modern and what it means to be Indian in a rapidly changing world.

What you are about to read is an imaginary three-way email exchange of questions and answers about the very real experiences of a designing costumes for the Hindi film industry. A young woman, let's call her Priti, is interested in costume and design and has approached a researcher and a designer to find out more about the field. Like many fans of Hindi films, Priti has long thought that costumes give a film some of its most vital visual interest, with outfits ranging from Indian-style clothing (contemporary and historical), Western-style clothing from evening wear to jeans and sportswear, fantasy costumes, down-at-heel costumes—everything from the sublime to the occasionally ridiculous. From time to time, Priti sees a costume in a film that she'd like to copy—a coat, say, or a shoe and bag ensemble. Priti is simply the most recent in a long line of film viewers who like to adapt film styles to their own tastes: Her mother and grandmother often went to their tailors and asked for versions of film costumes they'd just seen. But now Priti wants to know what's involved in bringing these visions to the screen in the first place.

From: Priti filmdressfan@##mail.com
To: Lovleen, Clare

I hope you don't mind me writing to you. I really want to know more about what a costume designer does in Hindi film. I want to write something about costume design for my student paper, in fact I've even thought of becoming a designer, but I'm not sure what it involves. So if you don't mind, I'd like to ask some questions and perhaps you'd help me out? I'm really interested in knowing more about the actual experiences of Ms. Bains since she's worked on such a wide variety of films. I guess my first question is who are designers, and what is their history in films?

From: Lovleen Bains
To: Priti, Clare

Happy to help. The serious costume designer emerged chrysalis-like in the 1980s. This was the time when international productions were also being filmed in India, using and training prospective Indian costume designers. It is remarkable that a country that produces up to one thousand films every year does not have any institute to teach the craft of costume design. Several costume designers have begun their careers in international co-productions shot in India. We also have students of fashion and textile design starting out as interns with costume designers. Film directors well-grounded in the language of cinema do value the work of a costume designer. However, it is a regrettable fact that costume designers in India are not given the respect commanded by other technicians, such as the cinematographer, production designer, sound recordist, editor, lyricist, choreographer, and so on. No one seems to care that India's first Academy Award was brought home in 1983 by a costume designer—Bhanu Athaiya, for Richard Attenborough's *Gandhi* (1982).

From: Clare
To: Priti, Lovleen

I think it's important to realize that filmmaking in Mumbai is quite distinct. On one hand it's not appropriate to compare it to Hollywood. Indian filmmakers have for years had to struggle to get even a fraction of the resources that Hollywood has at its disposal. And yet, for better or worse, how things are done in Europe and North America are regarded as the gold standard by most Indian filmmakers, so it isn't completely out of line to describe the particularities of costume production with reference to them. In the commercial Hindi film industry it has been impossible to identify anything like a costume "department," headed by a costume designer. Many stars in the past fifty years have preferred to hire their own personal designers, so any given film might list several "dress designers" in the credits (the most I ever saw was eleven for the 1994 film *Hum Aapke Hain Koun . . . !*). If you are designing for a single star, you'll get your directions from the director or even the star him- or herself. You may not have much to do with anyone else involved in the production. Before the 1950s, there weren't even any costume designers credited at all. Costumes were supplied either by an artist's personal tailor or by tailors hired to work on the set as filming went on. Alternatively, they might be made by dressmen or costumers in consultation with the director or art director or bought or borrowed from *dresswalas*.[1] Later on there might be a company designer for the other cast members as well as a designer for the dancers. You could say that costume design,

---

1. Costume shops.

except in the case of small, independent productions, was a somewhat ad hoc affair.

Since the late 1980s and 1990s, however, there have been more designers hired to oversee costume production all by themselves or in association with only one or two personal designers. There is more time dedicated to pre-production (preparing to start shooting the film), and there is—for lack of a better term—a unity of vision and more emphasis on cinematic realism. Some see this as the inevitable and very welcome move toward greater professionalism in the industry; others are nostalgic for the past, when filmmaking was a heroic enterprise carried out day in and day out in the face of material shortages, unreliable equipment, and uncertain financing. Costume decisions are not as likely these days to be derailed by insecure, demanding film stars or by plot lines that might change from week to week. Where personal designers used to be (and sometimes still are) a mark of the film star's prestige and power, now stars will agree to a single designer for a film because they are trying to project a seriousness about acting that coincides with the air of supposed professionalization that has enveloped the industry in the last several years.

From: Priti
To: Clare, Lovleen

In your message you mentioned the difference between small art films and commercial films. Can you expand on that difference? What distinguishes art films and commercial films and how does this affect costuming?

From: Clare
To: Priti, Lovleen

The small-budget, art filmmaking sector exists side by side with the commercial industry. It's in this sector where one usually expects to find more cinematic realism and subtle screen acting. Merchant-Ivory productions, for example, maintained a considerable footprint in Indian filmmaking for many years, starting with independent productions like *The Householder* (1963) and *Shakespeare Wallah* (1965). As much as the commercial and art film sectors seem to stand opposite one another, the two in fact regularly exchange acting and technical talent and thus form part of a larger fabric of media production in the country. The arrival in India of the multiplex cinema in the late 1990s has triggered the production of niche cinema alongside the blockbusters intended to attract audiences throughout the country.

From: Lovleen
To: Priti, Clare

The main difference between independent and commercial films is in the content, treatment of the characters—realistic or fantasy-oriented—and in the budgets. Most producers are independent filmmakers who raise the finance to make films. When a costume designer works on a low-budget film, he or she has to be prepared to work with a smaller team and limited resources, without compromising on the production values. This can be extremely challenging. I worked on a film in 2007 called *God Only Knows* that had an extremely limited budget. However, the costumes looked spectacular. Sometimes in a low-budget film the designer does not go on set during the shoot, especially if the shoot is on an outdoor location outside Mumbai. Instead, one or two assistants along with two or three dressmen manage the entire shoot. However, it is difficult to generalize, as this even happens in big-budget commercial films: The costume designer is not present on set but hands over the costumes to the production, at which point their responsibility ends.

From: Priti
To: Lovleen, Clare

Okay, thanks. I have a specific question for Lovleen, and that is how did you start in the industry? And what were the most important early lessons that you learned?

From: Lovleen
To: Priti, Clare

I became a costume designer by accident, not by design. It was destiny in the form of the dynamic filmmaker Ismail Merchant. I met Ismail in 1982 while he was filming for *Heat and Dust* in Hyderabad. It was a Merchant-Ivory production directed by James Ivory and produced by Ismail Merchant. I was a copywriter in an advertising agency and had been asked to help with the Hindi dialogue. That work was over in less than a week. I was actually visiting my husband, who was the second unit cameraman on the film. There was an English costume designer—Barbara Lane—and an inexperienced, non–English speaking Indian wardrobe assistant. The period English costumes, which were rented from a costume house in London, were to be brought down by a costume assistant from there. However, the Indian costumes were a mess. Barbara could not communicate with either the wardrobe assistant or the tailors and shopkeepers in Hyderabad.

So Ismail Merchant asked me to help Barbara. What started out as translating for Barbara and the local craftsmen stretched to researching period costumes in the famous Salaar Jung Museum (it helped that I had been a student of history as an undergraduate), overseeing the tailoring, keeping and maintaining costume continuity, working as on-set dresser. In effect, I was being trained in all the areas of costume design. It was physically very demanding: I don't remember walking—I used to sprint all over! But I loved what I was doing, every moment of it. Barbara then asked me if I could stay for the entire shoot. I readily agreed. *Heat and Dust* was my training ground. I was working with an immensely talented and efficient crew and cast. I got to learn the language of cinema—the difference between a long shot, a mid-shot, and a close-up and how that impacts the costumes.

From: Priti
To: Lovleen, Clare

Can you tell me more about how the costume designer gets hired and what are some of the things you have to bear in mind, apart from just thinking about the characters you are going to dress, from the practical point of view?

From: Clare
To: Priti, Lovleen

Before Lovleen answers, I think it's worth pointing out that there are a lot of organizational challenges to the designer's job. For example, extending shooting over film sets and locations requires the costumes to travel or be sourced from several locations; sequential scenes in the finished film are shot out of order, meaning that there has to be some way to achieve continuity; last but not least, a film is only completed in post-production, so a costume has to be visualized far beyond its momentary appearance on the actor's body while the action is shot. So there's a lot more at stake than just thinking about the right clothes for the film characters. Anyone who spends any time in or around the film industry knows that trust and reputation are important assets in an industry where uncertainty and contingency are unavoidable. No two films are the same and no costume regime either. A good relationship with the other filmmakers is very important.

From: Lovleen
To: Priti, Clare

A costume designer is approached for a film project either by the director or the producer. When the director initiates contact, the costume designer does not clinch the job until after the producer has worked out the financial side of things. If the producer first contacts the designer, the director gives final clearance on the creative aspects of the appointment. The director has to have faith and trust in the creative capability of his designer. Similarly, the producer has to provide financial, practical, and logistical support so that the designer can deliver. In other words, both the director and the producer have to be convinced of the designer's ability to design, execute, and provide the costumes required by the script. Sometimes, the director is also the producer; this was the case when Rakesh Omprakash Mehra hired me for the 2006 film *Rang de Basanti*. We had worked together earlier, so we knew each other professionally—the trust factor was already there. In the case of *The Rising: The Ballad of Mangal Pandey* in 2005, it was the producer Bobby Bedi who approached me. Here again, I had worked with him earlier. After a meeting with the director Ketan Mehta, it was decided that I would work on the project as the head of the Costume Department.

At this stage, the producer draws up a letter of appointment or deal memo formalizing the commitment. The detailed contract may take some time to be worked out. However, there are instances where the contract doesn't get signed at all! This leaves the costume designer in a very vulnerable position if payments are not made. Unfortunately, this happens quite often. Producers do not always honor their commitments once the work has been done, and even if one has a contract, the payment is not always made. But if one has a contract, one at least has recourse to the law, either directly through a lawyer or through the Association of Cine and Television Art Directors and Costume Designers (ACTADCD), which, in turn is affiliated to the Film Federation of India.

But ACTADCD hasn't always been willing to champion unpaid costume designers. It is only in 2013 that the association recognized costume designers as a separate category. Before 2013, although designers were members of this association, the name of the body was the Association of Cine and Television Art Directors. The words *costume designers* were added only after the Indian film industry had celebrated its centenary! Now the association is trying to fight for better working conditions for the designers. A standard format for contracts is being worked out, along with minimum wages for different categories of technicians. Also, the association is trying to convince producers to pay costume designers what they are owed.

From: Priti
To: Lovleen, Clare

I wanted to ask a follow-up question to Clare's message: What personnel do you work closely with as you put together the costume scheme?

From: Lovleen
To: Priti, Clare

Once a costume designer has committed to work on a project, the designer will talk at length with the director to get a detailed brief on each character. The costume designer must be able to understand the director's vision in order to help translate that vision onto the screen. It is imperative that there is a good professional rapport between the two. At this stage, there are also lots of close interactions with the other heads of departments—such as the production designer, director of photography, hair and makeup designers, sound designer, executive producer/line producer, and so on. The costumes have to fit into the world being created by this team of expert technicians; they cannot be made in isolation. The color palette is worked out together. For instance, in *Rang de Basanti,* the director of photography, Binod Pradhan, wanted me to use more bright blues and greens in the costumes for the contemporary sequences, in keeping with the lighting pattern designed by him. It was meant to contrast with the saturated earth colors used in the period sequences set in pre-partition India.

Similarly, in 2011, when I was shooting for the film *Mausam* in Scotland (one of the film's locations), there was a concert sequence where I carefully planned the colors after consulting with the production designer and director of photography, so that the cream tuxedoes worn by the members of the orchestra would be highlighted by the background and lighting, creating a stunning visual on screen. However, it must be kept in mind that, in the end, it is the director who is responsible for all creative decisions. And it is the producer who takes the call on budget-related issues. When I wanted the cream tuxedos for the orchestra, I had to use all my powers of persuasion to convince the producer to sanction the budget for them. So the costume designer has to work closely with both the director and the producer in different ways.

Once filming starts, all the costumes are labeled with the name of each character and scene. During the shoot, costume continuity has to be maintained by the costume department, and the costumes also have to be well maintained—laundered, ironed, mended, often within a few hours. This is where the dressmen are so important. Once the shooting is over, each costume is cleaned and carefully packed. These costumes also need to be preserved in case there is any re-shooting.

From: Priti
To: Lovleen, Clare

It seems like there is a lot of work to do once you commit to a film. I am not sure how one prepares to be a costume designer. Is there much in the details of costume design that a designer can try to master beforehand? How much is learning on the job?

From: Clare
To: Priti, Lovleen

Learning on the job is the experience of most designers in film industries around the world, in part because no two films are the same. The setting, the personnel, the story, and the look of the film will always vary, and in the commercial cinema, any of these elements may undergo modification even as the film is shooting. Costume designers build up their experience by solving problem after problem in one film after another.

From: Lovleen
To: Priti, Clare

It is important to remember that flexibility and unplanned changes are intrinsic to the nature of filmmaking. Once on *Heat and Dust* we were shooting on an outdoor location in Hyderabad, and suddenly the direction team decided to film a shot with our lead actress Julie Christie that was not on the day's shooting schedule. She was to wear a continuity costume—a white Lucknowi *kurta*[2] and white Aligarhi pajamas. I panicked, I did not have the pajamas on set. Julie Christie learned of my predicament. She asked me if I could provide something from my wardrobe to our makeup artist Gordon Kay. I fished out a *lungi*.[3] Now, Gordon was wearing white trousers and a white shirt. Julie turned to him and commanded that he take off his trousers and wear the *lungi* instead! Gordon sportingly gave me his white trousers. I set to work with a needle and thread and altered the trousers to fit Julie. She wore her costume and assured me that no one would know that she was wearing Gordon's trousers because it was a long shot. And sure enough, the shot was taken with no one else on set noticing the difference! If Julie Christie had not used her presence of mind and my rescue, the shooting would have been delayed. I may not have been blamed for not having the costume, but I would have still felt awful. A true professional knows that every delayed minute costs the producer a lot of money.

From: Priti

To: Lovleen, Clare

There must be changes in what specifically is planned for a particular scene. What about last-minute changes in costume needs? How do you deal with that? Also, I've heard that the Hindi commercial industry is quite chaotic, and I expect that makes things quite stressful.

From: Clare

To: Priti, Lovleen

An entire volume could be filled with stories of emergencies and crises told by designers working for stars in the commercial industry: So many have had to make evening dresses, sari blouses, dress shirts, and so on merely hours before a shoot begins. In the past (and even today, occasionally), last-minute orders for costumes were often dealt with by throwing all considerations of continuity and character logic to the winds. The pristine

---

2. A knee-length shirt-like garment.
3. A draped garment for the lower body, typically worn by men.

appearance of many costumes in commercial films comes from the fact that they may literally go straight from the tailor to the dressman's ironing board to the actor's body, with no time for any kind of washing or what people in the business call "relaxing" so that the costume looks like it might really come from the character's wardrobe. Ideally, more time and effort spent in pre-production will minimize these problems. But even the most professional production will still throw up last-minute costume emergencies. You cannot avoid breakdowns in communication, unforeseen delays, or last-minute changes to a schedule or to a costume. This is in the nature of filmmaking, and the costume designer has to learn to adapt.

From: Lovleen
To: Priti, Clare

It's certainly possible that the director may change his mind and throw a sudden requirement at the production team. It is then their job to provide the director with whatever is needed. When I worked on the 1994 film *In Custody* (*Muhafiz* in Urdu), another Merchant-Ivory production (directed by Ismail Merchant and filmed in 1993), I thought that I had worked out every detail of each costume. There was a scene in the film where the lead actor, Shashi Kapoor, was supposed to vomit. I thought that one or two costume doubles (duplicates) would be required for that sequence, to provide for retakes. However, when I checked with Ismail, he very emphatically said that no double costume would be required, as the scene would be shot in such a way that the vomit would fall on the floor and not on the actor's costume. So I did not make any doubles of that costume. The day we were to shoot the vomiting sequence, the first assistant director came to me while the shot was being rehearsed and matter-of-factly asked whether I had the double costumes ready. I informed him that I had been told by Ismail himself not to make any doubles. However, he was insistent that doubles were required, so I spoke to Ismail again; he sheepishly admitted that a double costume was indeed needed within the hour! I was shocked, but I couldn't question the director. The job had to be done, and I was the person who had to do it. So I rushed to the shop where I had bought the fabric, only to find it closed for lunch. Luckily, the rear door was half open, so I begged the shopkeeper to let me enter. He allowed me in, listened to my predicament and gave me the required fabric. I bought enough for two costumes, not just the one I had been asked for, and rushed to give it to the tailors for stitching. We were filming on location in Bhopal, and these were local tailors from the city, not film tailors from Mumbai who are used to working for erratic deadlines, under pressure, at a fast pace. But they rose to the occasion, and I had both the costumes stitched and "aged" (a process required to make the costume look used and worn and so realistic) in time for the shot. In the end, both of the doubles were used. This was another learning experience for me. After that incident, I quietly make doubles whenever I feel that the script demands it. I do not necessarily rely on the requirements given to me.

In the same film, there was an important song sequence featuring the lead actor Shashi Kapoor and the lead actress Shabana Azmi. Shashi Kapoor plays an aging poet and wears a beautiful but decaying embroidered shawl—an old family heirloom—all through the film. However, I had felt that he should be given another shawl for the song sequence as there was a change of mood in that particular sequence. Ismail did not agree, so I did not get another shawl. This scene was being shot at night. The wardrobe was set up in an isolated part of the *haveli*[4] where we were shooting. I was working there when suddenly Ismail walked in and started pacing up and down, looking very agitated. When I inquired if he needed something, he asked me whether I had another shawl for Shashi. Of course I did not, and I politely reminded him that he had told me not to get another shawl. He then asked me if I could somehow get another shawl anyway. I assured him that I would see what I could do. As soon as he left the room, I turned to my tailor and asked him to go on his two-wheeler moped to the home of a local shopkeeper who sold shawls while I telephoned the shopkeeper and requested that he give a few shawls to the tailor. Within half an hour the shopkeeper had brought the shawls himself. I selected two shawls and ran up the stairs to the set. One take had been shot, but it had not been okayed. The moment Ismail and Shashi saw the shawls, their faces lit up. One of the shawls was selected, and the shooting commenced. I felt elated that I had not let my director down!

Sometimes, the director, on seeing a location, changes his requirements for a particular scene. This happened while filming *Mangal Pandey*. As per the script, there were supposed to be four hundred soldiers of the East India

---

4. An old mansion.

Company army in one scene. However, once he saw the final location, the director Ketan Mehta felt that eight hundred soldiers were needed. It was the job of the line producer to convey this information to me, but it seems she "forgot." I learned of the situation just two weeks before the shoot. I was horrified, as I really felt that it would not be possible to have the costumes ready in such a short time. These were uniforms that included accessories such as leather belts with embossed buckles, embossed buttons, caps, badges, and shoes. I told the producer, Bobby Bedi, that it would not be possible to make eight hundred uniforms so quickly. I requested that he change the shoot date. Bobby said he couldn't, as he was bound by actor's dates, so I had no choice but to deliver the eight hundred uniforms on time. The problem was heightened by the fact that all the woolen fabric had to be dyed the same shade of red; the correctly colored fabric was not readily available off the shelf. My entire team at the production base got no sleep during those two weeks, maybe 2–3 hours at most, but we managed to do the seemingly impossible task of making the uniforms in time for the shoot.

From: Priti
To: Lovleen, Clare

So it sounds like a lot of things can change as a production goes on. But there must be things that can be done in advance. What can designers prepare beforehand so they can do their job better?

From: Lovleen
To: Priti, Clare

It is vital to do appropriate research, designing, proper planning and execution and timely availability of the costumes on the day of the shoot based on the shooting schedule. When a director is ready to shoot a scene, everything has to be ready, since to lose the opportunity to film costs money, and the exact conditions, even the actors' availability, cannot be guaranteed in future. But the most carefully executed preparations can go wrong. While I was working on the film *Rang de Basanti* there was an extremely stressful situation that was handled by my associate designer Rina. We were scheduled to shoot a candlelight protest in the Delhi winter. The first shot of the day was to be filmed at sunrise. In the scene, a Rapid Action Force (a special police unit) disperses the protestors. Their uniform included olive green helmets, which Rina had commissioned from a supplier. We had been promised delivery a good week before the shoot, but after some unforeseen delays, we were forced to plan to pick them up only a day in advance. When Rina went to pick up the helmets, she was shocked to learn that they were not ready. She went to every possible shop to see if she could pick them up from somewhere, even secondhand shops. The problem was that these were police helmets that could not be bought off the shelf but had to be specially made. Finally, she found a shopkeeper whose son wanted to become an actor. When he learned that we needed the helmets for a film shoot, he promised to procure them for us. And he kept his promise—he and his aspiring actor son reached our wardrobe base at 8 p.m. with two dozen police helmets. The only hitch was that they were khaki instead of olive green. So we rushed to the market and bought olive green oil paint and paintbrushes. My entire department along with the shopkeeper and his son sat up the entire night and painted the two dozen helmets. Had Rina not persisted and gotten the crucial helmets, I would have had to inform the director that the shoot would have to be postponed. In other words, I would have failed to deliver as per the schedule.

From: Priti
To: Lovleen, Clare

Apart from actually stitching clothes or draping fabric, are there other ways to obtain costumes? Is there anywhere in Mumbai that's like a costume supply outlet, like Western Costume in LA?

From: Clare
To: Priti, Lovleen

There is no source of costume "stock" aside from what is held by *dress-walas* or the costumes that are stored, somewhat haphazardly, in *godowns*[5] after a production ends. Generally this means that most costumes are made new for each production. In recent years, the explosion of a fashion retail market has boosted the option of shopping for costumes, although many trips continue to be taken outside the country to take advantage of better clothing sources.

---

5. Warehouses.

From: Lovleen
To: Priti, Clare

In period films, all costumes have to be specially made. In fact, sometimes, crew members also have to be given costumes so that their modern clothes don't stick out like a sore thumb and ruin the look. For instance, while shooting a huge festival scene involving 2,500 extras in *Mangal Pandey,* I had to provide *dhotis, angarkhas,*[6] and turbans to all the male assistant directors, the camera crew, lighting crew, and lead actor assistants as well as saris to the female crew members, as the scene was being shot with multiple cameras and cranes. I could not risk a pair of jeans appearing in a film set in 1857. This is why costume making for period films is much more expensive than it is for a contemporary film.

In a contemporary film, depending upon the characterization, one can buy ready-made clothes from shops. The character could be an urban, well-to-do, fashion-conscious person wearing branded jeans and T-shirts. In such cases, the designer might take the actor shopping so that the clothes fit well. Or the designer may bring clothes on approval from shops and have the actor try them on. This means the shop loans a selection of clothing, of which some will be chosen and the rest returned. Clothes such as jeans, jackets, and T-shirts are also bought from either Bangkok or London.

Rang de Basanti is set in contemporary India as well as pre-partition India. The contemporary portion constitutes two-thirds of the film, and the period part was just one-third of the film, but the budgets allocated reversed the equation, with the period portion taking up two-third of the budget! The contemporary clothing was very straightforward: lead actor Aamir Khan's character wears just three pairs of jeans, a couple of T-shirts, and two jackets all throughout the film. During filming, the stunt director demanded a double of one of the jackets, a leather one, one day before the shoot. This was a weathered jacket that had been bought in Bangkok! My associate designer Rina and I managed to find a jacket that looked similar, but it needed to be properly aged. Aging a costume requires a great deal of skill and care. If not done properly, the costume can get ruined. The production designer, (the late) Samir Chanda, helped me age the leather jacket in time for the action shot. This is an example of where filmmaking becomes teamwork.

---

6. Long coats.

While filming the contemporary portion, one can save money on the costumes worn by the extras. Usually, the person in charge of crowd casting works closely with the costume department. Once the costume requirement is conveyed to this person, the extras are told to come dressed accordingly and also to bring options with them. As a backup, the costume designer usually has a "bank" of costumes to be given out to any extra not dressed appropriately.

From: Priti
To: Lovleen, Clare

I really love the costumes in period films, they are always so elaborate and beautiful. What special considerations go into designing for historical films?

From: Clare
To: Priti, Lovleen

For period films, the designer needs to consider not only character and budget but also to recreate an historical era that will be convincing to the audience. Some periods are well documented visually and have been extensively explored in film. In other instances, in their research, designers draw on books, paintings, old photographs, and whatever else they need to inspire their designs.

From: Lovleen
To: Priti, Clare

When the film *Kama Sutra* was being shot in the ancient temple town of Khajuraho, I hired a team of fifteen local tailors. I also brought a master cutter with an assistant tailor from Mumbai, and together they churned out costumes for the shoot. This was because the pre-production time had not been sufficient to have the entire wardrobe ready before the filming commenced. As the film was set in fifteenth-century India, the research took a little longer than anticipated since there is little information on the pre-Mughal era. I managed to find something in the Bhandarkar Institute of Oriental Studies in Pune. There were descriptions of the clothes worn at that time but no visual references. And the entire writing was in Sanskrit, a language I had studied for three years in school as a third language, but did not know well enough to decipher these writings. I got the help of a Sanskrit scholar to translate the material into English. After reading the entire treatise, my design team and I prepared sketches of the different kinds of garments worn in the fifteenth century.

Various sketches were prepared for the lead characters. Once the look of each character had been finalized, fabrics were sourced, and the textures and color palette were selected. Then came the intricate task of fitting the design to the actor's bodies. The costumes were a combination of draped and stitched clothes. The two lead actresses, Indira Varma and Sarita Choudhury, were to be dressed in fitted short *cholis*[7] and skirts. However, since each body is different, each one had to wear a style that suited her and enhanced her appearance the most. We stitched twenty-five different samples of cholis in muslin cloth until we arrived at the perfect design for both. The entire process of execution was done on location in Khajuraho.

The men's costumes involved more draping—the dhotis, sashes, and turbans were draped by the team of expert dressmen. The only garment that required stitching was the short jacket. The dance dhotis worn by the two lead actresses were also draped. In fact, there was one dance costume that was made of pearls that had to be stitched on to the actress while she stood, the entire procedure taking about 30 to 40 minutes. The choli was made entirely of closely strung pearls with no fabric backing. Indira had to stand patiently almost like a statue while I stitched the costume to fit her perfectly. Her patience did pay off, as she looked stunning in it. It is one thing to make a beautiful costume, but the true test of a good costume is when the actor carries it the way it is intended. That is when the character comes to life, helping the director unfold his vision on screen.

From: Priti
To: Lovleen, Clare

Thanks for all this information! Do you have any last thoughts for me?

From: Lovleen
To: Priti, Clare

There is still so much to say! But I will try to be brief. So what do you need to know? Keep in mind that long hours are to be expected. Costume

---

7. Short, tight blouses.

designers work up to twenty hours a day at times, and when they are jug-
gling several film schedules at once they may be away from their families
for long stretches of time. They have to possess advanced management
skills in order to work within unrealistic budgets and to get the best out
of their team. They also need to have the insights and the tact of psychia-
trists in order to convince actors and directors that the costumes created are
indeed the most appropriate for the characters in the film. The people one
has to work the most closely with are the members of the costume team—
assistants, tailors, embroiderers, dyers, accessory makers, and so on. Since
filmmaking is teamwork, one has to have an extremely talented, hard-
working, resourceful, and reliable team ready to work long hours to help
meet what are at times unrealistic directorial demands and deadlines—all
this while maintaining a calm demeanor. The job demands a high level of
commitment to perfection. Each project is a learning experience—a voy-
age of discovery and an adventure. A costume designer is an artist who
also needs to have advanced managerial and motivational skills in order
to extract the best work in extremely demanding situations. Above all, a
costume designer has to work with passion—a passion that breathes life
into clothes and converts them into costumes that help the actor portray
the character on screen that reflects the director's vision.

Suggested Readings

To learn more about Hindi filmmaking and film costumes, these books are
   recommended:
Athaiya, Bhanu, *The Art of Costume Design*. Delhi: Harper Collins, 2010.
Dwyer, Rachel, *100 Bollywood Films*. London: BFI, 2008.
Ganti, Tejaswini, *Bollywood: A Guidebook to Popular Hindi Cinema*. New York: Rout-
   ledge, 2013.

11

Reflections from a Life on the Line: How to Be a Factory Worker

Caitrin Lynch and Warren Chamberlain

The monologue that follows is set in 2013 at Vita Needle Company, a suburban Boston factory. A family-owned business founded in 1932, Vita Needle makes hollow needles for medical and industrial applications, stainless steel tubing and pipes, and custom fabricated parts. The median age of the employees is seventy-four, and the oldest worker is ninety-five. There are workers in every "age decade" from the teens through the nineties; one of the striking things about this workplace is how people of such vastly different ages work together on joint goals. Seventy-three-year-old Warren Chamberlain has worked at Vita Needle for seven years at the time of writing. In this scenario, his boss Vincent asks him to work with a new employee, and Warren takes the request as an opportunity to reflect on his fifty years of manual labor, including twenty-seven years of building cars at the General Motors plant in Framingham, Massachusetts—before the plant closed down to relocate operations in Mexico. Warren offers the neophyte lessons on how to work in the service of the employer without losing oneself in the job.

What follows is in Warren's voice, and the imagined listener is a new employee named Brett, a recent high school graduate who will be trained on a variety of jobs on the production floor. This monologue is fictional in that it has never been spoken, but it reflects Warren's actual experiences and perspectives over a lifetime of manual labor. Most of it, including the use of informal slang alternating with a more scholarly tone, is in Warren's own language. Warren has always made time to read, discuss, and reflect on his social position and wider issues of economic justice. Back when he used to double up on work to get an unauthorized break on the automobile assembly line, he would read Karl Marx, Adam Smith, articles in *The Economist*, and more. We created the listener as a young person in his first job because Warren's reflections offer instruction on how to embark on a life of manual labor without going through the boredom, alienation, and depression that Warren endured until he figured out how to embrace the dignity of the work. Warren aims to pass on an optimistic, positive perspective, but with his invocation of work as "purgatory" and capitalism as a "beast," he conveys the complexity and depth of his relationship to work. While Warren is not simply a cog in the capitalist machine (to invoke George Orwell), he has felt ambivalence about how to be human while playing a role in that machine.

Warren's marked pride in his lifework is imbued with religious meaning and lessons he has taken from his family's membership in a fraternal order called the Grange. The Grange (formally, "The National Grange of the Order of Patrons of Husbandry") was formed in 1867 in the United States as an organization for farmers, and it still exists today, although its membership is dwindling. This monologue was created through numerous conversations between Warren and Caitrin, an anthropologist who has written a book about Vita Needle. In the process of reflecting on lessons to offer Brett, it became clear to us that the Grange has been an anchor to Warren. The Grange has an elaborate system of principles that a member masters successively in order to live a good life through doing good work. Using this format of successive principles that a worker adopts in the process of mastering a job, Warren lays out principles for Brett to embrace in order to have a successful life on the line.

Welcome to the Team

So, this is your first factory job? I have worked for more than fifty years in manual labor: building houses and cars, processing mail, and now making needles. We call it manual labor, as if there are no brains involved. But I've learned over my lifetime of work that body and mind together are what make for quality of work life, and that a quality work life means a quality life. I was raised in a Christian family, so I often think about work and life in religious terms. My Kingdom of Heaven is a dignified work life that allows me to enjoy myself and meditate on the meaning of life. I have created that Kingdom of Heaven on the assembly line, and I am here to tell you how you might do it for yourself.

I grew up working on a farm in this same town. Back then there were five dairy farms here; they are all gone now. Like you, I graduated from high school and went to my first job soon after: building houses on Cape Cod. My father taught me the importance of being absorbed in one's work and being in control in order to thrive at work and to stay healthy in mind and body. This was in the 1940s and '50s, but even back then we had machinery; one moment of hurrying or not paying attention could lead to injury on a farm. The same is true here. You'll hear that my first principle of working here is safety. And to be safe you really need to be relaxed: Don't be nervous! I can tell you right away not to worry about the boss, Vincent. He looks mean, but he's actually really nice.

I want to make sure you know some of the basics about what it takes to make a needle. First I'll give you an overview of the process, and then I'll tell you some principles I've pieced together for how to live a good life on the factory line.

A Primer on Making Needles

Think of anything that needs to go through a hollow needle with a pointed end, and you've likely thought of things we make here. There's air, water, glue, blood. Like that. We make needles for so many different things. I've heard that some of our needles were for robots to pick up soil samples on Mars, and some have been for doctors to squeeze anesthesia into an artery during open-heart surgery. One order was for scientists to tag salmon with computer chips to study where they swim, and others have been for taxi-dermists to embalm animals. I'll tell you about some of the tasks involved in making these needles. You will see all of this over the next weeks, and there will be a day when you start dreaming about the different tasks.

From start to finish, producing needles may include the following steps: pulling tubes (removing tubes from storage racks), cutting tubes down to size, taping tubes or needles together so the next operations can be done on multiple pieces at once, squaring off the bunch so they are all the same length, and sandblasting or grinding. Cannulas are the needle tubes. Those get sharpened to a first point; some also get sharpened to a second point. Some needle hubs are stamped with needle gauge size and customer name. Stamping was the specialty job of Rosa, who stopped working here earlier this year, a week before her 101st birthday. The hubs get drilled and reamed to make room for inserting the cannula, and then hubs and cannulas are connected together in what we call "staking" (I do a lot of that job). Final products are quality-tested and then brought across the room to be sent out. The packing and shipping might involve assembling multiple needles onto cardboard (a process called carding), then wrapping and packaging the cards, placing them in boxes, and shipping them out. Some orders will require bending of tubes or needles, flaring ends, gluing or assembling parts.

Other jobs involve receiving tubing that is shipped in, logging it, and putting it on the correct shelves. Keith and Miles design and make prototypes and customize machinery to produce those prototypes. Steve, Pete, and Gary process outgoing deliveries and receive incoming parts. Jobs move in a "progressive bundle system." One person works on a batch of needles or tubes and then passes the batch on to a coworker at the next step.

You'll notice that there is not an *assembly line* here. There is no mechanized line of products mid-assembly that moves by as we do our own tasks and keeps us working at an often-untenable pace. We are not Lucille Ball in the chocolate factory, shoving chocolates in her mouth, hat, and bra to hide evidence of falling behind. (I think of Lucy a lot because my cats are named Lucy and Ethel.) But even though there is no line like that, we need to keep up a good pace because our batch of finished work moves on to another person, and that person cannot do his or her job until we finish our tasks—and finish them well, with a high-quality product.

Vita Needle is known for producing small-batch jobs, so there are a bunch of orders being filled on the shop floor at the same time. Shop workers rotate in and out of jobs all day, so on one workday you may do three or four different operations. But there are some people who specialize in certain operations, which they are known to be good at. For good models take a look at Henry on staking, Flo on taping, and Jim on squaring. Except for one robotic machine, everything here is manual—even the moving of parts from one person's workstation to another, which we do in small wooden boxes made in a home woodshop in the 1960s by the husband of one worker. Take a look at the intricate tongue-and-groove joints of these boxes—no nails in that workmanship. That was real manual labor.

You'll be doing a lot of these jobs, but I know they've got you starting in drilling, which is why you're with me for the next few days.

Principles for a Life on the Line

Manual laborers like us can get much more out of making needles or cars or building houses than the end product itself (which we don't even get anyway, we are not the ultimate owners of what we produce). I have figured out some principles for doing this work. I didn't know about these for most of my work life. I figured it out much later, and I am hoping that if I tell you them now, you might have an easier time than I did. Think of it as my gift to you. We shouldn't all have to suffer.

I'll tell you about the principles in the order in which you can attain expertise in them: Safety, Expectations, Control, Routine, and Perfection. Nobody masters all of these immediately. The final principle, Perfection, is a goal to work toward over your career.

1. Safety

Safety is the most important principle when doing manual labor. If you feel rushed, tense, or afraid, you will get hurt. Don't let this happen. Instead, prioritize safety; this will then let you ease into later principles so you can be in tune with the assembly line and its expectations.

You can often find me drilling and reaming hubs so the cannulas can fit into them. I like this job because I have mastered it and because I can play games to beat my best record. You've heard of runners beating their "personal best," right? Well, shop rats do that too. Playing those games is really important—it gets you through the day. But if you're going to do that, you need to be really careful not to rush. There is a difference between working to beat your time and rushing carelessly. Timing is key, or you can end up drilling out your finger rather than a stainless steel hub. The boss won't like that, and neither will you. Also, in this job, you need to wear safety glasses so flakes from the drilling won't get in your eye. The company is obligated to provide them to you—just ask the boss and he'll give you a pair.

Safety starts with knowing the materials and process and taking charge of your space and time. You'll hear more about safety later, because safety is the essential ingredient in every other step of the game. It runs through all these principles. It is first, last, and always.

2. Expectations

Right away you need to find out what the expectations for productivity are at this shop so you can know what is the absolute minimum you can do without being fired, and the maximum you can do without getting hurt. Establishing this understanding for yourself early on will help you survive, and it will buy you time.

At General Motors, new guys would have three days to learn a job. In all my years training people, I knew only one guy who just couldn't get it. He'd get in the hole, and couldn't get out. When you get in the hole, you need to find the rhythm of the machine again. But this guy, if he got distracted, he could never get back the music. Most people could learn the job in a day, sometimes in a couple of hours. Then we'd have a few days to relax, because the supervisor expected it to take three days. But this one guy, he could never get the music back because he never felt the music. He got canned when the three days were over.

You've got to find the rhythm of the job. When I was training guys at GM, they wouldn't notice that I'd gradually stop helping out. I'd ease off, and eventually, they'd realize, "I just did five cars, and I'm all right." They didn't get nervous or worried, even though the line was moving and wouldn't stop for them. When you are drilling, there is a rhythm. Find it. Find the music. It's how you will cope with drilling over and over again for a four-hour shift.

You've got to figure out what the therbligs to your job are. Therbligs are the motions needed for the task. They include movements like holding, grasping, selecting, positioning. Each job you'll have here at Vita Needle will take different therbligs. Once you know what they are, you can concentrate on perfecting each. Like different dance steps. Ball change. Brush. Kick.

Therbligs were the idea of two management experts in the early twentieth century, Frank and Lillian Gilbreth—"therblig" is their name said backwards. (Their son wrote the book *Cheaper by the Dozen;* the family was run like an efficient factory.) A related idea came from an engineer named Frederick Taylor, who published a book called *The Principles of Scientific Management.* That book laid out Taylor's management principles, which people call Taylorism or "scientific management." I heard about it at work long ago, when people training me would tell me about something called "time and motion" studies, which came out of Taylorism. I'd be working and the industrial engineer (we'd call him the "time study guy") would stand by with a stopwatch to see how long each step took. The thing about therbligs and time and motion studies is that the managers end up breaking the job down until it's so simple that monkeys can do it. That makes it very boring and repetitive for us. So you really have to find some other way to occupy your time. That's why I would learn how to be more efficient, just for the fun of it. Regardless of the company expectations, I always operate my own time study. I control my time and space, including the ergonomics—down to the height of the stool.

I find out right away how many units the boss wants. But then, within those parameters, I develop my own time study to see what my capacity is relative to that standard. Can I exceed that standard to make time for myself? That's when I play games to beat my own record. At any moment I am focused on my own performance, just like I am in a bicycle race. It's a natural thing to play games and compete with yourself and others. When we were kids we'd say, "I can run to the ice cream parlor before you do." Hold onto that instinct, it'll do you good in here.

Vincent might tell you to aim for drilling one thousand pieces in four hours. You might find you can do it in two. Vincent doesn't need to know that. I take my phone and set a six-minute timer to do a sample time. (I learned this at GM.) If I can do fifty needles in six minutes, that's five hundred in an hour. If I can beat their expectation, I have an extra hour to play with. I can check my email on my phone. I can talk to Jim about politics; we argue a bunch about Obamacare and Social Security. I can talk to Flo about Vermont. I can dwell within those limits. Then, maybe for the heck of it, I'll start playing games. Can I max out my limit? Did my proficiency go up? The fun part is seeing if I can do it faster. I am playing games with myself and testing my own capacity. I don't have to do it; nobody is telling me to do that. I am already working at their expectations. But I want to maximize my own proficiency.

3. Control

Yes, the boss has things he wants you to do, but you are in control of how you do it. Don't let the system (or the bosses) take over your life; maintain control of yourself. Control your emotions, time, space, and process.

Be in control of your emotions. Don't let anyone make you nervous. The key is being calm and not rushing. You'll notice that almost everything that comes to you has the word "RUSH" on the work ticket. Ignore that. There are always things that have to be out by a certain date. Someone probably made a mistake somewhere so the job didn't get scheduled properly, and now we're supposed to rush. Don't worry about that. You need to allow yourself enough time to do the job, and you know how long that should be. Take your time and do it right. If someone comes along and says to rush a job, don't let that upset you. Just respond politely, "Right away, Vincent," but then do it at your pace. You are the master of your process; don't let other people control you.

You control your time and space. One of the great things about this place is that you can set up your own workstation and arrange the materials so they are comfortable for you. You might not be able to do that at other companies; we've got that advantage here.

When I sit down to drill, first I get a stool that is the right height for me. I'll walk around the shop until I find the right stool. Sometimes you might get in a turf war with someone, but usually you can find the right stool without bugging anyone. I also make sure I've got the light I need, and I usually turn on a fan, especially in the summer—it gets really hot in here.

Once I've got the chair, light, and air set, I get the parts. They are usually piled up at the end of the bench. Grab one of the wooden boxes containing undrilled hubs, and grab an empty box too. I am ambidextrous, and so I set it up so I go from left to right. I've got to set up the machine with the proper drill for the gauge of the particular cannula; you've got to adjust the depth of the drill and diameter of the fixture. Like this. The drill handle is on the right of the machine, the full parts box is on the left. The box for completed parts is on the right. You'll figure this out quickly, you've got to make sure to pull your finger out soon enough so you don't drill through your finger. Put the hub in the machine, it settles down snugly into a fixture that holds it firmly in place. Then use the handle to press the drill down. You know you're done when it stops, bottoms out. Then unwind the handle, lift it up, and take the completed hub out with your right hand. If you drop a hub, don't worry about it. I wait until I've dropped a few, then I get down and pick them up. Saving my old back, but it also saves some time.

Even though I've been doing this for almost ten years, and even though I am thinking about things like monetary reform, solar power, my wife's health, and my grumbling stomach when I work, I also am fully conscious of where my hands are at all times. When I was building cars at GM, even though it was twenty-seven years on the line, I never stopped being conscious of where my body was at any instant. Train your brain and small motor muscles; quality and productivity will come automatically.

I think of it like choreography, or like walking. You don't think about it after a while, but you do have a consciousness of it. If a dancer knows her moves from muscle memory, she can concentrate on the music to prompt her when to execute a move—and she doesn't need to concentrate on the move. If you know from memory the moves for drilling, you can pay attention to the machine but also you can devote your brain to higher pursuits. Your hands will work as a team. Don't move the right until the left starts to move. It's like a dance of the hands. Focus on where your hands are and where your fingertips are. Do not worry about getting job done. You should have a very narrow time focus: What am I doing in this moment? Coordinate your hands and eyes. Like walking. Like dancing.

4. Routine

You need to refine your own process and routinize the job so doing the job becomes habit. Then you will be liberated to concentrate on other things.

In the first days, I suggest you don't listen to an iPod. Eventually you can do that. But for now you really need to focus on what you are doing. Once you develop your routine, then you can listen to music without it interfering with your production. Jim over there listens to real estate investment programs on his. Steve has heavy metal music—I can hear it through his headphones. Someday that kid will regret all that music blasting his eardrums. But then he can work in here without earplugs, like some of the other old guys in here. If you are already deaf, you don't need earplugs!

If your back starts to hurt, stand up. Stretch. Walk around. Vincent won't care, and it's better to do that than to hurt yourself.

Once you've got yourself in control, which you'll feel within a few hours, you can start to routinize the job to improve your efficiency. You've got safety and quality under your belt; production will automatically rise. Some people think that we need to focus on production, and quality will come. But it's really the opposite. I learned this at GM. When I was first there, the bosses were always bugging us about production targets. More. More. More. I felt like I was in purgatory. I remember thinking I was being punished for something in my past. But in the 1980s there was a big policy shift at GM, an attempt to keep up with Japanese carmakers, and the company realized that quality was the way to productivity. I got trained in the new quality program. Suddenly I was doing work the way I wanted to do it, because I could focus on perfection, not on numbers.

I sing in a folk group in my church. I am always hearing music. Back in the auto plant, I'd feel the music. The transformers humming, the spot welders going. Bang boom. It was like a concert. You've got to get in the rhythm of that. You've got to go with the flow and stay on tune. I tap-danced as a kid. You learn a routine. Everyone is scripted. It all flows together, and the car comes out. The therbligs are like notes in music, or steps in dance. At GM people would walk by on a tour, and I'd pretend to be a robot. I'd work in slow motion. Lift left arm. Grab the gun. Swing body. Shoot. Turn. Repeat. I did this for fun. If you can't have fun on the job, it's not worth it.

I do that here too. I told you about creating extra time for myself by knowing the expectations. Then I can joke around with people, get on Facebook on my phone, shoot the breeze with Jim.

5. Perfection

The ultimate aim of these principles is perfection of self and of the product. In the process of creating the perfect product, you will also create a perfect self if you learn how to take advantage of the personal benefits of manual labor. Manual labor, when done correctly, can enable dignity, cultivation of character, and time for reflection.

Safety, Expectations, Control, Routine. If you can get those first four principles down, you will master your work. Once you've done that, you will have autonomy to do what you want. Your time for yourself expands. A few years ago, after I had left GM, I read a book called *Rivethead,* by a guy named Ben Hamper who worked at GM in Flint, Michigan. The guys in *Rivethead* were making themselves miserable unnecessarily with their basic attitude toward work. My attitude is that work is good, and it can be fun. Work is inconvenient, yes. But work is not bad. A positive mental attitude, in itself, is my tactic.

Those *Rivethead* guys thought of the job and the clock as enemies to conquer. I embrace them for what they can do for me. Hamper mentions the clock a lot, like in this example, where he describes sharing a job, unofficially, with another guy, in order to get a break on the off times: "When it was my turn to handle two jobs, I'd be so busy with my work that I wouldn't have time to agonize over the crawl of the clock. I patterned myself a brisk routine and the minute hand whirled by."

I also was trying to beat the clock—I did a lot of the same things that the *Rivethead* guys did. We also used to double up on work with coworkers. Gave me time for coffee and reading. But I don't think of the clock like the *Rivethead* guy does. I want to create more time on the clock. But I want that time for myself. Yeah, it can go by slow if you have an eight-hour shift, especially if it's Monday morning and you have a hangover. But that's when you've got to remember the lessons of this final stage: Perfection.

My approach is to get something out of this job for myself, to try to salvage something out of this job. It's all about having a positive mental attitude. You've got to find a silver lining in the cloud, instead of being miserable all day. My tactic is like the Law of Paradoxical Intent. Most people working in a shop like this want to be someplace else. They are not content with their situation, and they see this as a prison. But I tried to turn this inside out. I found that if you embrace the "pain" of being there, the "pain" goes away. At GM, I learned to make time for myself within the factory structure, so I could enjoy the time while I was there. I took it as a challenge to make time go faster, instead of sitting there and being miserable.

If I doubled up my workload, my attention was captured because I had to really focus; my production doubled and the time moved faster.

There were a lot of things I didn't like about building cars for hours and days and months and years on end. But there was no other job I could find that paid as well as this one did. I decided to face the inevitable and make the best of it. It's an attitude. You've got to derive good in your labors. It is an attitude that I learned from the Grange. Do you know about the Grange? My family has been involved with it for a long time.

One of my first childhood memories is of my father pacing the hall of our house as he drilled words of the Grange Manual into his head to recite them from memory at Grange meetings: "You may encounter difficulties. Overcome them, remembering that difficulties are but opportunities to test our abilities." I think of that expression when I encounter problems. These are opportunities to become creative and innovative. Some people go to gyms to challenge themselves. Some go to college. But you can do this in the context of work. Take a therapeutic approach to work. While you get paid to achieve someone else's goals, you can achieve your own goals. By perfecting what I am doing on the shop floor, I feel like I am not alone. I am living in a world that makes sense, and I am getting great meaning out of my time here on earth.

Sure, there are challenges here at Vita Needle. Sometimes the tools don't quite fit right. Just the other day, I was setting up my space to work, but someone had restructured the drill presses and now I couldn't adjust the drill up and down as much as I needed. There wasn't as much clearance to get the hub into the fixture. I tried different angles and approaches until it worked. Yeah, it can be frustrating. Somebody before you made a mistake, you need to correct for it. I could sit there and lament and complain and yell at somebody, or I could just make it work. That's when I remember that I am trying to go for Perfection. I'm pretty sure I will never reach Perfection, but I know there will be continual improvement. That keeps me going. And you can use a little of your imagination, your Yankee ingenuity.

Maybe you will make a game out of work. Pretend you are doing something else. You have to try to find amusement or self-edification in the process. Remember that you must satisfy your own needs. The real purpose of work should be to satisfy your own needs, not the needs of the business. Sometimes I might be spot-welding that car that a suburban mom will be driving, but in my head I am killing Nazis. (Remember, I was a kid during World War II.) Or, you can make work like a prayer life, meditative like a Buddhist monk. You can be welding a car and pretending to be a monk in a Buddhist monastery. The factory is a different kind of temple.

So, yes, you want to perfect the craftsmanship that you are doing. You want to create a perfect process and a perfect product. But it's not just about the *thing* that results. If you do it right, you are achieving perfection in the material world and in the spiritual world. I always remind myself that I'm in this for something else. Money is fine. What is more important is developing my own mental and motor skills. The boss doesn't care about that. But that doesn't matter. The boss gets his desired outcome (the perfect product), and we get ours (a perfect life). There is a win-win thing here: Give the people (or, your boss) what they want and need, they will get satisfaction, and you will get what you need in the process. Heck, you could even do the rosary with hubs, if that's what you want to do.

So, this final stage, Perfection, is in terms of manufacturing and the self. You want to produce the defect-free needle, the best quality as is humanly possible. Does the door fit properly on the car? Are there no flaws? The Kingdom of God is the perfect car door. But you also want to perfect your self. The Kingdom of God is within ourselves; that is where you find inner peace.

There is more to know and learn in life, even when working twenty-seven years on an auto assembly line, or twenty-seven years in a needle factory. The daily difficulties are there to test our abilities. We discover ourselves through experiences of trials and tribulations. I get a flat tire. How do I respond to that? My boss gives me an order marked "RUSH." How do I respond, when I know what I need to do to make the perfect batch of needles? "Right away, Vincent," I say, and then I pretend I'm shooting Nazis or meditating in a Buddhist monastery or moving my limbs like a robot.

Concluding Lessons

Brett, remember that you are not just making needles. You are educating your mind and elevating your character. In any work effort, we need to try to edify the person, to develop the higher qualities of the person. It's not in a fancy building like that college down the street. Even though it seems to be a crude setting, this is a free education. In fact, you are getting paid to learn.

You might be thinking, "Shut up, old guy. I know this is a dead-end job." Let me tell you, it's not. There are dead-end jobs out there, but this isn't one. This is a business where they let you think on the job. At some places, the worker has to keep his nose running to the ground. The worker is a wage slave and a debt slave. I have been that. I couldn't get a better-paying job than I had at GM, and it was close by to my home. Lots of people are in that same situation. There were times when I was depressed because I felt trapped in a job that was not regarded as good in our society, but it paid well. I was working a job that I respected but nobody else respected. I needed the money. It was lousy work, dirty and dangerous. But I also knew that all honest labor is honorable, and this was honest labor. I kept trying to find dignity in my labor, but I faced the prejudice in our society about being a manual laborer. I didn't have much self-esteem. Eventually I started to remember lessons from my childhood that my father taught me. Looking back, I think the Grange ideals insulated me in some respects from the dangers to a self of being a wage and debt slave. Remember that I bought myself time on the assembly time by producing ahead of the expectations? Well, with all that time I bought, what did I do? I read. I read about the economy. I read *Jonathan Livingston Seagull*. Jonathan tried to understand the true meaning of what he was doing. For the other birds, the object of flying was to get to the landfill to eat. But Jonathan saw flying as an art to be perfected. Not a means to an end, but an end in itself.

For me, it was about the *process* of building perfect cars, and now, perfect needles. When GM came around to the way I thought things should be, I felt vindicated. The way to approach the job properly is to seek continuous improvement. That is what *kaizen* is, the Japanese management principle that GM finally began to adopt and referred to as "Total Quality Management" (TQM).

With the new TQM atmosphere at work, and by reading and thinking about the higher principles from the Grange and from my church, I started to generate a new perspective on what was happening to me. Instead of killing me, the work made me stronger. Even if you are not worshipping the beast that we call capitalism, you are in its service. The goodness that is in you could easily be snubbed out by the powerful beast. You have to maintain your own sanity in the midst of this. We need to keep ourselves unspotted from the world. We need to keep ourselves from being overcome by the beast. You can only do that by being true to yourself and your own principles. That's how to maintain dignity, self-respect, and sanity while spending a lifetime building cars, needles, houses, or anything with your hands.

Acknowledgments

Thank you to Shannon Ward for participation in many of the conversations that led to this article and to Ilana Gershon and an anonymous reviewer for comments on an earlier draft.

Suggested Readings

On life on the GM assembly line, see:
Ben Hamper, *Rivethead: Tales From the Assembly Line*. New York: Warner Books, 1992.

On scientific management, see:
Frederick Winslow Taylor, *The Principles of Scientific Management*. New York: Harper and Brothers, 1911.

On The Grange ("The National Grange of the Order of Patrons of Husbandry"), see:
D. Sven Nordin, *Rich Harvest: A History of the Grange, 1867–1900*. Jackson: University Press of Mississippi, 2006.

On the 1980s shift of General Motors to "Total Quality Management," see:
Ellen Goldbaum with Herbert C. Short, "How Quality Programs Win Respect—and Get Results." *Chemical Week,* October 5, 1988.
John Holusha, "A Case Study of General Motors; Advice for Detroit's Humbled Giant." *New York Times,* December 7, 1986.
Francine Kiefer, "Drive for More Quality in U.S. Cars Is Catching on with Workers." *Christian Science Monitor,* June 16, 1983.
Cindy Skrzycki, "The Quest for the Best: U.S. Firms Turn to Quality as Competitive Tool." *Washington Post,* October 2, 1988.

On Vita Needle, see:
Caitrin Lynch, *Retirement on the Line: Age, Work, and Value in an American Factory*. Ithaca: Cornell University Press, 2012.

How to Be a Cell Phone Repair Technician

Amanda Kemble, Briel Kobak, Joshua A. Bell, and Joel Kuipers

Over the past decade, cell phones have become simultaneously more advanced and more vulnerable to a range of breakdowns. Sleek displays, fragile touchscreens, and increased use mean that the device that customers take everywhere can also break anywhere. In response to this, Americans have spent some $5.9 billion on iPhone insurance, repairs, and replacements since Apple released the first iPhone in 2007. Alongside this phenomenon artisanal repair shops and franchises across the country have emerged in North America. These stores position themselves as alternatives to established corporate consumer options, where customers have the opportunity to meet one on one with technicians and demystify the insides of their phones. In this way, the role of the repair technician marks a resurgence of the artisanal maker and brings "making" back into the equation of our engagement with electronics. Though the role of the repair technicians could be perceived as blue-collar, their work involves a combination of curiosity, patience, and creativity that large-scale manufacturing and assembly often erases or renders null. A day in the life of a cell phone repair shop technician reveals what it means to fix in a digital age.

September 21, 2012
Washington, D.C.
9:00 a.m.

Today, Apple released the iPhone 5. I waited outside the Apple Store in Georgetown, Washington, D.C., in the early morning while hundreds of Apple fans were patiently lining the brick sidewalks—some there since the night before. While each of the eager customers was envisioning their new phone, with its sleek edges and increased functionality, I was busy picturing all the cracked screens and dented aluminum casings. I come to every iPhone release so that I can drum up business for my store, which just opened in Washington, D.C. As one of the founders of the cell phone and electronics repair franchise Broken→Fixed, I hand out business cards embossed with the store's name and contact information to anyone who will take one. The shop is one of over forty stores in a franchise that I helped found in 2007 in the southeastern United States along with a group of people like me, entrepreneurial college graduates. After stopping by the major cell phone retail locations in the city to drop off additional cards to eager iPhone buyers (all of whom could become Broken→Fixed customers with just one spill of liquid or one fumble of their phone), I returned to the store with a new mission in mind: taking apart my own brand new iPhone 5.

Entering through the front door of the shop, I look over the waiting room—sleek black leather chairs facing a flatscreen TV, a coffee table strewn with copies of *Sports Illustrated* and *Good Housekeeping*—and I am about to head into the back room before I notice a vaguely familiar face standing next to the front counter. It takes me a minute, but then it clicks—it's the new technician we just hired for the store. Today is his first day, and I'm late.

"Hey, sorry I'm late. I was at the Apple store," I tell him, ushering him past the front counter, through the black curtain over the doorway, and into the back room. Damian, a fellow repair tech, glances up from his seat at the island of tables in the middle of the room as I enter, gives me a nod.

"I thought he'd want to wait for you, Aaron" Damien says, then goes back to the phone he's repairing. I pull up an extra chair over to my workstation on the other side of the island. On top of the work mat sits my toolkit, originally from the online repair store iFixit, but overflowing with additional tools—a new set of screwdrivers ordered online from China, a toothbrush for removing dirt and debris from disassembled parts, and a utility knife.

"So this is gonna be a little different today than most days, since the 5 just came out. So, we can get to the standard training the next time you come in, but today I was planning on taking mine apart." I pull a sleek white box out of my messenger bag and open the lid, revealing another sleek black "box": my iPhone 5. Without any official manuals or instructions, without the usual help or tips from my fellow repair techs, without numerous YouTube videos or online breakdowns, I have to take apart and put this device back together on my own. Not only that, I have to do it with someone watching.

"So before I start, I should tell you a little about the store and everything. And it's funny, because without the iPhone," I say, gesturing to the 5 sitting on my work mat, "we probably wouldn't be here. We'd never have been able to open this shop. Without broken iPhone screens, we wouldn't have a business."

Emergence of Cell Phone Repair in the United States

As I look over the new phone, I consider how much to tell the new technician. Our business began with the original iPhone, but a number of other factors came into place around 2007. As more and more people are buying smartphones, they're also having to get them repaired when they break. People think when they get a smartphone nothing will go wrong, they will always be able to carry them around, but really the actual devices break quite often. Part of the problem is in the design of the phones—larger screens on thinner units. But the phones also have increased functionality, so more people are using them all the time. When they do break, people come in here feeling like they are missing part of themselves. They always want their phone repaired as soon as possible to access their personal data.

Our business for cell phone repair really grows out of the DIY repair communities that have existed for a long time in the United States. We all know people who prefer to fix things themselves—because it's cheaper, because they want to do it themselves to learn, because they don't trust other people to do a good job, or because they don't want to feed into consumer practices of simply throwing something out when one thing stops working and buying something new. But we're much different than the type of repair you'd think of in the nineteenth and twentieth centuries. We don't get manuals with each phone model. We're fighting against the manufacturers who don't want us to know how to repair what they produce, but we figure out a way to do it anyway.

The new technician may not need to know all this though—the first day we just try to introduce the techs to the business. I turn to him and say, "We opened up our first shop in Washington, D.C., in 2012. There were already one or two other cell phone repair shops in D.C., and more have shown up since, but none do it like us. Some have technicians who respond to calls and drive to people's homes. Others are brick-and-mortar stores or kiosks in malls. Some repair businesses are side activities in shops devoted to other things. But we bring a level of professionalism and customer service to an industry that customers often think of as 'sketchy.' For every repair we do, we want to make sure the customer's happy—even if that means we might lose money. Without customers, we don't have a business."

"So did you guys not really start your business until smartphones came around?" asks the new tech.

"Yeah, exactly," I say nodding my head enthusiastically. "Without cracked iPhone screens, we would never have been able to open our first store, let alone the forty stores we've opened across the country in the last five years. I'll tell you why: the cost of iPhone screens and the structure of U.S. contract plans allow repair businesses to have competitive pricing options for repair compared to phone replacement through the carriers or manufacturers. U.S. contract plans subsidize the cost of the smartphone itself, charging a couple hundred dollars at most for what is, at full retail cost, a $800 phone. They do this by locking customers into a two-year contract, so that the higher cost of the plan (compared to pay-as-you-go) subsidizes the lower cost of the phone. This means that customers don't often know how much the phone itself costs. They only realize this once they break their phones and try to replace them. Without an upgrade, they would most likely have to pay full retail cost for a new phone. Or, if the provider offers repair, customers have to send their phone away for several weeks. This is where we enter the game, offering repairs of both aesthetic and functional breakdowns for much less than the cost of replacing the phone."

Repair: Craft, Blackboxing, and the Bricoleur

"Does this make sense?" I ask, pausing to read the face of the new tech. There's a steep learning curve in the repair shop, and I'm just trying to get him up to speed as soon as possible.

"Yeah. I'm glad to hear customer service is the most important to you guys. I've taken apart computers and stuff, but not as many cell phones. I guess if you like repairing one thing, you'll get to know all the others eventually, right?" he asks.

"Yeah, definitely," I affirm. "You'll definitely get the hang of phones with practice. I'm also telling you this because I think it's important for technicians to understand the repair landscape. As repair technicians, we operate in a frontier of sorts, forging a space for legitimate and viable business outside of accessible big-box companies and cellular phone providers. We aren't part of the cell phone's traditional supply chain, but we're still hooked into it. We need to connect with cell phones' suppliers for parts, but we're doing a type of work that most cell phone suppliers do not do, at least not for individual customers. We also occupy a space between problem-finding and problem-solving, made all the more difficult by the devices we have to repair, and the ways that companies will hide the design, people, and labor that produce the cell phones."

At this point I see Damien look up from the Samsung Galaxy he is fixing. "I think you lost me at frontier, Aaron." The two of them laugh and I realize that the new technician's eyes look a bit glazed over. I realize I should probably stop talking and walk him through the repair soon. Now that I've explained all this, I cannot help but continue to think about the sorts of changes in the last two decades that made electronics repair possible. The other store owners and I always reflect on how it was standard practice for electronic devices to have manuals enclosed with them until the 1990s, helping owners figure out how devices worked and how to repair them. When corporations moved away from producing these manuals, they were signaling their disinterest in repair and their commitment to a disposable economy. Without these manuals, it is hard for customers to know how these devices are put together and how they work. This creates a space for us to step in, we diagnose the problem and fix the device. In the process of repair, we rely on our experience, constant practice and our own set of tools and techniques. We hope that these tools and techniques will help us to uncover the device's problem, especially when all the customer can say is that "it won't turn on." But telling a customer what is wrong with their phone is not enough; repairing is what keeps the business running.

I turn to the new technician, and try to reassure him, "There's a lot of problem solving involved but over the course of repairing thousands of phones like I have, you develop a certain technique that allows you to try to predict where problems will occur. As you learn the style of each particular cell phone brand, you can make better and better guesses as to where the cables may be connected, which parts might need more force to move, and which parts are frustratingly fragile. Each step in the repair sequence becomes familiar, each iPhone with its predictable cables and connectors, each HTC requiring delicate and tedious glass removal, exposing an easily breakable LCD."

The new technician nods his head, "I've heard HTC phones are the worst. Like the engineers who made them wanted to make all the arrangements as complicated as possible."

Damien and I laugh in agreement. "It's true. But you're always going to be nervous and careful with a model that you have never repaired before. We learn to gather information that gives a clue to the 'correct' way to repair but we also have to rely on trial and error, being willing to risk a little bit, to try to find an ideal way (in terms of accessible parts and tools, and your own method) to complete the repair. Yet, go too far, get too careless, and the device may break, losing the company money—not just in the lost profits of the repair, but also in the purchase of a new phone for the customer—and leaving you feeling like a failure. We always walk along this tightrope with each repair, every time we pick up a screwdriver and remove a screw."

After this long speech, I decide I've imparted enough verbal wisdom. It's time to actually start the repair. Ever since I was a kid, I have enjoyed taking things apart, from lawnmowers to old computers. Not all our technicians have backgrounds in electronics or repair, but they usually have

Figure 12.1 A technician disassembles an iPhone 4S and performs a diagnostic test. Photograph by Briel Kobak.

this kind of keen interest in how to break things apart and put them back together. Even though I've had two years of experience repairing phones, my hands shake as I place the phone on my work mat and pull out my screwdriver. I put the screwdriver back down, and pick up the phone again, looking it over, moving it around, trying to make sure I'm not forgetting anything before I start. It's even worse having this new tech here to witness everything—I don't want to look like an idiot in front of a new hire. I consider calling one of my good friends, a manager at another store in the franchise, to see if anyone else has tried to open up the iPhone 5. We all keep in touch with each other pretty frequently, usually by phone and email, to update each other on new fixes and techniques or half-jokingly compete over store profits. I decide against it though, partly hoping that I'll have the first story to tell about opening this new phone.

I try to focus and decide to lay out all of my tools around the device so I don't have to rummage around for them mid-repair. I pull out the Phillips screwdriver I'm sure I'll need, as well as my red plastic spatula and suction cup. I pick up the phone and rest it on its head, with the back casing facing me, then pick up my screwdriver. Taking a deep breath, I remove the two Pentalobe screws on the bottom of the phone and drop them on the workstation. We all deal with our screws differently. I have made a small sketch of the phone and placed my screws down near where I remove them in the actual device. I've learned far too early the frustration of mixing up my screws. I grab the suction cup and position it at the bottom of the screen, near the home button, pushing down to seal it. With the phone in my left hand, I use my right hand to start to pull the suction cup up, careful not to pull too hard, or I could rip the cables at the top of the phone. I take hold of my bright red spudger—one of my favorite tools that I got working for a different repair company and have held onto ever since (and had to hide from my coworkers to keep them from "borrowing" it). I wedge it between the LCD display and the rest of the phone, and slowly slide the spudger along the gap. But as I reach the right side of the phone, I feel resistance. I carefully continue to pry, unsure of where the resistance is coming from. I pull gently on the suction cup to see how far I can separate the screen, but I instantly encounter more resistance. I pull again, feeling with my left hand to try to locate exactly where the problem is, feeling it the most at the middle right of the midframe. I set the phone down on the table and stare at it for a few beats. And then it hits me: I forgot to remove the SIM card!

These are the small things that can have huge consequences: a SIM card left in, a cable pulled too hard, a nick in the battery. This is why technicians have to learn by doing. Just watching a repair won't help you get a feel for how the repair should be going, when to give a little extra force, or when to know that you need to proceed carefully. While watching a breakdown video or having some inside tips about the phone would definitely be helpful in this case, a lot of the job requires knowing when something's working and knowing when it isn't. And the only way to really get a handle on that is to keep repairing as many phones as possible.

"Shit," I say out loud.

"What's wrong?" Damian asks, looking up from the phone he's working on. The new tech lets out a worried sound.

"I forgot to take out the SIM," I say exasperatedly. "This is why you always have to be careful and always be focused. You don't want to fuck up," I tell the new tech.

It's such a small thing, but something that could easily cause problems. But now that I've discovered the problem, I can fix it. Pushing down on the suction cup, I snap the screen back into place, undoing all that careful prying and lifting. Out of my toolkit I grab my SIM key (although a paper clip would work just as well) and insert it into the hole on the right side, easily popping the SIM card out.

"Alright," I mutter. "Take two."

Normally, Damian and I would joke around while we both worked, talking about crazy customers or our families or gossiping about new devices and repair methods or tricks. Or I would talk the new tech through the repair. But not today. Today, I am trying to focus only on this, because if I mess it up too bad, I'm out of luck. Since the iPhone 5 was just released, there will be almost no chance for me to get replacement parts for anything I break. If anything goes wrong, I'll have an $800 paperweight for at least a couple months until factories start supplying parts to third party vendors.

Thankfully, being very, very good at repairing other iPhone models really helps. It's how you start to learn the ways one company puts the phones together a certain way, a way that is going to be different than any other company's design. Apple generally makes their phones pretty straightforward to repair, and their ubiquity makes quality parts available at a good price, often coming as a discrete package—LCD and glass come together as the full display. So it's a simple "pop one off, pop the new one on" situation (well, not really that simple). Whereas the phones we in the store almost all hate—HTCs—make you do a lot of work to separate the glass from the LCD, which makes the LCD much more vulnerable during repair. These are the things that you learn as you open up more phones; they can give you an idea of how to proceed with a new one. But you can never be totally sure that you know exactly what you're doing. Sometimes, you just have to keep going, having faith that you're not going to break anything and that you're being patient and cautious enough to get through that first repair blind. We only have ourselves to rely on for these repairs. There's no one else to help us.

Because we're essentially shut out of the big box companies that manu-facture these phones, we not only have to steadily learn tricks and secrets for each brand, but our position as technicians also means that we have to get to be super creative to figure things out. It's how we develop our trade secrets, quick fixes, and new techniques that make the repair more success-ful. One of the things I've learned since starting to repair phones is that you shouldn't discount trying out something different. Everything can become a tool and might be able to help you in finishing the repair or getting you out of a jam with parts. Knowing how to improvise and use everything at your disposal, especially when you don't have the insight of the manufacturer, this is what enables us to come up with strategies and fixes that we might otherwise never have thought about.

Warranty and the Concealment of Labor

I put down my screwdriver and decide to take a short break before diving back in. I turn to the new tech, eager to explain more about what we do and how we do it.

"Technicians have to be careful," I say again, it's something I'll never get tired of telling new techs. "We don't want to show any trace on the phone that anyone has repaired it. If we do, we risk the chance of voiding someone's warranty. And trust me, you don't want to do that to the customer. If the company refuses to honor the warranty, we normally pay for a new phone just to keep the customer happy.

"So when we work on a phone here, we must make sure we do not pull off any stickers that say 'Do Not Remove' or strip any screws—"

"What does removing the 'Do Not Remove' do?" interjects the new tech.

"Nothing technically to the phone," I explain. "Except void the warranty. It's one of Apple's ways of trying to discourage repair and tinkering. Even though we do so much back here, we have to use our skills to make our own work undetectable. That means fingerprints have to be scrubbed off the metal shields, and every screw must be returned to its original place. Leaving screws out is a tell-tale sign that someone's been in the phone, and that they were sloppy enough to either lose a screw or forgot to put it back in. And at Broken→Fixed, we aren't sloppy."

The new guy looks a little nervous, so I go on. "Our store layout also helps hide the work we do, but in this case, it's for our own good. Customers normally deliver their phones to the front desk while the work takes place back here, behind a curtain. Actually, in our very first store, we didn't have any partitions or separate rooms. People got so nervous and anxious about seeing their phones being worked on, they were always freaking out. We realized that cell phones are way too intimate, they're like extensions of the people in a way, filled with so much personal information. So customers feel particularly vulnerable when a phone is broken. Some customers come into the store just losing it, and we have to work carefully to provide a positive customer experience and make them feel at ease. That's why we have to be fast, but perfect—speed not only means we've got skill, but it also means that anxious customers don't have to part with their device for too long. And believe me, you don't want to keep an anxious customer waiting any longer than necessary."

I hear the bell ring several times at the front desk. I leave behind the iPhone 5 and the new tech in order to greet the customer out front.

"It got wet," the customer says cryptically, handing over an iPhone 4S with a blank screen.

Water damage is always a bit of a guessing game. Not just because we often cannot reverse the corrosion that results from the metal oxidizing, but also because customers sometimes choose not to disclose the real circumstances regarding the incident. The fewer details provided regarding the water damage, the more likely I am to assume that the phone has suffered "potty damage." Those phones I handle with gloves and douse in rubbing alcohol. When I first started repairing cell phones, I would try to find out what kind of water so I'd know the extent of the damage and what to expect. Now I prefer not to ask.

"Okay, so with water damage we normally take a twenty-four-hour diagnostic period to see what sorts of issues are happening inside the phone," I explain, promptly placing the phone onto the counter and out of my hand.

"But I can't do anything without my phone," the customer replies quickly.

This kind of reaction is common. One of our franchise's biggest concerns is providing a happy customer experience, so we just have to gently stress to the customer that leaving the phone here will ultimately benefit him or her in the long run. "We could try to get it to you by the close of business tomorrow. Will that be fast enough for you?"

"Is there some sort of loaner phone you guys give out? Or maybe you could just replace the screen and leave the water damage to chance?" he asks.

"We really would not recommend ignoring the water damage. And I'm sorry, but we don't have any loaner phones to give out. I strongly suggest waiting so that we can take a look and know for sure what parts of the phone have been affected by the water."

I can tell he is thinking about the payoff of leaving the phone. There are a few moments of silence. "I'm thinking, I'm thinking of taking the risk to see if it works. I could just wait for an upgrade if something goes wrong," the customer says. But after a few more pensive moments, he agrees to leave it with us and says he'll see us tomorrow.

I head into the back with the phone. "One of the most difficult parts of this job," I tell the new tech, "is to make customers realize how much their phone is worth. With the whole upgrade process, people think their phones cost a fraction of their actual retail price. So we do our best to explain how much they can save by choosing repair."

"Yeah, when I told my friends about this job, they didn't realize there other good options for fixing a phone besides insurance or warranty," says the new tech.

I'm not surprised to hear this at all. I explain, "Like I said before, some repair shops have the reputation of being 'sketchy.' Unhappy customers will post on Yelp that they are not totally trustworthy. But our franchise has worked to make our practice seem more legit. We do our best to present ourselves well with company t-shirts, sleek waiting rooms, and separate back rooms where all the repairs happen."

"We're also super careful with parts. I think that's something repair customers worry about a lot. When we opened one of our first stores, we just got all the parts from eBay. After a while though, when we started to be a bit successful, we actually got contacted by a Chinese vendor. That's pretty common. There are guys who just scour the web looking for tech businesses opening up. So now we actually work with a vendor linked to a number of different outsource factories. Each one has their own thing— Foxconn makes the motherboards, other guys are in charge of the glass, the batteries, and LCD displays. That company outsources a bunch of parts, like the glass and LCD. A lot of those factories do the same thing for other companies like HTC and Samsung as well. Our franchise actually has a distribution center now that we order all our parts from so that individual stores don't have to worry about contacting vendors" (see figure 12.1).

I continue, "With this 4S, we won't have many problems, though. It's the most popular model of phone that we see, and our distribution center keeps us well stocked on all the parts—the front glass, the back panels, and the LCD displays. When customers ask why a certain repair costs so much, we explain by breaking down the cost of the part and then the cost of the labor. For example, the iPhone 4S front screen costs $149.99. We charge $100 for the part and $49.99 for our own work."

Staring at the new phone, I am a bit worried about how we are going to supply these new iPhone 5 parts. I tell the new guy and Damien, "The first few months after a release, we just expect to have very few customers willing to pay what we are able to afford in parts. By the time another model comes out, though, we normally find a supplier that has parts for a price that feels adequate for customers when combined with our labor costs."

"I love the feeling of finishing a phone and having it look like it just came from a manufacturing site. As much as we like to get creative around here, we like to provide customers with a phone that looks—and functions—like brand new."

Conclusion

I stop talking and focus on my own phone again. The front screen and the back panel are lying next to each other on the mat. Immediately I notice a few differences between the 4S that I was just working on and this new model. The LCD screen and front glass are fused like the 3GS, there's an extra bracket on the home button, and the battery comes out like in the 4. I decide not to take it apart any further because I worry about damaging my brand new phone. Putting the phone back together at this stage will be easy.

I begin by threading a cable between the front screen and back panel and replacing all the different screws back into their original locations. I snap the display back into position and replace the two bottom screws that always punctuate an iPhone repair. I take a breath and hold down the home button. As the Apple logo appears on the screen, I breathe a sigh of relief. It still works!

As the day nears closing, the new tech turns to me and asks, "What is the single best advice you can give to a new tech?"

There's a lot to that answer. I begin by saying, "Being a repair technician requires so much more than just knowing the phone's composite parts—it requires patience; never giving up, yet knowing when to take a break; using all the available resources at your disposal, in whatever way you can make them work. It also means you have to take some risks, figure things out on your own because you have no other choice. It's not like the phone manufacturers are printing out manuals or blueprints. It means you have to trust your own instincts and touch—you learn when to ease up and when to apply a little force. It sometimes means you have to believe in some superstitions, things beyond your control, and know when it's time to give up. Sometimes a phone just has some bad magic, and there's no way you're bringing it back to life."

The new tech nods his head in understanding. I finish by emphasizing the most important point: "But the job isn't just about the phone; it's about making a customer happy, a customer who feels like he's just lost his whole life when he drops the phone in water, who feels like he can't survive without the phone. It's about bringing phones back to life for the customers, data and parts, without them ever truly realizing the challenge you face in the backroom and all the ways in which you work to restore what was broken."

Acknowledgments

In this piece we draw on our ongoing work in the Washington, D.C., metro region on the repair of cell phones to make an idealized portrait of repair. To do so, we have used our interviews and experiences with cell phone repair technicians in a number of stores. We would like to thank the technicians and owners at all the repair shops we worked with, as well as the Smithsonian Institution's Grand Challenges Consortia Understanding the American Experience and World Cultures for funding the *Fixing Connections: The Art and Science of Repair* project (2012–2014).

Suggested Readings

For ethnography of repair and repair websites, see:
Joshua Bell, Joel Kuipers, Jacqueline Hazen, Amanda Kemble, and Briel Kobak, "'We're Almost Like Therapists for People with Electronics': Fetishization, Cell Phones, and Repair." Paper presented at Wenner-Gren workshop Linguistic and Material Intimacies of Mobile Phones, Washington, D.C., June 4–7, 2013.

Tim Dant, "The Work of Repair: Gesture, Emotion, and Sensual Knowledge." Lancaster
    E-prints, 2009. Available at http://eprints.lancs.ac.uk/26893/1/work_of_repair_3.pdf.
Julian Orr, *Talking about Machines*. Ithaca: Cornell University Press, 1996.
Andrew Skuse, "Enlivened Objects: The Social Life, Death, and Rebirth of Radio as
    Commodity in Afghanistan." *Journal of Material Culture* 10 (2005): 123–36.

For DIY movements, see:
Matthew B. Crawford, *Shop Class as Soulcraft: An Inquiry into the Value of Work*. New
    York: Penguin Books, 2010.
Christopher M. Kelty, *Two Bits: The Cultural Significance of Free Software*. Durham,
    NC: Duke University Press, 2008.
Morgan Meyer, "Domesticating and Democratizing Science: A Geography of Do-It-
    Yourself Biology." *Journal of Material Culture* 18, no. 2 (2013): 117–34.

For craft and the bricoleur, see:
Michael Herzfeld, *The Body Impolitic: Artisans and Artifice in the Global Hierarchy of
    Value*. Chicago: University of Chicago Press, 2004.
Claude Lévi-Strauss, *The Savage Mind*. George Weidenfield, translator. Chicago: Uni-
    versity of Chicago Press, 1962.
Richard Sennett, *The Craftsman*. New Haven, CT: Yale University Press, 2008.

For blackboxing and fetishism, see:
Bruno Latour, "On Technical Mediation—Philosophy, Sociology, Genealogy." *Com-
    mon Knowledge* 3, no. 2 (1994): 29–64.
Karl Marx, *The Marx-Engels Reader*. Robert C. Tucker, editor. New York: W. W.
    Norton, 1978.

13

Becoming a Professional Wrestler in Mexico City

Heather Levi

Mexico City, also known as the Federal District, is the capital of Mexico. Over the course of the twentieth century, it grew from a relatively small city of five hundred thousand to a megalopolis of twenty-one million, making it the most populated urban area in the Western hemisphere. In addition to being Mexico's center of government, population, and economy, it is the center of Mexico's entertainment industries, among them professional wrestling.

Professional wrestling, called *lucha libre*[1] in Mexico, originated in the United States. It was not practiced in Mexico until 1933, when Salvador Lutteroth, promoter and founder of the Empresa Mexicana de Lucha Libre,[2] brought a group of wrestlers from Texas to Mexico City. The sport—the "entertainment"—quickly gained an audience in Mexico

---

1. Literally "free struggle" or "free-style wrestling," lucha libre usually refers to professional wrestling, similar to the kind practiced in the United States in organizations like the WCW.
2. Mexican Company of Lucha Libre

and by the 1940s was adapted to Mexican tastes through changes in costuming and technique. In the 1950s, lucha libre was integrated into various forms of Mexican mass media. *Luchadores*,[3] especially masked wrestlers, became the subjects of comic books and movies. For much of the twentieth century it was Mexico City's second most popular live sporting event.

I trained in lucha libre in the late 1990s. My teacher, Luis Jaramillo Martinez (a.k.a. Aguila Blanco) was unfailingly generous with me, teaching me lucha libre technique and talking to me about the life of the luchador. When we first met, he gave me a short speech about what he considered lucha libre to be. In the piece that follows, I take on the voice of a trainer like him, advising someone like me, a novice, as she considers a career in lucha libre. The majority of luchadores are men, but women have participated in lucha libre since the 1940s. Even though he is addressing a female student, a trainer would normally use masculine grammatical forms and pronouns when talking about wrestlers in general, so I have done the same here.

You want to be a luchadora? Well, I can teach you. I can teach you, but I'm not going to teach you the clown show they put on TV. If you want to learn, I can teach you the real, Mexican lucha libre. Is it the same as it is in other countries? Well, yes and no. We have our own style. In Japan, they wrestle hard, it's a very hard style, hard blows. The U.S.? Well, most of us have worked in the U.S. from time to time, and that's a lot of fun, because U.S. wrestling is pure *show*. There's more of what they call *power moves*, but mostly it's a lot of talk. If you want to be a luchador, though, it's not a lot of talk, and it's not just show. People see us, and they say, "Oh, that's just circus, somersaults, and theater." But that's not true. We are athletes. To be a luchador, you have to have the body of a luchador. You have to look the part, so when people see you in the street, they don't say, "Oh, there goes a bicyclist." They say, "There goes a luchador!" Or, in your case, a luchadora.

Well, to get that body, you have to train. Like I said, I can train you, but you don't have to train with me. You can go see other trainers in other gyms.

---

3. Professional wrestlers. A male wrestler is called a *luchador* (plural *luchadores*). A female wrestler is a *luchadora* (plural *luchadoras*).

Almost any gym in any *barrio popular*[4] in Mexico City has someone who gives classes in lucha libre. Be careful though; not all of them know what they're doing. They don't know the secrets of lucha libre, or they don't want to show you if they do. They'll just teach you a somersault or two, have you jump off the ropes around the ring, and they'll tell you that's lucha libre. But it's not. The first time you get into the ring, you'll get hurt. If you train with me, you don't have to get hurt. Nobody ever has to get hurt.

Not everybody can be a luchador, though. We have a saying here: "A luchador isn't made, he's born." That's why, if you look at who the stars are, most of the really big stars were born into the *familia luchistica*.[5] No, really . . . look how many wrestlers are son-of-somebody or somebody-or-another II. They were practically raised in the arena, so of course they could be luchadores! And I'll tell you something else. Luchadoras? Well, luchadoras who get married, they almost always marry luchadores. No other husband would understand. He wouldn't understand the schedule, the dedication, the hours in the gym, the travel . . . he wouldn't understand. But if you are a luchador, then it gets into your blood. You'll see. It's like we say: "*La llevo en mi sangre.*"[6] If you're born into a lucha family, then it's there in your blood. But even if you aren't, even if you are a foreigner, it gets into your blood. If I go a day or two without anybody throwing me, without at least a fall or two, I just don't feel right.

So, like I said, you could train with me. I'll train you, but you don't have to train with me. But you should go to a gym where the teacher is a real luchador. There are several here in Mexico City. "Charles Bronson" (he was a wrestler—he looked like Charles Bronson, so that was his character), he has a gym near Metro Pino Suárez. You could go to the Nuevo Jordán, near Metro Salto de Agua. That's mainly a boxing gym, but there's always at least one or two really good luchadores giving classes. Ham Lee has a gym too, up north of Metro Tlatelolco. If you want to train with a luchadora, I hear that Irma Gonzalez is still training people, and she must be over seventy years old now. Oh, there's a lot of places. Or you could go directly to the CMLL, the Consejo Mundial de Lucha Libre.[7] They don't

---

4. A working-class or lower-class neighborhood.
5. Lucha libre family.
6. "I carry it in my blood."
7. World Council of Lucha Libre.

always train novices, but sometimes they do. If you train there, well, that gets you in the door at least.

The Consejo, the CMLL? They used to be called the Empresa Mexicana de Lucha Libre (EMLL), but they started calling themselves the "Consejo" (Council) in the 1990s. I guess they thought it sounded better. Anyway, they are the oldest lucha libre *empresa* in Mexico. An empresa? That's a business that has an arena and hires luchadores. There are all different sizes, but the CMLL is the biggest. The CMLL owns the two biggest arenas in Mexico City, Arena México and Arena Coliseo. They also own arenas in Puebla, Guadalajara, Acapulco, . . . lots of places. The AAA is just as famous now, because they're on television, but they don't have an arena. They just promote events all over the country in different arenas, and then they broadcast them. When you see lucha libre on television, it's either the CMLL or the AAA, but that's not all there is to lucha libre! Anyway, I'll tell you more about that later. You're just getting started, after all.

So, say you find a teacher. Maybe it's me, maybe it's someone else. You want to know what you will need to do, what you will learn. You want to learn the secrets of lucha libre. Well, if you train with me, I will teach you the secrets of lucha libre, but I'm not going to tell you all of them now. I'll tell you how it is, though. The first thing is, like I said, it's not just turning somersaults. It's not acrobatics. The first technique I'll teach you, though, is how to do a front roll, which is basically a somersault. But then you'll learn the three-quarters roll, the backwards roll, the rear breakfall, the *plancha*,[8] and the *salto mortal*.[9] If you think those are just for show, you're wrong. Those are techniques! Those are the secrets of lucha libre. You can use them to escape from a lock or fall without getting hurt. You're going to practice them over and over and over again. You'll do twenty, thirty, a hundred in a row! You'll do them until you don't get dizzy anymore.

The second thing is that you have to be in good physical condition. I know people say all kinds of things about luchadores, but we really are athletes, and you really have to train in the gym outside of class. You should run, because you need to have endurance. You should also lift weights. The most important areas to train are your legs and your neck. Finally,

---

8. Literally, iron. In U.S. professional wrestling the move is called a flying crossbody.

9. Literally, mortal leap. A technique in which the wrestler jumps into a somersault in mid-air and lands on his or her back.

Figure 13.1 A *luchador* executes a *salto mortal* too late to pin his opponent.
Photograph by the author.

you also have to learn the real core of wrestling: the art of joint locks. In lucha libre, we use locks from lots of different sports. We use techniques from Greco-Roman wrestling and Olympic wrestling, but we also have techniques that came from judo and jujitsu. Some of the most important locks were made famous by great wrestlers in the past. There's the *de a caballo*,[10] that El Santo liked to use. Fray Tormenta, the priest who used to wrestle, he invented the *confesor*.[11] The more you know, the better wrestler you'll be. You'll also learn the stuff that the public likes to watch: how to do aerial moves off the ropes, how to do flying kicks and *planchas* and *tijeras*.[12] But none of that is as important as learning your rolls and your joint locks.

When we practice, you'll line up just outside of the ring with the rest of your classmates. Yes, the ring is the same as a boxing ring. Whoever is the most advanced will be at the head of the line. The newest student will be at the back. I'll call the first student into the center of the ring and show him the technique we are going to practice first. Then I'll leave the

---

10. Literally, on horseback. In U.S. professional wrestling the move is called a Boston crab.
11. The confessor.
12. Scissor-legs.

ring, and the next student will enter. The first student will take my role, and the two will perform the technique together. Then the first student steps out and the third steps in until, finally, the newest student takes my role with the most advanced student. After that, I'll demonstrate a technique that logically follows from the first one. Eventually, all the students will take both roles practicing a short sequence of techniques, one after the other.

Well, that's how we teach the basics. If you're like most people, you'll need to train for about three years before you'll be ready to try your luck as a professional. First, though, you'll have to have a character. Don't start clowning around and acting when you're starting your classes, though. For the first couple of years, you just need to learn the techniques. But at some point, you'll think about your character; that's where the magic of lucha libre comes in.

The first thing you need to decide is whether to wrestle as a *rudo*[13] or as a *técnico*[14]—a good guy or a bad guy. In any match somebody has to be the rudo and somebody else has to be the técnico, otherwise it's not really lucha libre. The rudo, well, the rudo has to break the rules sometimes. The rudo gets to cheat. But there's more to being a rudo than that. If you're a rudo, you have to learn to move like a rudo; you have to move roughly, brusquely. You might hit or kick your opponent more than you would if you were a técnico. You don't have to know as many locks, maybe, and you don't have to do as many moves off the ropes, but you have to make the public hate you. But you can't make them hate you by attacking them, the audience. No, you have to make them hate you by attacking the técnico, and by the *way* you attack the técnico. If you are the rudo, every insult from the audience will be applause to your ears.

As for the técnico, well, he's the good guy. He's the one who obeys the rules, who respects the referee (at least some of the time). But the técnico has to make the audience cheer for him, love him. He has to know how to use more spectacular, elegant moves, whether it's escaping a jointlock or doing a flying *salto mortal* onto an opponent. He has to be charismatic. The técnico has to know more locks, more techniques than the rudo, but the rudo . . . the rudo is the one who brings real flavor to the lucha libre.

---

13. Ruffian.
14. Technician.

Whether you decide to be a rudo or a técnico, well, that's usually a matter of temperament. Usually when you're training, you'll find that you are more comfortable with one role or the other. It has to do with the way you move, the way you like to enter the ring and face your opponent. It has nothing to do with how you are in real life! I know some técnicos who are really sons-of-bitches, and some of the nicest guys I know are rudos. When they are in the ring, though, it's another story. You'll know which you want to be; you'll feel it in your bones. Of course, the best wrestlers can perform both roles, and they sometimes change roles over the course of a career.

Once you know whether you're a rudo or a técnico, you'll want to start thinking about what your character is going to be. There are a lot of different kinds of characters. Some people—say they're from somewhere in *la provincia*.[15] Everywhere outside of Mexico City is *la provincia,* but say they are from the state of Durango. Well, the symbol of Durango is the scorpion, so maybe they'll call themselves "The Scorpion" or "The Scorpion of Durango" or something like that. Or if they want to be another animal, well, a lot of wrestlers are cats or tigers or jaguars or eagles. The Aztec warriors, they would wear jaguar masks or eagle masks into battle, so it's kind of like being an Aztec warrior. Some wrestlers pick a character from the movies or comic books or television and go as Astroboy or Underdog. Then there are the ones who call themselves angels or demons or saints, like the two most famous wrestlers of all time, El Santo[16] and Blue Demon. By the way, you might want to pick a name that's in English or sounds like English. A lot of luchadores do that, even though they're Mexican.

It doesn't pay to get too attached to your character if you're going to be a professional. Whatever you come up with, you will use it when you are working in small empresas or freelancing, but you won't get nearly enough work to make a living. If you're really lucky, you might get a chance to be recruited by one of the big empresas, but unless your character already has

---

15. The provinces. In Mexico City, this term refers to all of Mexico outside of Mexico City.

16. El Santo (Rodolfo Guzmán Huerta) was the most famous and best-loved luchador in Mexican history. His career lasted from 1948 until his death in 1983. He and his silver mask became icons of Mexican popular culture through his work in the ring and, more importantly, through his work in cinema. Over the course of his career he starred in over fifty low-budget action movies in which he saved Mexico or the Earth itself from a variety of monsters, criminals, and extraterrestrials.

big fan base, they will probably assign you a different character. It's important to be flexible when you're starting out.

If you make friends with a big star, and he doesn't have any children or nephews going into the business, you can ask to use or buy a version of his character. That way you can start out with something of a following. Be careful not to use someone else's character without their permission, though! That's just not done, and if the luchador has registered his character, he can even sue you.

Once you have your character, you will need to think about your costume. The first and most important decision you will now make is whether you will be a masked wrestler or not. Plenty of wrestlers don't bother masking. I've heard some people say that it's just the ugly wrestlers who mask themselves. But a lot of people feel like the magic of lucha libre lies in the mask and the mystery of the masked wrestlers. Don't think you can get away with being a lousy wrestler just because you're masked, though. As we say, "The mask doesn't make the luchador, the luchador makes the mask."

If you decide to use a mask, it's a big responsibility. You have to go to great pains to preserve your anonymity. You must never let anyone except close friends and family know who you are, and you must swear them to secrecy. It's a burden. El Santo, the most famous wrestler ever, he never showed his face in public to anyone until just before he died. They say that when he would work in the United States, he would travel masked and only show his face to the immigration officers in a closed room. He unmasked himself on television in an interview, this was back in 1984. He showed his face to all of Mexico. A few days after the interview was broadcast he died, suddenly. A heart attack.

Anyway, once you've decided on your costume, and whether to mask, you need to go to someone who makes equipment for lucha libre. You could go to Deportes Martínez; they've been doing it since 1934, but they are expensive, and a lot of wrestlers starting out find someone else to make their costume. At a minimum you'll need tights or shorts, boots, and a singlet of some kind. You might also want a mask, a cape, and maybe something that covers your arms too. That's up to you.

Once you've trained for about three years and your teacher says you're ready and you have your character and your costume, you're going to have to take an exam and get your license. Yes, you have to have a license if you want to wrestle professionally! The licenses are issued by the Commission of Lucha Libre. The members of the Commission are appointed by the governor of the Federal District (except for the secretary, who is appointed by the president of the General Directorate for the Promotion of Sports). So in order to be a luchador, you have to take the exam. It's given every few months over by the Velodromo, where the commissioners have their offices. Right now the president is a luchador, El Fantasma. Back in the '60s, '70s, '80s it was that writer, Luis Spota. Anyway, once you get there they'll give you a medical exam. Then you have to go through the real exam. You have to demonstrate your physical condition, your mastery of the various rolls I talked about before, and then you have to show that you've mastered three kinds of wrestling: Olympic wrestling, wrestling to submission, and professional lucha libre. Only then will you be granted your license. Be aware that the judges will be more demanding if you intend to be a masked wrestler, because nobody wants a mediocre wrestler to hide their shame behind a mask. At the end, if you pass, you'll get your license, with your photo, and the designation "with mask" or "without mask."

After that you might think you've got it made. Now you're going to be a big star on television, and everything like that. Well, think again, because you still have to find someone who will hire you. If you are hired by one of the big empresas, like the CMLL or the AAA, then you will probably get regular work. You might not be paid very much, but you'll work pretty regularly. In order to get into the empresa, though, you need what we call a *palanca*,[17] someone who can ease your way in. If you come from a family of luchadores, well, then you probably have someone who can get you in the door at least. If you have a trainer with connections to the empresa, that's another way you might get in. Otherwise, you're going to be working for the smaller empresas, and there are fewer and fewer of those. The most likely thing that will happen is that you will be working for a promoter, and your promoter probably won't have his own arena. They are located throughout Mexico City and the surrounding area. You're going to have to pay a lot of dues.

Whether you start in a big empresa or not, you have to conduct yourself as a professional. That means arriving on time to the arena. That may sound easy, but you know how big this city is. It can take two hours to get

17. A lever.

from one place to another. Not only do you have to arrive on time, but if you are a masked wrestler, you have to arrive with your mask already in place. If you have a car, you can put it on in the car. If you don't, well, you're going to have to figure out how to put on your mask without anyone seeing you or guessing who you are. (By the way, your promoter will care a lot about how you get to the arena, but he won't care at all about how or whether you can get home afterward.)

Being a professional means upholding an ethic. A luchador never tries to injure his opponent. He takes the joint-lock as far as he needs to but no further. Sometimes people lose control or get angry or get sloppy, and that's when someone gets hurt. A luchador who hurts his opponents, though . . . well, he's not going to be in the business for long. But you never really know what's going to happen once you get in the ring. You might expect one thing, and then something else happens. Sometimes you have to swallow your pride. You have to know that sometimes you will win, and sometimes you will go under, But we can talk about that later.

Your first professional match is sometimes called your "baptism," and your first opponent or opponents are your "godparents." We might be opponents in the ring, but outside the ring we are all comrades. We are family. That's just the way it is.

An event usually consists of five matches. The first two are usually between novices. That's also where they usually fit matches between women or matches between minis. Minis are luchadores who are smaller than most men. Some are dwarves, some are just guys from Chiapas or Oaxaca. They're just small. Sometimes women or minis get to do the third match. The last two matches feature bigger stars.

Here in Mexico, although we have one-on-one matches and two-person tag teams, we also like to do what are called *relevos australianos,*[18] three-person teams with a captain and two partners. In general, a match is decided by two falls out of three. A fall is counted when one wrestler pins the other's shoulders to the mat while the referee counts to three, or when a wrestler can't escape a joint lock and openly submits to his opponent. In relevos australianos a fall is counted when one team pins or joint-locks either the team captain or both of his allies. Those are the usual matches.

---

18. Australian relays.

Some matches are more important or dramatic than others. If you work for a big empresa, your bosses might decide to put you in contention for a championship belt. If you wear a mask or have long hair, you might find yourself in a *lucha de apuesta,*[19] a match in which one wrestler bets his hair or mask against another's. If a wrestler loses his hair, then a barber comes and shaves his head right then and there, in front of the public. If a wrestler loses his mask, then he has to take it off and let the announcer tell everyone his name and hometown. Once he loses his mask, though, he can never wear that or any other mask again.

The thing with lucha libre is, it's a hard life. Unless you get to be a big star, you'll probably struggle. If you work for the CMLL or the AAA or one of the other big empresas, then at least you'll have steady work and a union. If you get to be a really big star, like El Hijo del Santo or Mil Máscaras, you might even be able to work as an independent. If you can't get into a big empresa, though, you probably won't be able to be a luchador full time. You'll get a gig here, a gig there. Sometimes you'll get paid pretty well, sometimes you'll just get a sandwich and a soda. Freelancers work for a promoter, but the promoter has to work with the arenas and the big empresas too. Most freelancers have a day job. There's no way to live off of just wrestling if you are freelance.

If you do work for an empresa, though, it's still a hard life. Stars work four or five nights a week. Imagine if soccer players had to play that often! Imagine if boxers had to box four nights a week! And you'll have to travel. In a way, it's great; you might spend time in the U.S. or Japan. Back in the 1980s lucha libre was popular in Kuwait, so a lot of wrestlers got to go to Kuwait, and they made a lot of money. But it's also hard. You'll be on the road a lot. You'll have to wrestle in the Federal District one day, Monterrey the next, then maybe you'll have to go down to Guadalajara. It's not easy.

After a while, as you get older, it will get harder. Some people can do this a long time. El Santo was over sixty when he retired. So was Irma Gonzalez. Her career lasted fifty years! But not everyone can do that, so don't think that just because you're going to be a luchador means you don't need an education. If you get hurt or you get older and you just can't take the abuse in the ring anymore, what will you do then?

---

19. Betting match.

A lot of wrestlers have something to fall back on. They'll start a business or study accounting or something so they can get a job. But it's hard to leave the *familia luchística*. Like I said, it gets in your blood. So there are some jobs that you can do to stay in the business, even if you're not wrestling anymore. Some retired luchadores teach classes; that's what I do. I don't go into the ring anymore, but I also have my little store. Luchadores who work for the Consejo, though, they sometimes have other options. Like what? Well, for example, some ex-luchadores sell concessions in Arena México or Arena Coliseo. You don't have to be an ex-luchador to work there, but a lot of the concessionaires are. Some luchadores get administrative jobs in the Consejo or the AAA.

And then, some luchadores become referees. Referees are really important. Outsiders don't realize how important they are. Now, referees are part of the show, just like the wrestlers, so referees have to have their own personas. They tell the wrestlers when to enter the ring, and when they have to leave it. The referee's job is to make sure that the wrestlers follow the rules and to decide when one side has won a fall or won the match. Of course the referee can't always enforce the rules against the rudos, and some referees like to favor the rudos, but I don't think that's really part of the job. Luchadores are *supposed* to respect the referee (although they don't always).

But there are other parts of the referee's job that the public doesn't know about. If the match is going slowly and the audience is getting bored, the referee might tell the wrestlers to pick up the pace. The most important responsibility of the referee is to stop the match if a wrestler gets injured. Like I said, nobody has to get injured, and a professional will never intentionally injure his opponent, but sometimes something goes wrong. When the luchadores are in the middle of a lucha, sometimes they don't even feel pain. They've got so much adrenaline that when they get hurt they don't always realize it. If that happens, the referee's job is to stop the match and get the injured luchador out of the ring. So if you're lucky and you have a long career, when you're ready to retire you can just start working as a referee, and you won't have to leave the arenas.

So, that's about it. If you want to start, we can start on Monday. Wear shorts. You should wear Lycra shorts, sneakers, something light. You're going to sweat. If you want to train somewhere else you can train somewhere else, but I'm a great teacher, and I was taught by great teachers. So

if you want to learn the real Mexican lucha libre, not the clown-show you
see on TV, then you can come back on Monday.

Acknowledgments

My thanks to Luis Jaramillo Martinez (Aguila Blanco), my classmates, and
the entire *familia luchistica*.

Suggested Readings

On apprenticeship and communities of practice in general, see:
Jean Lave and Etienne Wenger, *Situated Learning: Legitimate Peripheral Participation.*
    New York: Cambridge University Press, 1991.

On Mexican Lucha Libre, see:
Heather Levi, *The World of Lucha Libre: Secrets, Revelations, and Mexican National
    Identity.* Durham, NC: Duke University Press, 2008.

For a photographic study of luchadores, luchadoras, and their world, see:
Lourdes Grobet, *Lucha Libre: Masked Superstars of Mexican Wrestling.* Federal District,
    Mexico: Trilce Ediciones, 2005.

On the training of professional wrestlers in the United States, see:
Sharon Mazer, *Professional Wrestling: Sport and Spectacle.* Jackson: University Press of
    Mississippi, 1998.

On the training of wrestlers in a different context, see:
Joseph Alter, *The Wrestler's Body: Identity and Ideology in North India.* Berkeley:
    University of California Press, 1992.

The Pains and Peaks of Being a Ballerina in London

Helena Wulff

Ballet is transnational, more so than many other occupations. This means that in the ballet world, dancers move easily between classical ballet companies in different countries. Work routines are the same everywhere—daily morning class, rehearsals in the afternoon, and performances in the evening. All dancers know the approximately two hundred ballet steps and their French names. Different versions of the classical ballets are similar enough to be learned in a short time. This is why a Royal Ballet dancer from London can go to Stockholm or New York on short notice, should there be an emergency because a leading dancer is suddenly injured before a premiere. When it comes to funding and employment laws, though, the Royal Ballet in London and, for instance, the Royal Swedish Ballet in Stockholm are very different. According to Swedish employment law, Stockholm dancers have the right to get a permanent contract that lasts until retirement in their early forties, and they cannot be fired unless they refuse to work. They also have ample parental leave, which even some of the men use. In London, dancers are appointed for one year at a time; the contracts are renewed—or not—once a year. Most women dancers postpone having babies, since they know that they will not easily get back into the same shape afterward, and it is unheard of for men to take paternity leave. The Royal Ballet is funded through public subsidy to some extent, but it also depends to a great deal on private and corporate sponsorship. In the United States, major ballet companies such as American Ballet Theatre and New York City Ballet are almost entirely funded by private donors and corporate sponsors. Donors and sponsors have a say when it comes to repertory and touring, and they can also influence casting.

A ballerina at the Royal Ballet in London thus has more in common with a ballerina in New York than with one in Stockholm because of similarities in funding systems and employment laws in the United States and Britain. With the regimented work routine, strict hierarchy, and relative lack of opportunities for promotion in the ballet world, there is not much room to wriggle anywhere, but even less so in Britain. The most British aspect of being a ballerina in London has to do with the relatively rigid class system in Britain, with royalty on top and the lingering legacy of the British empire—all of which is prevalent in the British ballet world. Drawing on my extensive research in the ballet world including the Royal Ballet, here follows a story from a composite London ballerina´s point of view.

"So what is your day job?" people ask. As if we didn't work at all during the days. As if dancing on stage at night is all we ever do. When we actually work incredibly hard six days a week, starting with early morning practice in daily class, then rehearsing in the afternoon and, more often than not, performing until late at night. We work when other people are free to come to watch us, during weekends, evenings, and holidays. Also, mind you, we work with our bodies. This means that we are totally dependent on the state of our bodies, on how fit we are. We always have to keep improving. Coaches and colleagues keep telling us: "You are only as good as your last performance!"

All this makes us different than other people. We are vulnerable, and I don't think this is really understood by people outside the theater world. We are exposed on stage. Now that I have been a principal dancer with the Royal Ballet in London for so long, and get leading roles that require

Figure 14.1 *The Sleeping Beauty.* Copyright Alexander Kenney, Kungliga Operan.

a lot of acting, I know that the audience sees right inside me, sees my passions and my griefs. I use my personal memories of momentous experiences when I dance. It can be anything, from the breakup with my first boyfriend and falling in love with the man I later married to the death of my mother. On a bad day, when I'm slightly off, or when I am in pain from injuries, this used to be amplified on stage. Now that I have extensive experience of dancing on stage, I can dance on auto-pilot, so to speak. I can do an okay performance anyway, no matter what kind of day I am having. The audience does not necessarily notice that I'm not in good form. We have a saying in the ballet world about the importance of constant training:

> If you miss class once
> you will notice.
> If you miss class twice
> your colleagues (or teacher) will notice.
> If you miss class three times
> the audience will notice.

For a peak experience, though, I have to be in top form. Thing is, you cannot plan those extraordinary experiences. They happen infrequently, rarely lasting a whole performance, and they can strike during a rehearsal. This is when everything works, when my movements and the music merge. I do not have to think about the technique or what I look like, the steps are effortless. Liberated, I create new ballet artistry. Such exceptional moments of peak experience occur not only to dancers but to other artists as well, and scholars and craftspeople. I am, of course, recognized as a leading ballerina, but for those who remain unknown (and are never mentioned in reviews or featured in the media), which actually are the majority of dancers, it is these moments of peak experience that make it all worthwhile. This is the reward for practicing all the time for decades, often enduring pain from injuries. Bodily pain is expected in the ballet world; you cannot improve your technique without pain from training. But when we push our bodies too hard or in the wrong way and the result is an injury, then the bodily pain is devastating and becomes mental pain as well. Not being able to dance is the worst thing that can happen to a dancer, even if it is only for a limited period of time. To us, it is very painful to be held back in our career, we might miss important performances and opportunities to shine on stage. All dancers have to endure injuries. Many if not most dancers are injured sometime or another. Some are injured so badly they have to stop dancing prematurely. This threat is traumatic to everyone involved, since dancing is our whole life.

Mental pain can occur because of worry over upcoming casting, expected promotions, or a premiere. When I was a new principal dancer and was cast to do Princess Aurora in *The Sleeping Beauty,* I was delighted at first, but as the premiere approached I started panicking. Would I really manage? What if I made a mess of the whole thing and brought shame on Britain's premier ballet company? And my mother, after having made all those sacrifices to get me into ballet, what would she think? So I went to the company physical therapist, who was also trained as a psychologist. I fell apart in her office. She picked up the pieces, put me together again. When she said that I had been selected to do Aurora because the ballet management knew I would succeed, only then did I feel confident enough to do it. On the night of the premiere I was ready. It went very well. And the critics, well, they raved.

The way we perceive the world outside the theater and the studio is through ballet and ballet culture. We spot movement everywhere around us where non-dancers do not necessarily notice anything in particular. We think of repeated movements in terms of rehearsal, especially when children learn a bodily skill such as walking, swimming, or cycling. Outside the theater, we identify ballet stories and roles in everyday situations. Like the way my husband looked when I came back late from a party he had not been invited to: He looked as evil and threatening as Rothbart, the magician in *Swan Lake*.

We think of ballet and the ballet world all the time, especially steps in the productions we are doing at the moment, how to execute them. If we are partnering, we discuss how to dance together, issues of timing and spatiality, how to make enough space for the other dancers on the stage. Often we dance with high speed across space, and it's vital not to crash into someone or cause an accident. In partnering, rapport and technique are key. When a male dancer lifts me high above himself and holds me there, I have to trust him completely. Also, when I run into his arms and he is supposed to swing me around, then put me into position with one leg stretched behind without losing balance, we have to practice trust and technique, "rescuing," as it is called.

Most of the time, we do not say anything on stage, there is no need. But because the music is very loud, we can actually talk without the audience hearing or noticing. This is useful when doing difficult combinations of steps that might potentially be dangerous. You can remind each other to be prepared for a high jump or a quick pirouette or that you will soon need more space. I normally remember steps, but it's good to know that my partner can remind me, if I forget. It is more common, though, that a dancer makes a mistake, and then being able to talk on stage is essential. If the mistake is made by a dancer in the long line of the corps de ballet, it normally passes without any drama.[1] But when a leading dancer or a soloist does something wrong, other dancers have to adapt. Then we can agree verbally on how to save the situation. Failing to save a situation on stage might result in injury. I know of a few instances when dancers have been seriously injured on stage and were not able to get off stage; they just lay there. Then the curtain has to go down. Usually, the performance continues after a short break when an extra is called in. I have even heard of a dancer in Amsterdam who fell into the orchestra pit and died.

---

1. The term "corps-de-ballet" refers to the group of dancers in a ballet company. They move in unison and form the background for the principal dancers.

Comic incidents also happen on stage, by the way, without the audience noticing. They are in most cases not harmful to our bodies but might potentially break the spell. I will never forget a performance of *Romeo and Juliet* when I was doing Juliet and my friend John was doing Romeo. We have known each other since ballet school when we were ten years old, and we have always been close. (John likes my husband, and I have always liked his boyfriend.) So there we were, deep into the highly charged love pas de deux, which ends with us kissing and then going in different directions across the stage.[2] The audience was totally with us. But as we parted, having kissed for real, while the music was getting very tender—a string of saliva grew longer and longer between our mouths. Fortunately, we were able to control our giggling on stage, but it escalated into loud laughing when we came back to the wings.

Ballet in Britain

What does it mean for me to be part of the Royal Ballet? Since World War II, the Royal Ballet has been the premier national ballet company in Britain. The Royal Ballet rose to fame at the same time that Great Britain was losing its imperial power. British people responded to this with a combination of apprehension and responsibility. Many embraced a nationalism that, for instance, was expressed when the Royal Ballet went on tours abroad in the 1950s and 1960s. According to former dancers with the Royal Ballet, they were taught that they were "ambassadors of Britain." This is still the case. When we go on foreign tours or individual dancers do guest performances abroad, we are told that we are representing Britain. This includes an awareness about Britain's glorious past. We are also invited to dance at international sports events, such as at the closing ceremony of the London 2012 Olympic Games. For us, it is always a great honor to be asked to dance at national celebrations such as the Queen's Diamond Jubilee. We are pleased to be part of the top tier, the best of British art and culture.

---

2. The term "pas de deux" refers to a dance in classical ballet performed by two dancers, a man and a woman. In contemporary dance, it is called a "duet" and can also be performed by two men or two women.

As for the repertory of the Royal Ballet, it mostly consists of classical ballet productions such as *Swan Lake,* the ballet of ballets, and *The Sleeping Beauty.* They build on European folk tales. We take special pride in mounting productions by British choreographers, both late legendary ones and those who are active now. The Royal Ballet also does contemporary ballet and experimental dance by choreographers from abroad. When it comes to the background of the dancers in the Royal Ballet, like any national ballet company, dancers in the Royal Ballet are not all British anymore, even though many dancers from other countries have attended the Royal Ballet School before auditioning for the company. There is now a great diversity of national and ethnic backgrounds in the Royal Ballet, and while many ballerinas were born in Britain, some come from Brazil, Spain, Argentina, Russia, Ukraine, and France. There have been a few black male principal dancers with the Royal Ballet, but not yet any black ballerinas. In this respect, the Royal Ballet does not reflect the ethnic diversity of contemporary British society. As to the Royal Ballet dancers' class backgrounds, the company reflects what contemporary British society looks like.

There is a misunderstanding outside the theater that ballet is an elite activity only, that dancers and audience members are all upper-class or upper middle-class. The truth is that the ballet world contains the entire class system, with the majority of people being upper working-class or lower middle-class. In the Royal Ballet, only a few ballerinas are from upper middle-class backgrounds. What happens is that when upper-class dancers realize that they are never going to be promoted to principal dancers, they quit. This means that the dancers offer cultural capital for their audiences, even if they themselves are not necessarily very familiar with Western high art and culture. Also, the audience is diverse classwise: yes, premieres are attended by dignitaries and movie stars, but ordinary performances attract ballet lovers who come to see the dance, not to be seen by others in the foyer. We dancers, we want everyone to see our dance, regardless of class. We want to touch people, mesmerize them!

We are invited to receptions and dinners with wealthy donors, prominent politicians, famous artists, and other "glitterati," not least the Royal family, often in connection with tours and guest performances but also premieres at Covent Garden. Like most major national ballet companies in monarchies, the Royal Ballet has a royal patron, Her Majesty the Queen. I remember when Princess Margaret (the Queen's late sister) was our patron. She was a true ballet lover. She would never miss a premiere. Covent Garden's gilded auditorium with soft red velvet and sparkling crystal chandeliers would be full, doors closed, orchestra in place, and then a moment of breathless silence. As the conductor lifted his baton, the sign for the musicians to start playing "God Save the Queen," the audience rose and sang to her. The Princess always looked happy as she walked in, waving demurely with her white gloved hand, before she took her seat next to dazzling flower arrangements. She also often came to watch general rehearsals, or just stage rehearsals when we were in costume, but still just danced to piano music played by a pianist rather than to the orchestra. The Princess would sit there on her own, in the middle of empty stalls, only attended to by a waiter in tails serving her a cocktail. By the way, it is well known that Princess Margaret mixed with artists and dancers, and such collapses of class are common in the ballet world.

As we are on one-year contracts in the Royal Ballet, there is great anxiety every spring when the contracts are being reassessed. You are called in for a talk with the ballet director, which I must admit is nerve-wracking. This is presented as an opportunity to have an impact on your career, but it never seems to work out that way. Rather, the ballet director provides an evaluation of your progress, or lack thereof, during the season. As far as I know, only leading dancers or up-and-coming ones who are already the favorites of the ballet director are able to identify roles they wish to dance or promotions they are hoping for—and get them! Luckily, I am one of the few who gets to choose what to dance. That is the way it works when you have a big fan following and the critics adore you. My following includes some wealthy donors who sometimes sponsor certain ballet performances. They enjoy arranging parties and want to get to know you. I have to admit, though, that I don't appreciate those parties. They often take place late at night after you have been on stage for three hours and you are completely exhausted. All you want to do is go home and go to bed. But since the donors pay the bill, you have to dress up and smile and reply to their, well, silly questions about ballet. What I really hate is when donors and other fans do not understand that when they meet me, they are not meeting the Swan Queen in *Swan Lake* or Princess Aurora in *The*

Sleeping Beauty! All these adults who cannot separate fiction from reality! At least, I have never been the target of stalking, like one of my older colleagues was.

Work as Vocation

I had a lot of energy when I was a child. I played the piano, but I couldn't sit still. So my parents sent me to a local ballet school. Some children are sent to ballet school for the opposite reason, because they are shy and need to be more comfortable in their bodies. I saw ballet on television. I had a dream I was going to be a ballerina. We start our vocational training already as children, and the decision to do ballet as a career is made early. This commitment is necessary to make it in the ballet world. This is work as vocation. My ballet teacher said I was very talented and suggested that I audition for the Royal Ballet School. I got into the company when I was eighteen. I became a soloist and then a principal dancer, our highest rank. There are about a hundred dancers in the company and only fifteen principal dancers. In the past there were a few prima ballerinas, and a couple of prima ballerina assolutas. To reach the top in this very competitive world, you have to be absolutely superb both technically as a dancer and also artistically, you have to find your own expression. For this it is not enough to be determined and tough, you also need to be sensitive and to be able to express fragility on stage.

Like for many dancers, my breakthrough came unexpectedly. I had been asked to start learning a leading role, the Swan Queen, as a preparation to do the role at some later point. Then the day before the premiere, the dancer who was cast to do the Swan Queen was injured during a rehearsal. Late at night, the ballet director phoned me and asked if I could dance the Swan Queen the day after. I accepted, of course, honored and scared. In the ballet world, the show must go on! Cancelling a performance is the worst thing that can ever happen. Not only is it expensive, as much money is lost, but it is also a loss of face for the company, not good for our reputation. I rehearsed all day before the premiere in a state of fright. Toward late afternoon, I felt a bit better, as if I was beginning to find the role—or roles, rather, as this actually requires the dancer to do two roles, a good swan and an evil swan.

The story is about Princess Odette, who has been turned into a swan by Rothbart, the magician. She and her companion swans can only be brought back to human existence if a man swears true love to her. Prince Siegfried falls in love with the Swan Queen and expects her at a ball. But it is the magician and his daughter Odile who appear, she dressed up as a black swan. Her dancing imitates that of Odette but is harder and flashier. Siegfried is infatuated by Odile and proposes to her. When Siegfried realizes his mistake, he is heartbroken. *Swan Lake* has different endings: in our production, Odette and Siegfried die together.

On the day of my sudden debut, after having finished rehearsing in the late afternoon, I had a body massage and then went home for a rest. But it was difficult to relax. I had some food, pasta, and went back early to the theater for warm-up class. There were flowers and good-luck cards on my dressing room table, even a couple of small soft yellow toy bears. One of my friends had found a ballerina doll. According to tradition, you are not supposed to respond to these gifts, you shouldn't say thank you or anything at all when someone wishes you good luck before a debut or an important premiere. If you do, the performance might go badly. And just to make sure, the very words "good luck" should be avoided, and transformed into another expression such as "toi toi," "merdre," or even "break a leg," which of course is exactly what should not happen.

With my makeup and hair and headdress of white feathers in place, the tutu on, I went down to the stage to watch the first act from the wings. My entrance was not until the second act. I stepped into the box with resin, and as I put it on my shoes (to avoid slipping) I could sense the familiar sharp smell. I saw dancers going out on stage and taking their positions behind the closed curtain. There was the cacophony of the orchestra tuning their instruments. Then I bent down and knocked three times on the floor—an old tradition we ballerinas have—for the floor to hold.

As is the custom, my entrance was met with a loud applause, much louder than I had expected, it almost threw me backward. But it carried me through the first steps, and then I just continued throughout the whole performance. Everyone was very supportive. The corps de ballet girls were there for me, doing their parts beautifully, and my Prince, he was an excellent partner. There was just one moment of horror, when I spotted a dancer who used to be my friend at ballet school in the wings. She was standing in a space she knew I had to look at when I turned. And she was making faces. I had heard about this, how an envious dancer tries to get a competitor who is on stage to lose her concentration. But I managed to keep my composure and danced on and on.

Tricks of the Trade

When I teach master classes to women ballet students and young dancers, I give a little lecture in which I talk about tricks of the trade, how to get ahead in this very competitive career.

A ballerina is a top dancer, more important than the big group of corps de ballet, now also called artists or dancers. To make it as a ballerina, you have to take the bodily and mental pain. There are, again, the physical hardships, the pain involved when growing up and constantly forming, some say forcing your body into the formalized ballet steps. What happens is that this disciplining of our bodies makes them agile and suited for ballet, yet more prone to injuries that result in bodily pain. And there is mental pain. If you start succeeding and are selected to do solos and leading roles early, and then if this goes very well, then you will be appointed a principal dancer, like I was, rather unexpectedly and long before my colleagues and friends from ballet school. This causes envy, and you lose friends. I don't think anyone in the ballet world suffers from success, but being promoted does come with harassment in some form or other. In ballet very few reach the top and are really able to develop their dancing (and acting) accordingly. You leave the majority of dancers behind to do what is called "corps work," which means forming long lines or other patterns of dancers who all look the same, are usually dressed in white tutus, and do the same steps in total unison. Margot Fonteyn, our British prima ballerina assoluta who famously danced with Rudolf Nureyev, had a remarkably long and acclaimed career. She really was a lovely person and my role model, but not everyone is that generous. I have had to learn that your colleagues' envy is a sign of your success.

The ballet world is infamous for being extremely competitive, especially for women dancers, a competiveness that is sparked by casting or promotion disappointments. I have witnessed incidents in which women have fought like screaming cats in the corridor outside the studio until they must be separated by force. But not all harassment is so public, it can take many forms. One of our top ballerinas was on maternity leave. When she came back, she was not as fit anymore, which was a source of sorrow for her. After her comeback performance and subsequent luke-warm reviews, she received anonymous letters saying that she should stop dancing. And there was a feature article celebrating her posted on the notice board next to one of the studios backstage, but someone anony-mously altered it. The words "thinks" and "our greatest ballerina," which appeared in different places in the article were underlined in red in order to emphasize an ironic reading of them. It did not take long before the ballet director saw to it that the "revised" article was taken down, and he also had a short talk with the company about collegiality and aging in the ballet world.

Cases of competition between women are, again, more common than between men. But there was the acid attack in January 2013 at the Bol-shoi Ballet in Moscow that occurred between men. It was such a shock to us all, and it was, of course, all over the news. The dancer who arranged to have acid thrown in the face of the ballet director, Sergei Filin, had been annoyed that he had not become the artistic director of the company instead of Filin. I have never heard of anything as cruel as that taking place here in London, at the Royal Ballet, or anywhere else, not even in New York, where ballet is said to be even more competitive than here.

There are many stories and rumors about competition in the ballet world. One legendary notion is to put broken glass in the tip of some-one's toeshoe. I doubt that this ever happened, perhaps once a long time ago. No one I have met has actually seen this or even known of a specific person that had been the target of such an awful assault. Competition will always be there, it is part of the game, but we prefer healthy competition that drives dancers to surpass themselves. Unfortunately, it is films such as *Black Swan,* which is about a dancer pushed to dance to her death, that form what people outside the ballet world think about us. You see, there is so much collegiality and camaraderie. Working together with your bodies creates bonds. Many times when I have danced really badly and come back crying in the wings, other dancers have comforted me.

When I was a young dancer, older dancers were always very helpful with tips about how to dance certain roles. Older dancers also advised me about how to handle difficult coaches and directors, which mostly meant doing as they say, especially when I was just starting out. You have to find a way to get them to notice you both on stage and in the studio. One trick is to dance slightly off-beat when you are in a long line. If you are a strong stage personality, they may think you are the only one who is doing it right.

Finally, you have to burn for ballet to make it as a ballerina. The intensity is relentless. This is why older ballerinas often urge younger dancers to "get balance in your life," meaning to set aside time for family and friends. In the real world of ballet, injuries and drawbacks in casting and promotions create pain, but it is those moments of peak experience that we aim for.

Suggested Readings

On peak experience, see:
John Blacking, "Towards an Anthropology of the Body." In *The Anthropology of the Body,* ed. John Blacking. London: Academic Press, 1977.

On cultural capital, see:
Pierre Bourdieu, *Distinction: A Social Critique of the Judgement of Taste.* Cambridge, MA: Harvard University Press, 1984.

On flow, see:
Mihaly Csikszentmihalyi and Isabella Selega Csikszentmihalyi, eds., *Optimal Experience: Psychological Studies of Flow in Consciousness.* Cambridge: Cambridge University Press, 1992.

On pain, see:
Mary-Jo DelVecchio Good, Paul E. Brodwin, Byron J. Good, and Arthur Kleinman, eds., *Pain as Human Experience: An Anthropological Perspective.* Berkeley: University of California Press, 1992.

On ballet rivalry, see:
Miriam Elder, "Bolshoi Ballet Director Suffers Acid Attack." *The Guardian,* January 18, 2013.

On disciplining the body, see:
Michel Foucault, *Discipline and Punish: The Birth of the Prison.* New York: Vintage, 1979.

On the transnational ballet world, see:

Helena Wulff, *Ballet across Borders: Career and Culture in the World of Dancers.* London: Berg/Bloomsbury, 1998.

On experiences of peak and pain in ballet, see:

Helena Wulff, "Experiencing the Ballet Body: Pleasure, Pain, Power." In *The Musical Human: Rethinking John Blacking's Ethnomusicology in the Twenty-First Century,* ed. Suzel Ana Reily, 125–142. Aldershot, U.K.: Ashgate Press, 2006.

On ballet history, see:

Helena Wulff, "Ethereal Expression: Paradoxes of Ballet as a Global Physical Culture." *Ethnography* 9, no. 4 (2008): 519–36.

On ballet funding, see:

Helena Wulff, "Ballet Culture and the Market: A Transnational Perspective." In *Dancing Cultures: Globalisation, Tourism, and Identity,* ed. Hélène Neveu-Kringelbach and Jonathan Skinner, 46–59. Oxford, U.K.: Berghahn, 2012.

Afterword

Jean Lave

In *Situated Learning: Legitimate Peripheral Participation* (Lave and Wenger 1991), my coauthor and I laid out a way of talking about changing practice, work, and learning that was partly developed around the notion of "communities of practice." In the book, we left it as an intuitive concept that addressed the "histories and developmental cycles of complicated, heterogeneous collective practices" and encompassed groups that "reproduce themselves in such a way that the transformation of newcomers into old-timers becomes unremarkably integral to the practice" (122). In the years since this book was published, our notions have been taken up in diverging ways. On the one hand, these ideas have been employed by people working together in jobs where they are trying to change their own practices. On the other (very different) hand, these ideas have also been used prescriptively, principally by management in corporate settings as a "how-to" manual for creating and "managing" communities of practice. Nothing could be farther from this corporate idea of a "how-to manual" than this book.

When chapters in this book present "how-to manuals," they do so in order to elucidate ways of participating in (what I would call) communities of practice. That's because the focus in these how-to manuals is on the complicated things people need to do in order to do their jobs, tasks that are too surprising to be prescribed in advance. And they do not find it possible to talk about people *doing* work without talking about the heterogeneous others with whom they must engage.

Academic or educational or business management efforts to write formal job descriptions (beforehand and from above) compose these descriptions as if "the job" were a limited series of tasks requiring specific knowledge and skill, tasks that can be easily listed. They also assume that everything the job doer needs to know is taken care of when the individual has mastered those tasks. Well, no wonder there is this big residual category to hide the mysteries of actual practice, called "tacit knowledge." (The term has more interesting meanings when it is not being invoked to cover up the chasm between what a job could conceivably be about and what actually goes on in practice.)

In a way this book is all about the stuff you can't learn about from reading the other kind of "how-to" manual, the one with step 3.4.a. followed by 3.4.b. and 3.4.c. and so on. Life—including working life—doesn't work that way. Harold Levine, an anthropologist who did some research on "mild mental retardation," once handed me a list he'd found, two columns of instructions, intended as a step-by-step guide for a person with learning challenges. Harold's question to me was, "Whatever do you think this is a guide *for?*" I couldn't figure it out until more than half way through the list: lift the lid, stand in front of basket, pick up the basket, take things out of the basket, put them in. . . . I suddenly realized: Oh—this is about how to do a load of laundry. I doubt that anyone could actually do the job based on a job description like that.

So how come a list of instructions or lessons or exercises is not adequate for learning how to do a job? What's great about the "how-to" manuals in this book is that they just plunge into showing what people engaged in a job do. In the authors' descriptions and analysis lie answers to questions about, well, if your individual worker's task list is not sufficient, what else is the worker doing? It turns out that they are moving among several different contexts and are engaged in numerous different working relations with a very disparate array of other folks, trying to make different parts of doing the job serve as support for other parts. Many of these necessary social relations, which you encounter while doing the stuff without which you cannot do your job, aren't obvious until you actually do the job.

Actually there is no way to do your job (as one person) by yourself. Having read this far in the book, you already know that. One way to sum up a bunch of interrelated observations in these studies would be to say that they all address jobs by looking closely at the communities of practice of which they are a part. Several propositions together may help to convey what that includes and implies: Communities of practice involve heterogeneous co-participants. That makes the person doing a job a *partial* participant in ongoing work. The same is true of everyone else.

Second, there has to be a community of practice there if you are going to participate in it. An ordinary, messy, complicated situated practice doesn't just arrive ready-made on the world stage—there is a backstory, a community of practice that is historically made, and since history doesn't suddenly stop when we get to the present, the community of practice is ongoing—and changing.

One way to see history of/in the present is to notice the different ways in which it is concretely embodied. So, for one thing, while working at a job you may want many of the same things as other generations of participants who have come along before or after you, but at the same time you have different experiences, perspectives, and stakes in how the practice goes on and should change. The chapters on being a village court magistrate in Papua New Guinea (chapter 4), on being a traveling musician in Bolivia (chapter 7), on how to be a professional wrestler in Mexico City (chapter 13), and on being a ballerina in London (chapter 14) all consider changes in the job over time, as well as the intergenerational tensions that accompany change in communities of practice.

For these, and other, reasons, what you do, in the midst of *doing* a job, often seems to pull you in contradictory directions. So one wonderful effect of these how-to manuals is to give you a sense of where change is happening and sometimes where those tensions lie. Given that there are changes and social tensions in most jobs, *improvisation* is necessary and endemic.

The notion of contradictions I am describing might seem hard to understand. But another thing these how-to manuals do beautifully is draw attention to how complex jobs involve contradictions. Almost any job you can imagine is complex, and when described in static terms the job just appears complicated, not contradictory. But contradictions emerge precisely as we look at people in action *doing* jobs. For instance, as a magician in Paris (chapter 3), amateurs often innovate elaborate illusions, while professionals use a limited repertoire of tricks. You might expect that as a practitioner a professional should be doing the highly skilled stuff and that the amateurs should be working on simple card tricks. But what happens is just the opposite—dumbed down senior performances, virtuoso juniors. Here's another contradiction: magicians need colleagues who they trust, and yet colleagues are also competitors. You are caught in both trusting and not trusting, working with and working against the same people. Further, magicians must practice endlessly in order to create wonder, but the more they engage in repetitive routine, the more they lose that sense of wonder themselves. What a dilemma—in practice! In chapter 5 we learn that chaplains in airports and hospitals where they are not ministers have more job security than they would as church pastors, yet they have to avoid religious doctrine in favor of spiritual conversation. Their job is to "make religion more like other kinds of work and, at the same time, to set it apart." (Wouldn't you want both?) They sound like simple choices to be made—on paper. In working, doing the job, excluding either one for the other seems wrong—but to work requires that you do so. You *cannot* do everything at the same time. In every one of these contradictory circumstances—call them lived dilemmas—whatever way you decide to go, it is probably unstable over time, as you shift back from one way of dealing with a dilemma to instead emphasize another way (for example, innovate and don't innovate, create illusion by losing it, treating your job like work—but also not like work). That suggests that life involves more "dilemma management" than problem solving. And that is one of the very useful conclusions about doing jobs brought home across the chapters in this book.

Further, this being the ordinary state of affairs when doing jobs, here's a piece of "how-to" advice from me. It's best to try not to feel you are bad at your job if you cannot turn contradictory issues into mere solvable problems. To feel better, it is useful to figure out the contradictions in your job and deal with them openly (proudly even—though that might be a bit more difficult). Out in the open, they are easier to follow and address thoughtfully, and less likely to run *you* rather than the other way around (The needle factory worker giving advice to a novice expresses this vividly in chapter 11).

Up to this point the term "jobs" has been employed to characterize the practices of people working in all of the how-to manuals. But bringing them together under one umbrella term raises a really interesting question: How appropriate is it—in what sense(s) does it *make* sense—to treat all these jobs/people/places/practices as alike as well as different? After all, the book as a whole is inspiring because the manuals give rich accounts of heterogeneous specific jobs. That is, these manuals describe jobs that are NOT alike; even "the same" job in two places isn't the same job. The chapter on how to be a doctor in Malawi (chapter 1) offers an eloquent example as does the chapter on how to design film costumes in India (chapter 10) or how to be a journalist in Buryatia (chapter 8). The "umbrella" does look sensible on some grounds, however. For one thing, these manuals stick to a common focus on *the people doing the jobs.* The book also excludes, on purpose, employers imagining what ideal employees *should* do—a hazardous exercise according to the argument at the beginning of this Afterword. (I would probably exclude experts', and vocational educators' attempts to imagine the ideal subordinate/subaltern as well.)

We do sometimes catch glimpses of the work job doers must engage in when dealing with powerful participants who are paying, managing, regulating, and exercising power over them. For instance in some chapters "old timers" advise new apprentices about how to handle the constraints and conditions of their jobs (and their tensions). When conditions of employment, bosses, regulations, or issues of workers' accountability come up, we see them *from the point of view of those doing the work.* There are not a lot of jobs in the world today that don't involve boss-employee, management-labor relations. Even in a multitude of historical moments, differently articulated with all sorts of states, nations, cultural worlds, and local practices—it's hard to leave traces of capitalism and its hierarchies out of accounts of How To Do Jobs. The jobs have this in common.

While delivering the message that doing jobs is always a specific, heterogeneous, collective proposition, the chapters sooner or later get to specific ways in which capitalist political-economic relations of our historically arranged "here and now" shape all kinds of labor practices. They do so in broadly contemporary global capitalist ways, yet not in successfully standardizable ways. Ilana Gershon argues in the Introduction that the "belief in the ever-increasing similarity of workplaces is misplaced." Indeed. Her point, and mine, is that those "broadly contemporary global capitalist ways" are always instantiated in different specific historical articulations of class, race, gender, and other deep social divisions. So all jobs are affected by their insertion in capitalist practices, but these interrelations come about *differently* in different times, places, and practices. I'd use this collection of "how-to" manuals to try to suss out both commonalities and differences, amid questions about just how, in particular concrete ways, jobs are produced and lived in ways that are caught up in the logic of capital-state relations, production, and the creation of surplus value. Telling us about how to do different sorts of jobs reveals a lot about the complex relations that make up these "situated practices" as well as about participants' ways of working.

There are lessons in these how-to manuals about the limitations of power and possibilities. National policies around immigration reward some kinds of *laborers* less than others, just for being who the others aren't. The rewards for some kinds of *jobs* are also less (or more) than for others. Marx's labor theory of value says that employers pay their employees wages that are not in equal exchange for the value of what they produce, but only enough to cover what their employees need in order to survive and sustain their families' lives. (The difference goes to owners/managers as profit.)

Gershon finished her introduction by explaining that she intends the book as a gift for young people. I think she is too modest, in two different respects. First, with unemployment at 6.2 percent, surely many not so young people are also wondering about how to do different jobs, whether it might be their first job, or one in a series of different jobs across decades (increasingly common in the United States and elsewhere today). Second, behind these "light-hearted ethnographic fictions" there is dense ethnographic research work, visible in how vividly these how-to manuals illuminate the practices of people participating with others in making their ongoing lives. They are rare products of long effort, often years, by ethnographers and others doing *their* jobs, as witnesses and participants in those lives, who then go on to more long-term work to make sense of what they have found in the field. (See my suggested readings list and all the contributors' suggested reading lists for good how-to manuals for ethnographic research, and good examples of ethnographic research.)

The focus on doing jobs in these chapters offers a powerful way into a whole host of social, cultural, political-economic facets of the social worlds of which they are a part. I have rarely encountered such an original and creative way of inviting us all into examples of real work that feel close to our own experiences of working and at the same time gives us the gift of a book that makes it possible to see how to understand practices of working in deeper and more interesting ways.

Suggested Readings

For good how-to manuals for ethnographic research, see:

Charles Briggs, *Learning How to Ask: A Sociolinguistic Appraisal of the Role of the Interview in Social Science Research*. Cambridge: Cambridge University Press, 1986.

Allaine Cerwonka and Liisa Malkki, *Improvising Theory: Process and Temporality in Ethnographic Fieldwork*. Chicago: University of Chicago Press, 2007.

Jean Lave, *Apprenticeship in Ethnographic Perspective*. Chicago: University of Chicago Press, 2011.

CONTRIBUTORS

Lovleen Bains is a Mumbai-based film costume designer. Her career spans thirty years and includes work on films large and small, including *Heat and Dust, Mausam, The Rising: The Legend of Mangal Pandey, God Only Knows,* and the critically acclaimed *Rang de Basanti.* She has been nominated for many awards and has won India's National Award for Film Costume Design for *Muhafiz (In Custody)* in 1993.

Chiwoza Bandawe is a social psychologist who has been on the faculty at University of Malawi and University of Cape Town and has served as dean of students for the University of Malawi College of Medicine. He is now senior lecturer in the Department of Mental Health there. He also writes a weekly column, "Life Tools," for one of Malawi's national newspapers. His ongoing research interests include cultural aspects of human behavior and the effects of poverty on health decision-making.

Joshua A. Bell is a cultural anthropologist and curator at the Smithsonian Institution's Museum of Natural History. Combining ethnographic fieldwork with research in museums and archives, his work broadly examines the shifting local and global network of relationships among persons, artefacts, and the environment. Since 2000 he has worked with communities in the Purari Delta of Papua New Guinea.

Michelle Bigenho is a professor of anthropology and Africana and Latin American studies at Colgate University. Her work has been published as articles, book chapters, and in two monographs: *Intimate Distance: Andean Music in Japan* and *Sounding Indigenous: Authenticity in Bolivian Music Performance*. Performance as a violinist has significantly shaped her fieldwork encounters in Peru, Bolivia, and Japan, and she has participated in numerous recordings with the Bolivian ensemble Música de Maestros. She is currently working on a collaborative project about intellectual property, intangible heritage, and indigeneity in Bolivia.

Warren Chamberlain is currently employed at Vita Needle Company and is a native of Needham, Massachusetts. He was employed in the automobile industry for twenty-seven years and retired from the General Motors plant in Framingham, Massachusetts. He now lives in Holliston, Massachusetts, where he serves on the town's planning board. Warren is interested in urban planning, community development, public transportation, conservation, and agricultural preservation and is a member of The Grange. He is married and has two grandchildren.

Melissa Demian is a research fellow with the State, Society, and Governance in Melanesia program at the Australian National University. She is a social anthropologist specializing in the anthropology of law and has conducted fieldwork in Papua New Guinea periodically since 1996, in both village and urban settings. She has published on topics such as the village courts, land disputes, customary law, and child adoption in Papua New Guinea.

Ilana Gershon is a cultural anthropologist with a wide-ranging set of interests, from Pacific diasporas to how new media affects highly charged social tasks, such as breaking up or hiring in the United States. She has published a book comparing Samoan migrant experiences in New Zealand and the United States, *No Family Is an Island: Cultural Expertise among Samoan Migrants in Diaspora*. She has also written about how people use new media to end romantic relationships in her book *The Breakup 2.0: Disconnecting over New Media*. Her current research addresses how new media affects hiring in the contemporary U.S. workplace.

Kathryn E. Graber is a linguistic and sociocultural anthropologist focusing on Russia and Mongolia. Her research on media and ethnic politics in Buryatia has appeared in *Language and Communication, Inner Asia,* and *Culture, Theory, and Critique* as well as Russian publications. She is currently working on her first book and teaching as an assistant professor in the Departments of Anthropology and Central Eurasian Studies at Indiana University.

Graham M. Jones is an associate professor of anthropology at MIT and author of *Trade of the Tricks: Inside the Magician's Craft,* an ethnographic study of the French magic scene.

Amanda Kemble is a PhD student in anthropology at the University of Michigan. She graduated with her BA in anthropology from the George Washington University in 2012. Her research interests include the mediation of religious language and the formation of pious subjects in the Arab Muslim world.

Briel Kobak completed her BA in anthropology from the George Washington University in 2012. Briel is currently pursuing a PhD in anthropology at the University of Chicago, focusing on branding, circulation, and the commodity form.

Corinna Kruse is a lecturer at the Department of Thematic Studies— Technology and Social Change at Linköping University in Sweden. She is interested in processes of knowledge production, particularly how knowledge is produced, moved, translated, and used across contexts—especially when knowledge is in the form of forensic evidence. She is the author of the articles "Producing Absolute Truth: CSI Science as Wishful Thinking," "The Evidence Doesn't Lie—CSI and Real-Life Forensic Evidence," and "The Bayesian Approach to Forensic Evidence: Evaluating, Communicating, and Distributing Responsibility."

Joel Kuipers is a professor of anthropology and international affairs at George Washington University. He has undertaken research on authority and evidence in communicative practices, ethnography of reading and writing, scientific argumentation and reasoning, medical discourse, video ethnography, and Southeast Asia.

Carrie M. Lane is an associate professor of American studies at California State University, Fullerton. She is an anthropologist of American culture and teaches courses on work, community, and ethnographic research methods. She is the author of *A Company of One: Insecurity, Independence, and the New World of White-Collar Unemployment* and is currently writing a book on the growing field of professional organizing.

John Law is a professor of sociology in the Faculty of Social Sciences at the Open University. In addition to authoring *Aircraft Stories: Decentering the Object in Technoscience,* he has written a wide range of publications in the areas of noncoherent methods: people, technologies, and animals; biosecurity, agriculture and disaster; and alternative knowledge spaces.

Jean Lave is a social anthropologist and professor emerita at the University of California, Berkeley. She is also the founder and director of the Slow Science Institute in Berkeley. Her research has focused on craft apprenticeship, math practices in everyday life, social practice theory, and critical theory more generally, in hopes of challenging conventional convictions that limit our understanding of how learning happens. Her books include *Cognition in Practice, Apprenticeship in Critical Ethnographic Practice, Situated Learning: Legitimate Peripheral Participation* (with Etienne Wenger) and (with Dorothy Holland) *History in Person: Enduring Struggles, Contentious Practice, Intimate Identities.*

Heather Levi is an assistant professor of anthropology at Temple University. She received her PhD from New York University in 2001. She is the author of *The World of Lucha Libre: Secrets, Revelations and Mexican National Identity.* Her research interests include street musicians in Mexico City and LGBTQ community responses to marriage equality laws in Mexico and the United States.

Marianne Elisabeth Lien is a professor of social anthropology at the University of Oslo. She is the author of *Marketing and Modernity* and has published widely on food, nature, invasive species, and aquaculture, based on fieldwork in Norway and Tasmania. Her book on salmon, *Becoming Salmon: Aquaculture and the Domestication of a Fish,* will be published by the University of California Press in 2015.

Caitrin Lynch is an associate professor of anthropology at Olin College and the author of *Retirement on the Line: Age, Work, and Value in an American Factory Retirement on the Line* and *Juki Girls, Good Girls: Gender and Cultural Politics in Sri Lanka's Global Garment Industry.*

Loïc Marquet has been a professional close-up magician for fifteen years in his hometown, Paris.

Winnifred Fallers Sullivan is a professor and chair of the Department of Religious Studies and affiliate professor of Law at Indiana University Bloomington. She is the author of *The Impossibility of Religious Freedom, Prison Religion,* and *A Ministry of Presence*.

Christopher Swift is a former president of the College of Health Care Chaplains in the United Kingdom and is author of *Hospital Chaplaincy in the Twenty-First Century: The Crisis of Spiritual Care on the NHS*. He is head of chaplaincy in the Leeds Teaching Hospitals and has affiliations as an honorary member of staff at the University of Leeds and Leeds Metropolitan University.

Claire Wendland is an associate professor in the Departments of Anthropology, Obstetrics & Gynecology, and Medical History & Bioethics at the University of Wisconsin–Madison. She worked as a practicing physician on the Navajo reservation for many years before turning to medical anthropology. Her ongoing research focuses on medical expertise in African settings and explanations for maternal mortality.

Clare Wilkinson is an associate professor in the Department of Anthropology at Washington State University Vancouver. Her research focuses on the nexus of art, media, and culture in India. Since 2002 she has been studying labor and creativity in the Mumbai film industry. In addition to many articles, she has published two books: *Embroidering Lives: Women's Work and Skill in the Lucknow Embroidery Industry* and *Fashioning Bollywood: The Making and Meaning of Hindi Film Costume*.

Helena Wulff is a professor of social anthropology at Stockholm University. Her primary research interests are the anthropology of communication and aesthetics; she has undertaken a wide range of studies of the social worlds of literary production, dance, and visual arts in a transnational perspective. More recently, she has included the anthropology of literature in her research interests by focusing on contemporary Irish fiction writers and their work. Among her publications are the monographs *Ballet across Borders: Career and Culture in the World of Dancers* and *Dancing at the Crossroads: Memory and Mobility in Ireland*.